A Moseley Miscellany

# Also by Sangharakshita

**Books on Buddhism**
The Eternal Legacy
A Survey of Buddhism
The Ten Pillars of Buddhism
The Three Jewels

**Edited Seminars and Lectures**
The Bodhisattva Ideal
Buddha Mind
The Buddha's Noble Eightfold Path
The Buddha's Victory
Buddhism for Today – and Tomorrow
Creative Symbols of Tantric Buddhism
The Drama of Cosmic Enlightenment
The Essence of Zen
A Guide to the Buddhist Path
Human Enlightenment
The Inconceivable Emancipation
Know Your Mind
Living Ethically
Living with Awareness
Living with Kindness
Living Wisely
The Meaning of Conversion in Buddhism
New Currents in Western Buddhism
Ritual and Devotion in Buddhism
The Taste of Freedom
Tibetan Buddhism: An Introduction
Transforming Self and World
What Is the Dharma?
What Is the Sangha?
Who Is the Buddha?
Wisdom Beyond Words
The Yogi's Joy
The Purpose and Practice of Buddhist Meditation

**Essays and Polemics**
Alternative Traditions
Crossing the Stream
Forty-Three Years Ago
The FWBO and 'Protestant Buddhism'
Going for Refuge
The History of My Going for Refuge
The Priceless Jewel
Was the Buddha a Bhikkhu?
Beating the Drum

**Memoirs and Letters**
The Rainbow Road
Facing Mount Kanchenjunga
In the Sign of the Golden Wheel
Precious Teachers
Moving Against the Stream
Travel Letters
Through Buddhist Eyes
From Genesis to the Diamond Sutra
Dear Dinoo
Early Writings

**Art and Poetry**
The Call of the Forest and Other Poems
Complete Poems 1941–1994
In the Realm of the Lotus
The Religion of Art

**Biography**
Anagarika Dharmapala
Ambedkar and Buddhism

**Miscellaneous**
The Essential Sangharakshita *(anthology)*
Peace is a Fire
A Stream of Stars

# Sangharakshita
# A Moseley Miscellany

## Prose and Verse 1997-2012

Introduction and notes by **Kalyanaprabha**

**Ibis** Publications

Published by
**Ibis Publications**
The Urgyen Annexe
Adhisthana
Coddington
Ledbury
Herefordshire
HR8 1JL

© Sangharakshita 2015
Design: Dhammarati

British Library Cataloguing in Publication Data
A catalogue record for this book is available from
the British Library

ISBN 978-1-909314-68-9

# Contents

# About the Author

URGYEN SANGHARAKSHITA was born in 1925 in South London and christened Dennis Lingwood. On reading *The Diamond Sutra* during the summer he turned seventeen, he realized he was a Buddhist 'and always had been'.

He was conscripted in the Second World War and travelled to India, Sri Lanka, and Singapore. He returned to India, living as a homeless ascetic, meeting the gurus of the time, and meditating and reflecting intensively on the Dharma. He received monastic ordination in the Theravadin tradition and was given the name 'Sangharakshita': he who is protected by, or is protector of, the Sangha.

For fourteen years he was based in Kalimpong in the eastern Himalayas where he came into contact with and received teachings and initiations from leading Tibetan Buddhist teachers. Dedicated to spreading the Buddha's teachings as widely as possible, he taught and wrote extensively, becoming known to many in the Buddhist world East and West as editor of the *Maha Bodhi* journal. Through his contact with Dr B. R. Ambedkar, he went on to play a highly significant part in the Dharma revolution inaugurated by the great Indian leader in 1956.

Sangharakshita returned to London in 1964 at the invitation of the English Sangha Trust and in 1967 founded the Friends of the Western Buddhist Order (FWBO). The following year he performed the ordinations of the first members of the Western Buddhist Order. The decades that followed were dedicated to establishing a thriving Buddhist community in the modern world. In 2010 the FWBO and its Indian counterpart, TBMSG (founded 1978), were renamed the Triratna Buddhist Order and Community, now an international Buddhist movement with over sixty Centres on five continents.

It has been said that Sangharakshita combines an understanding of East and West, of the traditional world and the modern, and that he has been able to distil from the ancient principles discerned by the Buddha the practices best suited to modern men and women who seek to practise the Buddha's teaching. He has particularly emphasized the decisive significance of commitment in the spiritual life, the need for a 'new society' supportive of spiritual aspirations and ideals, and the paramount value of spiritual friendship and community. As a lover of art and a poet, he has made explicit the connection between art and spiritual life.

Now entering his tenth decade, and having completed the task of handing on his responsibilities to senior disciples, despite impaired vision and infirmity, he continues with literary work, as well as attending to correspondence and meeting with people who come from all over the world to 'Adhisthana', Triratna's headquarters in rural Herefordshire, UK, where he is now based.

KALYANAPRABHA has been a member of the Triratna Buddhist Order since 1989. For fourteen years she was editor of the magazine *Dakini* (later renamed *Lotus Realm*), an international Buddhist magazine for women. She was a member of the Taraloka Retreat Centre team and helped set up a Dharmaduta training course in Birmingham for people interested in teaching the Dharma. She has lived in Manchester, Berlin, and Birmingham, working with others to run Triratna Centres and teach the Dharma. In recent years she has worked closely with Sangharakshita to enable him to continue his literary output. She lives in Great Malvern.

# Acknowledgements

Texts in this book written after 2001, when Sangharakshita became partially sighted, were dictated to his personal secretaries. Khemavira (secretary 1999–2006) was in office at the time the book review 'Asian Commitment' was composed as well as the poems in Section IV. Dharmamati (2006–2009) recalls writing down 'An Apology'. Vidyaruchi (2009–2013) was amanuensis for *My First Eight Years, Reveries and Reminiscences, Looking Back,* and *Poems II.* (When a temporary improvement in his vision allowed Sangharakshita to write a little each day by hand, Vidyaruchi typed it up.)

The author was able to read – and offer corrections – to the notes and the Introduction through his current secretary, Ashvajit, who read incoming emails and attachments, and wrote replies in a clear format making communication between Sangharakshita and myself very easy.

Information for the notes concerning people and events in the history of Triratna was supplied in part by quite a number of Order members from the UK and abroad who responded readily to requests for help.

Paramartha and Mahamati, both of whom lived at Madhyamaloka for some of the period 1997–2012, read an early draft of the Introduction. Nityabandhu went through the text and notes for *Terra Incognita.* They all gave useful feedback and encouragement.

The publication of this book rests especially on the generosity of Shantavira, Ibis Publications' much-valued subeditor and typesetter, who once again worked tirelessly on the text; and Dhammarati, who has designed many books by Sangharakshita, and brought his skill and creative inspiration to this one. Dharmashura readily took on proofreading. The helpful team at Windhorse Publications in Cambridge undertook printing and distribution.

Grateful thanks to all these people who together made it possible to bring out this book.

Finally – and most of all – gratitude to Sangharakshita. Our collaboration to bring out his writings is work that is deeply satisfying, leading me sometimes to deeper understandings or giving a glimpse of a new vision of life. I hope all those who read these pages will profit from them, each in their own way.

Kalyanaprabha
Great Malvern
21 April 2015

*References to Sangharakshita's memoirs have been abbreviated in the notes as follows:*
*FGDS: From Genesis to the Diamond Sutra,* Windhorse Publications 2005
*FMK: Facing Mount Kanchenjunga,* Windhorse Publications 1991
*ISGW: In the Sign of the Golden Wheel,* Windhorse Publications 1996
*MAS: Moving Against the Stream,* Windhorse Publications 2003
*PT: Precious Teachers,* Windhorse Publications 2007
*RR: The Rainbow Road,* Windhorse Publications 1997
*TBE: Through Buddhist Eyes,* Windhorse Publications 2000

*The font used in this book does not support Pali and Sanskrit diacritics or the Polish stroke-L. We have therefore omitted Pali, Sanskrit, and Polish diacritics.*

# Introduction

Moseley was once a village on the edge of Birmingham, with its own stately home, Moseley Hall. Though now a suburb of the city and part of that great sprawling mass of human habitation and industrial development known as the West Midlands, it still has something of a village feel to it. At one time, long before the hall was built, there must have been a chantry where priests sung masses for the souls of the dead, for there is now a Chantry Road, its large houses standing back from the road, front gardens planted with flowers and shrubs, and a few mature trees; and back gardens that run down to Moseley Park with its lake – or pond as locals call it – with its ducks and swans, its trees and bushes, and open spaces – a secret garden in an urban landscape.

It was to a three-storey Victorian house in this road, a house with a large and half-wild garden, a house built by the Blackwell family towards the end of the 1800s, that Urgyen Sangharakshita, founder of a growing international Buddhist movement, came to live in the spring of 1997. He was seventy-one years old and had already begun the process crucial to the survival of that movement of handing on his responsibilities to his senior disciples. As it turned out he was to live in Chantry Road for sixteen years: the longest time he had been based in any one place in his whole life.

He did not move to live there alone, of course, but with a company of friends and disciples, some of whom had moved in soon after the property was purchased in 1994. Paramartha, with whom he had recently completed a 'world tour', visiting a number of the movement's Centres, came with him and together they moved into the 'granny-flat' above the garage at 'Brackley Dene'. The garage itself was turned into a library to store Sangharakshita's large and precious collection of books. The upper floors of the main house accommodated the men's community (there was a women's community nearby), while the ground floor, with its kitchen and easy access to the garden, had three large rooms suitable for seminars and meetings. Beneath were an office and a shrine room.

The name Sangharakshita had given to the new place was 'Madhyama-loka', the Middle Realm. It was to be a sort of spiritual headquarters of the movement which, in the year he moved, turned thirty years old. Gathering together in one place, under one roof, some of the senior Order members to whom he would be handing on the last of his responsibilities, would, he hoped, allow them to get to know one another more deeply so that they might be better able to work together in the future.

Standing back and surveying those sixteen years that Sangharakshita lived at Madhyamaloka, they seem to fall into three more or less distinct phases or, you might say, chapters. The first, 1997–2000, sees the Madhyamaloka community coming together and the 'College of Public Preceptors' with its Council establishing itself. During this time Sangharakshita was active on many fronts, continuing to visit Centres both in the UK and abroad, giving talks, conducting seminars, meeting people; and engaging in literary work including writing his memoirs, completing his translation of the *Dhammapada*, composing book reviews for the *Times Higher Education Supplement*, and so on. He read extensively and kept up his cultural interests, visiting art galleries and occasionally the theatre.

And then, in August 2000, on an occasion marking his seventy-fifth birthday, at a gathering of Order members in a hall at Aston University in central Birmingham, Sangharakshita handed on what he considered to be the last of his responsibilities – at least, the last of those responsibilities that could be handed on: he handed on the Headship of the Order. To whom did he hand it on? He handed it on to the eight members of the Preceptors College jointly.

No doubt he had plans – to do some of those things which his duties had not left him time for before. He was now free to come and go, to spend time at Madhyamaloka or time away. His programme for the spring of 2001 included a visit to Belgium and a ten day tour in Germany. But such freedom was not to continue very long. Less than a year after handing on the Headship, unexpectedly and dramatically, as he recounts in these pages, his vision deteriorated and suddenly he could no longer read or write.

Despite this major setback, undaunted, it seems, in the face of this adversity, he gradually found ways to continue his literary and other work. Once more he was visiting Centres and giving talks such as those given in June 2002 at the London and Manchester Buddhist Centres on creativity in relation to art, meditation, friendship, and institutions. In September he visited Buddhafield in Devon, and attended the opening of the new Sheffield Buddhist Centre. A few months previously, in May that year, he ventured into *terra incognita*, spending ten very happy days in Krakow for the launch of the Polish translation of *A Survey of Buddhism*.

But life had not yet finished dealing out a series of heavy blows. In October 2002 Sangharakshita began experiencing the extreme insomnia that was to lead him into 'a season in hell', an experience about which he writes so movingly here. (Yet even that dreadful season brought some compensations in the form of dreams and visions of other, one could say heavenly, worlds. And perhaps an even greater compensation was the blessing of friendship, also an essential part of that time.) But there was more to endure. Some months after the insomnia had set in, 'the good ship FWBO' hit stormy seas and there was unrest among some of its passengers and crew. About that, too, we can read something in these pages, taken from the log-book of the captain. And still there was more to be endured. In the summer of 2004, Sangharakshita suffered a heart attack and was detained in hospital for a week. I recall cycling over from Moseley one hot day to visit him, one of several visitors who came and sat beside their friend and teacher for a short time. Perhaps we all wondered, what was going to happen now....

Within a single lifetime one can discern cycles that mirror the great cycle of birth, death, and rebirth – and sometimes dramatically so. There came to Sangharakshita in due course a new lease of life. Sleep returned, and though his energies were not all they had been before his insomnia and the heart attack, nevertheless he once more enjoyed reasonably good health for one of his age. And so the third period begins, the longest one, from perhaps 2005 or 2006. It sees Sangharakshita mostly at home at

Madhyamaloka, though for a few years he was still making some trips away. I was living in Berlin when he visited in 2008 and gave a talk at the Centre there, the Buddhistisches Tor. He spoke to a full house on the Six Distinctive Emphases of the FWBO, a theme he spoke on at several Centres during this period. In 2010 he and Paramartha went searching for traces of his Suffolk ancestors. (You can read about what happened in *Looking Back*.) People continued to come and see him at Madhyamaloka, and he continued with his wide correspondence and some substantial literary work: *Living Ethically* and *Living Wisely*, books based on teachings he had first given during a seminar on Nagarjuna's *Precious Garland* in 1976, were put together at this time and published in 2009 and 2013 respectively. Between 2009 and 2012, through intensive discussions, chiefly with Subhuti (the first Chair of the College of Public Preceptors), he issued a series of papers, written by Subhuti and carefully checked by him, papers that laid down as clearly as possible some of the basic principles, the key ideas, the common practices and so on, on which the Triratna Order and movement, now and into the future, was to be based.

So in this third period, too, there was much significant and creative output; and though he could no longer read, he kept up his interests in culture and in the wider world through audio books and the radio – 'Mr Wireless' – as reflected in several of the poems in this volume. Yet most characteristic of this time, I think, is a contemplative mood. I think of Sangharakshita as I sometimes caught sight of him from a window in the main house, taking his morning walk round the garden (which by now had been beautifully landscaped by Sanghadeva and planted with flowers and shrubs). I see him as he passes the great cedar tree, moves slowly through the ivy archway, past the lavender beds and along the holly hedge before coming up along the other side of the lawn towards the pond and the miniature box-hedge knot gardens. Or again, I see him before my mind's eye in his room, the 'room with a view' – a view over the garden – a room in which he spent so many hours, seated in his red armchair with its white lace-edged antimacassar, there in the very modest space that served as his and Paramartha's sitting and dining room, the walls to the left lined with books, on the right a bookcase on which stood Buddhist images. He is looking towards the door on which hangs a picture of the Egyptian god Thoth and sitting, just sitting quietly, until there comes a gentle knock.

I used to be one of those who gave that gentle knock. In the summer of 2010 I began working with Sangharakshita as his – I suppose one could call it 'literary assistant' – and I well remember leaving my little flat (I lived in an attic over the garage of another house on Chantry Road), making my way past the front gardens and the large old houses with their curious architectures, and turning into the drive of Madhyamaloka; going through the main house and then along the little passage that connected it with the granny-flat. Pausing to take off my shoes, I would tip-toe upstairs, past the Buddha rupa where the stairs turned a corner (occasionally incense was burning) and along the landing on whose walls hung a photograph of a statue of Anagarika Dharmapala, and pictures of Thomas Carlyle and John Ruskin. 'Come in!' would ring out in answer to my knock. And in I would go, take up my seat opposite, and after a few personal exchanges work would begin.

It was a seat in which many others also sat – indeed, many readers of this volume will have sat there, coming to see their teacher – seeking clarification or blessing or reassurance or simply contact; or occasionally wanting to argue or complain.

And it was in this room that Sangharakshita sat for so many hours reflecting, contemplating, listening – listening sometimes as the poet listens, listening 'for the inevitable word'. Poems came to him in two phases: the first, 1999–2003, and again, quite unexpectedly, in 2009; poems of such diverse subject matter: from the hatred that led to the destruction of the Twin Towers to the experience of dementia; from the Arthurian legends to the all-important difference between the Brahmas and the Sages. These poems tell us much about the mind of their author. One poem stands out in a particular way: 'The Wind', written in February 2009 and communicating something fundamental about Sangharakshita's whole life. As such it has found its way to the very start of this collection. The earlier group of poems then comes towards the middle, and the 2009 set is at the end. Thus the miscellany begins and ends with poetry and in the middle – at its heart – you will find poetry as well.

But before going on to say any more about the contents of the book I had better say something about its title, a title chosen by the author. I have said something about Moseley and you will probably have worked out that all these writings belong to Sangharakshita's Moseley period. They constitute, in fact, writings from that period that have not appeared elsewhere in book form. But what exactly is a 'miscellany'? Though readers of past ages would have had no difficulty recognizing the term, some of today's readers may need a little help. A miscellany is simply a collection of writings of different kinds by one or more authors. Apparently in medieval times a miscellany might include recipes and legal documents as well as verse and prose. This miscellany does not include any recipes but it does include part of a Will as well as a wide variety of writing, from the poetry I have already mentioned to the prose about which I will say more below. Miscellanies were at their height during the eighteenth century when a great many were published. As the eighteenth century is the century of Dr Johnson, one of Sangharakshita's Five Literary Heroes, it seems fitting to make a connection, through the title, with that literary era.

To get back to the contents of this modern miscellany: between the two sets of poems, making up the second half of the book, are four quite distinct kinds of writing. First comes *Looking Back* which has already been mentioned. It tells the rather extraordinary story of how Sangharakshita came across the Lingwood Family Papers on the very first day of his search for traces of his paternal ancestors. Based on what he discovered in those papers, he writes about the lives of some of those great and great-great etc. grandparents, his Suffolk forebears, and concludes with some reflections. (What, I wonder, might be discovered should someone go looking for his mother's Hungarian ancestors? Perhaps one day somebody will....)

Then comes a change of mode with nine book reviews: eight short ones first published in the *Times Higher Educational Supplement* between 1997 and 2002; and the substantial review of Stephen Batchelor's

*Buddhism Without Beliefs* in which Sangharakshita questions some of the views behind Batchelor's ideas, at one point calling upon no less a person than Lewis Carroll's Alice to help make the position clear.

Ayya Khema became a good friend of Sangharakshita towards the end of her life after they both attended the European Buddhist Union Congress in Berlin in 1992, to which they had been invited as Western Buddhist teachers. His personal tribute to her was published – in German translation – in the *Gedenkschrift* (commemorative volume) brought out after her death in 1997. It appears for the first time here in the original English.

Among the collection of poems written in 2009 there was one, 'An Apology', which, Sangharakshita told me, did not really count as a poem. Rather, it was 'a kind of manifesto'. In those few lines are expressed the shame of modern man who has desecrated his own planet and caused harm and destruction on so many fronts. The last line is perhaps most surprising of all.

These, then, are the writings that come between the two groups of poems which together constitute the second half of the book. But what of the writings that come between the initial poem, 'The Wind', and the first set of poems? It is time to say something about those.

It is common in old age to recall with vividness the experiences of childhood. In *My First Eight Years*, his 'mosaic of memories' written in 2010, Sangharakshita recounts some of his own childhood memories with something of the child's simplicity and directness so that one finds oneself transported to the South London of the 1920s and 30s; and into the child's mind – a child whose experiences were, I think, exceptionally vivid. These recollections supplement those recounted in 'Giants and Dragons', the first chapter of his memoir *The Rainbow Road*. The reader will notice I have not added many notes to this text, not wanting to interrupt with too much extra information the atmosphere that belongs to early childhood.

A reverie is said to be a composition suggestive of a dream-like or musing state. In such a state thoughts and images, memories and ideas, arise and lead on to others by way of association. To engage in reverie might also be said to be an old man's occupation. But if that old man has spent a whole life in the Dharma, what then? In the eight *Reveries and Reminiscences*, composed when the author was eighty-five and eighty-six, we find out. Each begins with a memory, a thought, or an idea: 'Above the mantelpiece of my study…'; 'Every language is unique …'; or 'How big is God?' – a question he had pondered as a boy. Having posed the question, we are led on to consider how 'big' and 'great' are sometimes not distinguished, the one coming to stand for the other, and so to the Bamiyan Buddhas that were blasted by the Taliban. From there it is a short step to a consideration of what Sangharakshita calls 'principled vandalism' and iconoclasm. Having taken his reader to London's National Gallery and the Brighton Pavilion for further examples of such vandalism, and with a brief glimpse of two men jumping on Tracey Emin's Bed in the Tate Modern, we are brought with a wonderfully unexpected U-turn of thought from the negatively destructive to the positive, and so to the world of Madhyamaka Buddhism. In a single short piece we find memory, observation, critical comment, art, and Dharmic exposition all present.

Yes, in the course of these eight pieces the reader is given a glimpse into Sangharakshita's mind. Sometimes when reading them I felt as if I had wandered into a cathedral: far above, the lofty vaults supported by mighty pillars; below, the crypt with its treasure of ages, and everywhere side chapels, each with its own particular icons and precious objects. Just as the gaze in a cathedral can roam freely upwards to great heights and down again, along the aisles and nave and into the nooks and crannies, so as I entered the world of the *Reveries*, it seemed I was in touch with a freedom to roam with the author, ideas, images, intimations, teachings – world within world yet all coherently opening one into another: now we were in his mother's kitchen in the 1930s, now at an incense burning party in the 1960s, and now in the esoteric world of a Mahayana sutra beyond all time and space – all within a few paragraphs. So that at the same time as communicating something transcendent, these pieces bring us close to the author personally, the tone is almost intimate so that one feels one has come in and sat down opposite him in his room with a view, and is now listening as this friend and teacher shares his latest musings.

But these eight pieces are not just *Reveries*; they are also *Reminiscences* and, particularly in the first three, we are able to read Sangharakshita's own account of notable times in his own life and in the life of the movement he founded; and the development of a notable friendship.

These, then, are the pieces which together make up this miscellany of writings, prose and verse, written during Sangharakshita's time in Moseley.

Perhaps we are left with just one question: is there anything else which connects all these diverse writings? I think perhaps there is. If there is a single note to which everything in the author's life returns, it is the wish to spread the Dharma as widely as possible. Spreading or communicating the Dharma may be done, you could say, in two ways. There is giving the teachings, explaining the principles, clarifying Right View (and challenging Wrong View). His verbal and written teachings are very many and there are plenty to be found – in less traditional guise, perhaps – in this collection. But there is also personal example. The example of one whose life is dedicated to the Dharma is not an example of idealized perfection standing above and beyond the highs and lows, the happiness and sorrow, the complexities of human life; rather it is the example of one who, within that human reality, goes for Refuge to the Three Jewels that lie in a sense beyond it. In the present collection we are privileged to get a close-up view of one who very deeply indeed goes for Refuge to the Buddha, the Dharma, and the Sangha. In letting ourselves come into contact with him, we may come away changed.

# The Wind

# I

## The Wind

A wind was in my sails. It blew
Stronger and fiercer hour by hour.
I did not know from whence it came,
Or why. I only knew its power.

Sometimes it dashed me on the rocks,
Sometimes it spun me round and round.
Sometimes I laughed aloud for joy,
Sometimes I felt a peace profound.

It drove me on, that manic wind,
When I was young. It drives me still
Now I am old. It lives in me,
Its breath my breath, its will my will.

**My First Eight Years:** A Mosaic of Memories

# My First Eight Years: A Mosaic of Memories

## Neighbours and Early Friends

Our nearest neighbours were the Hartnells who lived in the flat below ours. There was old Mrs Hartnell, her son Fred, and Fred's wife Florrie. There was also Roy, a ginger-haired dog of medium size and no particular breed who was very much a member of the family. Roy liked to lie on the tiled area before the flat's twin front doors. My sister and I had played with him since our earliest years, for he was a good-tempered old dog and never minded how much we tugged at his collar or fondled his soft, velvety-brown ears. He was also a dog of regular habits. At 4 o'clock every afternoon he would go padding up the road to Marsden's Dairy, which was on the corner, only five or six doors away, from whence he would return carrying in his mouth a bar of Nestlé's Milk Chocolate. This he would deposit at the feet of Mrs Hartnell who would remove the wrapper for him and tell him he was a good boy. On Friday she would go to the dairy herself and settle the week's bill on Roy's behalf. Mrs Hartnell was indeed a kind old lady. The horse who drew the milk float got his daily lump of sugar as regularly as Roy got his bar of choco-late. Our family photograph album contained a snapshot of the horse with his forelegs up on the pavement taking the sugar from Mrs Hartnell's outstretched hand.

I remember her very well. Auntie Hartnell, as my sister and I called her, was a widow, and always wore black. (I remember being told that old Mr Hartnell was ill, but I have no recollection of his funeral.) Of medium height, she was slightly built, had a yellowish complexion, brown eyes, and a head covered with small dark curls. She was certainly very kind to Joan and me. When she made a fruit trifle, for example, there would always be a portion for us, which she would bring up to us in two cut-glass tumblers. She was also concerned that we should not be upset or frightened, so that when, one sultry July afternoon, there exploded overhead the mother of all thunderstorms with continual loud rumblings and crashes of thunder and repeated brilliant flashes of lightning, she insisted that we be brought down to what she seemed to think was the greater security of her kitchen, where she distracted us with tea and biscuits until the storm was over.

Uncle Fred was fairly tall, and rather thin. He had a pale, bony face, and thinning hair brushed straight back. He was a bespoke tailor, and I sometimes wandered down to see him at work in the Hartnell kitchen, slipping through the communicating door in the hallway, which was usually left unbolted. More often than not, I found him sitting cross-legged on the kitchen table, which was set lengthwise against the room's only window for the sake of the light. I do not remember him ever talking to me, but he sometimes gave me a piece of tailor's chalk to play with. My father knew him quite well, for they had grown up together, and gone to the same school, the turquoise cupolas of which could be seen from our front gate. (It was to this same school that I started going, unwillingly, when I was four years old.) My father thought Fred Hartnell a milksop, averring that when he was a boy his mother mollycoddled him to such an extent that in the morning she used to sit on the toilet seat to warm it for him before he got up. He also told me that as a young man Fred had been quite a dandy. When he went out he wore pin-stripe trousers, a black tailcoat, and spats, and sported a top hat, on account of which he had been nicknamed the Duke of Selincourt, Selincourt being the name of the street in which we lived. Thus attired he had courted and won his wife Florrie, though how and where was not known, having apparently led her to believe that he had money in the bank and a house of his own. It was, therefore, a cruel disappointment to her when she discovered, after the wedding, that he lived with his parents in a rented ground floor flat in Tooting, and that this was her new home. The marriage was not a happy one. There were frequent quarrels, which from time to time were so violent, and so loud, that my father had to go downstairs, taking advantage of the communicating door, and try to calm things down.

While I have vivid mental pictures of old Mrs Hartnell and Fred, I have no such picture of Florrie Hartnell. I do, however, remember her as being dark-haired and olive-complexioned, which in later years suggested to me that she may have been of Italian, or partly Italian, descent. Despite her unhappiness, she was kind to my sister and me, so that it is all the more unfortunate that she should have been the unwitting cause of the most unpleasant experience of my early childhood. Playing one day in the porch, I chose to press my cheek against the wall between the two front doors, at the same time spreading out my arms, as though in an embrace, until my fingers touched the doors, both of which were half open. Auntie Florrie was at home at the time, and happening to notice that the front door had been left open she closed it, thereby trapping my hand between the door-jamb and the hinged side of the door. On hearing my shrieks of agony, she opened the door to see what was the matter, thus freeing my hand, the third finger of which was crushed and bleeding. The upshot was that for the next two weeks or more Auntie Florrie came upstairs every morning to change the dressing on my injured finger, sitting with me at the kitchen table to do so. I well remember the sessions. First I immersed my finger in a tumbler of hot water so as to loosen the old dressing prior to its removal. This was the most painful part of the proceedings and took a long time. Eventually, however, it was over, and the finger could be examined for signs of improvement and given a fresh dressing, after which I would be free to go and play.

The Harveys lived a couple of doors away, in the direction of the school. There were four of them. The one we saw the most was Mrs Harvey, who was at home all day and could often be seen in their tiny back garden or leaning from their upstairs back window as she hung out her washing. She was a tall, well-built woman, who wore gold-rimmed spectacles, and whose smooth, ginger hair was pulled back into a bun. Mr Harvey was jovial and portly, and wore a gold watch-chain across his capacious stomach. A printer by trade, he was generally to be seen only at weekends. The couple had two teenage sons. As they were much older than us, Joan and I had little or no contact with them, and I do not even remember their names. As the grandest family in the street, the Harveys commanded a lot of respect. They did not own a car (nor did anyone in the street, or even in the neighbourhood), but the family enjoyed regular outings in a chauffeur-driven hired car, on which occasions the children of the neighbourhood would gather round the car and watch their departure with great interest.

The Harveys were not only the grandest family in the street. They were also probably the most literary. At least they took in the popular weekly, *Everybody's*, and when they had finished with it they passed it on to us. I do not remember if my parents read it but I certainly did. I particularly enjoyed the short accounts of striking events in the lives of famous people. These were written in what I later came to recognize as a journalistic style. Thus it was that a French king's discarded mistress 'scrawled on a sheet of scented parchment, "I have seen the man in black,"' rather than the more straightforward, 'wrote on a piece of paper,' etc. The Harveys had also taken in, week by week, the successive parts, sixty-one in all, of Harmsworth's *Children's Encyclopaedia*. When they learned that I had been diagnosed as having valvular disease of the heart, they very generously gave me the entire set. For this kind act they have my undying gratitude. For the next two years and more the *Children's Encyclopaedia* was my constant companion, turning what might otherwise have been a period of gloomy imprisonment into a time of enrichment and enjoyment, and opening up for me all the treasures of the human spirit.[1]

At a gate midway between the Hartnells' flat and Marsden's Dairy, there often stood, immobile, a stout, middle-aged woman in a pinafore. She never spoke to anyone, and so far as I remember no one ever spoke to her. It was as though she was waiting for someone who never came. This was Mrs Hoare. Joan and I were very conscious of her presence at the gate, for one side of her face was entirely covered by a reddish-brown birth mark. Rather unkindly, we called her 'fishpaste-face', for the birthmark was of the same colour as the fishpaste we had for Sunday afternoon tea, along with watercress, celery, and winkles.

The neighbour who was on the most intimate terms with us, in a sense, was red-faced Thomas Whitehead. He was close to us on two counts. Not only was he my godfather, he was also a close friend of my grandmother, and the two old people used to go on outings together. Being a little pitcher, and having a little pitcher's proverbially long ears, I knew that Uncle Tom had asked my grandmother to marry him, promising that if she did so he would make me his heir. She had no difficulty resisting this temptation. She had buried two husbands, she told him bluntly, and she had no wish to bury a third. Uncle Tom therefore remained a bachelor. He lived on the other side of the road, almost directly opposite us. He lived with his niece Barbara, a small, thin woman with lank brown hair, a long red face, and a long red nose who always looked as though she had been crying. I often visited him in his room, the attraction being not so much Uncle Tom himself but the stuffed fox with a pigeon in its mouth, which occupied a glass case against the wall. I longed to possess this wonder, for the collecting instinct was already strong in me, and I believe my godfather had promised that the fox should be mine one day.

Uncle Tom often came to see us, being very much part of the family, especially at Christmas and on birthdays. On my own birthday he would seat me on his knee, tell me to hold out my hand, then slowly count into my palm as many half crowns as he felt disposed to give me. My father always paid this birthday money into the Post Office savings account he had opened for me soon after I was born, as he did with any money I was given when I was young. Forty years later, when I returned to England after an absence of twenty years in the East, I withdrew all the money. By then it amounted to a tidy sum, for my father had had the interest made up at the end of each year, and Uncle Tom's money went towards financing my 1966 travels in Italy and Greece. By then my godfather was long dead. He died when I was five or six and I disgraced myself in the eyes of the family by demanding, when I was told of his death, 'Shall I get the fox now?'

For the first four years of my life my playmates were Joan, who was fifteen months younger than me, and a lively little girl of my own age called Frances who lived next door to Marsden's Dairy. Later, my friends were boys of my own age who were in the same class as me at school or who lived in the same street. My principal friends at this time were

Gerald Inkpen and Robbie Rudd. Gerald lived in the next street, and I was often at his house. His mother and mine were friends, so that whenever my mother went to see Mrs Inkpen, who was a Rechabite,[2] I would go too, a circumstance which must have facilitated the development of my friendship with Gerald. He was taller than me, though no older, and we swapped cigarette cards and comics, roamed the streets together, and played with each other's lead soldiers and Meccano sets. Robbie Rudd lived in a ground floor flat at the end of the block, as an American would say. His father was a policeman, and he had a much older sister called Ivy. My mother and his mother were *not* friends. Littler pitcher that I was, I knew that Mrs Rudd had run away with another man, returning to her husband three weeks later rather worse for wear, and the other women who lived in the street tended to avoid her. Robbie said nothing to me about this, of course. He was a dark-haired boy of my own age, reserved rather than shy, and fond of reading. Since he lived so near, I saw more of him than I did of Gerald, so that his parents and sister were used to seeing me around. On entering their kitchen one day I saw four or five black kittens crawling about on the floor. I had not seen kittens before, and the sight of the helpless little creatures gave rise to an emotion I could not then have described. It was compounded of surprise, delight, curiosity, and pity. I have always loved animals. During the four years before, and the four years after, my confinement to bed, I had a variety of pets. They included two guinea pigs, a pair of green budgerigars, two white mice (soon there were forty of them), and half a dozen lizards caught on Wimbledon Common. Later I had a frog, and a toad who liked to have his neck scratched.

When my two years of confinement to bed were at length over, and I was able to lead a more or less normal life, I discovered that Gerald and Robbie were no longer around. Robbie's parents had moved to a council house in another part of Tooting, and what had happened to Gerald I never learned. I therefore had to make new friends. This was not easy, as I was not allowed to run, or even to walk fast, and therefore could not join in sports or games. A few friends I did make, however, mostly among my classmates. There was Leonard Westward, who was better dressed than most of the other boys, Alec Havell, who had a hare lip, Owen Wheeler, who liked to run round the playground with out-stretched arms pretending to be an aeroplane, Freddie Timmins, whose father was the local chimney sweep, Douglas Nicholas, who was a cry-baby, and whom I once rescued from a group of boys who were bullying him, and ginger-haired Raymond Parratt, who collected American postage stamps. I, too, collected postage stamps, but not American ones, and I wondered why anyone would want to collect the stamps of a country as uninteresting as America. I favoured the more exotic varieties, such as the orange-and-purple, high denomination stamps, with the king-emperor's head in the middle, that came affixed to the parcels received by the family from Uncle Dick, my mother's youngest brother, who was stationed in India.

In 1936 I moved with my parents and my sister to a council house in the same part of Tooting where Robbie now lived. It was not long before we resumed our friendship, which lasted until, in the second year of the War, I was evacuated to North Devon.

## In the Classroom

Mrs Davis was my teacher when I was in the top class of the Selincourt Road Infant School. She was stout, grey-haired, and motherly, and like the other teachers she wore a housecoat to protect her dress from the clouds of chalk dust that flew from the blackboard whenever it was wiped clean. Her housecoat had a pattern of brown leaves and yellow flowers, and I have a mental picture of her in it as she sat at her desk in front of the class trying to thread a needle. Her eyes bulged as she focused her gaze on the eye of the needle and the tip of the thread, and I could see that the whites of her eyes were yellow.

The upper half of the classroom door was glassed in like a window, while across the lower half of the window there hung a short curtain. One day Mrs Davis painted this curtain with broad vertical stripes of all the colours of the rainbow, as it seemed. This gave a touch of brightness and gaiety to the rather drab classroom, as no doubt she had intended.

I did not learn very much while I was in Mrs Davis's class. I have vague recollections of white cards printed with such sentences as 'the cat sat on the mat', of our chanting the multiplication tables in unison, of scripture lessons, and of our teacher reading to us some of the Enid Blyton stories, none of which I remember, a fact that suggests I did not find them very interesting. One autumn afternoon she wrote on the blackboard the lines:

> *Please to remember the fifth of November,*
> *Gunpowder, treason and plot.*

She did not tell us anything about Guy Fawkes, or about the nature of the famous plot, but she did want to know if anyone could read the words 'remember' and 'November', pointing to them with her ruler as she put the question. I was the only one who could do so, for some of the other children were still struggling with 'the cat sat on the mat', whereas I had no difficulty with words, and by this time was reading such classic children's books as *Black Beauty*, *The Water Babies*, and *The Swiss Family Robinson*.

We had no formal singing lessons, but in the course of the term Mrs Davis taught us a few songs. One song touched me deeply, but it was not the simple tune that affected me so much as the words. The song was a lullaby, sung by a mother to her baby, and the second verse ran:

> *Sleep and rest, sleep and rest,*
> *Father will come to thee soon;*
> *Rest, rest, on mother's breast,*
> *Father will come to thee soon;*
> *Father will come to his babe in the nest,*
> *Silver sails all out of the West*
> *Under the silver moon.* [3]

When we came to the words 'silver sails all out of the West' I experienced a thrill of intense delight, and there flashed upon my inner eye a vision of bright silver sails. What was more, those silver sails came not from a particular point of the compass but from somewhere beyond all geography. This was one of my earliest experiences of the magic of poetry, as well as of my capacity to match its images with vivid mental pictures of my own.

Although there were both boys and girls in Mrs Davis's class, I do not remember any of the boys. On the other hand I do remember two of the girls. Indeed, I remember them extremely well. Daphne Taylor was an ash blonde with green eyes, white skin, and a slightly prominent nose. Sometimes we shared the same desk, and on one memorable occasion we simultaneously bent down, as if searching for a fallen pencil, and under cover of the desk kissed each other on the lips. Daphne's lips were deliciously soft, and meeting them with my own was definitely a sensuous, even sensual experience, though not at all sexual. I liked Daphne, but I was much fonder of her friend Gladys Gown, who was as shy as Daphne was forward. Whether I knew it then or not I was in love with Gladys. A little taller than Daphne, and quite slim, she had straight fair hair, blue eyes, and a small nose and small mouth. I thought of her constantly. So much so, that at night, in bed, I used to pretend that my big teddy bear was Gladys and would hug him for a few minutes before going to sleep. I called this ritual "Gladys's love".

Shortly after moving from the top class of the Infant School to the bottom class of the Junior School, and from the care of Mrs Davis to that of Miss Browne, I came down first with scarlet fever, then with chicken-pox, and spent three weeks in hospital. When my mother came to take me home one of the nurses told her that my pulse was unusually fast and that I should be taken to see a doctor without delay. The result was that I was found to be suffering from valvular disease of the heart and my parents were told that I must be put to bed and kept absolutely quiet, this being the standard treatment at the time for my condition. For the next two years, therefore, I was confined to bed, seeing no one except my parents. This was followed by six months in a wheel-chair. I was then deemed well enough to go back to school. I had not forgotten Gladys, and looked forward to seeing her again with great eagerness. I went back to Miss Browne's class, which was the Junior School's top class, but Gladys was not there. When I did see her I received a shock. She wore a navy-blue beret and a short black coat, and was not only taller than before but so thin as to be positively skinny. What was worse, in their black stockings her thin legs looked like the black hairy legs of a spider (not that I disliked spiders). I fell as quickly out of love as I had fallen *in* love three years earlier. It was one of the biggest disappointments of my young life.

## Outings

We were up 'in the gods' together. There were six of us: my mother, Joan and I, and my mother's friend Margaret and her two children – Rita, who was the same age as me, and Mavis, who was the same age as Joan. We were up there with our bottles of lemonade and our buns. It was Christmas time, we were at the Wimbledon Hippodrome, and I was seeing my first pantomime. From where I sat I had a clear view of the stage far below. The pantomime was 'Shock-headed Peter', a character of whom I had not heard before. I do not remember what the story was, but I well remember the small figure of the pantomime's eponymous hero. He wore a black jacket with a belt, and black breeches, and he had an enormous shock of white hair. On the stage there was also a well. As I watched, Peter jumped into the bucket that hung above the well and *disappeared from sight*. I was overwhelmed by feelings of indescribable horror and dread. It was as though Peter had descended into unfathomable Tartarean depths and was lost forever. I expect he reappeared later on in the pantomime, but of this I have no recollection. For me his disappearance must have been absolute, and the feeling of horror and dread must have persisted for some time. I do, however, remember the pantomime's 'principal boy'. I remember her singing 'Whistling in the Dark', a song which evoked in me an eerie feeling of loneliness and desolation.

Christmas was also the time when Joan and I visited one of the big department stores in Tooting Bec, or Balham, or Brixton, to meet Santa Claus. It was always our mother who took us, for our father detested shops and shopping. Dazzled by the myriad lights and deafened by the noise we would push our way through the milling crowds to where Santa

Claus sat or stood at the entrance to his magic grotto, his sack of presents beside him. He was dressed from head to foot in red, and his abundant white beard reached down to his waist. In return for our sixpences he dipped into his sack and gave Joan a pink package and me a blue one and we were allowed to enter the grotto, where we saw not only more lights but all manner of wonders, from Santa's sledge and his two reindeer (were they real?), to huge Christmas trees hung with tinsel and silver bells and topped with a glittering star or no less glittering fairy. On reaching home we would open the presents Santa Claus had given us. One Christmas Joan's contained a small celluloid doll, mine a tin whistle.

Although our father never took us to see Santa Claus, he certainly took us out – particularly me. One grey Saturday afternoon he took me to see a football match. We went with Uncle Jack, my mother's brother, who was a staunch Fulham supporter. The match was at White City, a name that conjured up a vivid mental image for me. Though for much of the time I sat perched on my father's right shoulder, which I was still small enough to be able to do, I could see little or nothing of the game, with the result that I did not enjoy the outing. Moreover, there was a drizzle of rain, and I felt cold and wet. I must have expressed my dissatisfaction to my father afterwards, for he did not take me to a football match again. My first football match was therefore also my last.

A black ditch, and across the ditch a wooden plank. My father and I had to walk over the plank in order to get to Figge's Marsh and to the fair that was in progress there. It was a new experience for me, and as we wandered in and out of the good-natured holiday crowd, I with my hand firmly in my father's, I took in eagerly the unfamiliar sights and sounds. Roundabouts whirled to the music of the mechanical organ, the riders of the brightly-painted wooden animals screaming with laughter; swinging-boats carried people high into the air. We passed coconut shies and shooting galleries, passed purveyors of bright pink candyfloss and vendors of balloons. I was particularly attracted by the stalls where, for a single penny, one could win a big box of chocolates. These stalls were circular in shape, the proprietor standing in the middle, entirely surrounded by his counter. On the counter there was laid out a tempting array of large and small boxes of chocolates. From behind a barrier one tossed a penny on to the counter, aiming for one of the boxes of chocolates. If your penny landed on the box and stayed there, it was yours. With pennies supplied by my father I made several attempts to win one of the boxes, but even if it hit the box I had chosen it bounced or rolled off it onto the counter. As we turned away from the stall, my father and I, a man walked past carrying an enormous teddy bear he had won. Some people were luckier than others, it seemed.

The fair at Figge's Marsh was a new and exciting experience for me, and it is not surprising that I should have vivid memories of it, but I have an equally vivid memory of an experience of a very different kind, albeit one still connected with the fair. My father and I happened to pass by a small tent, and seeing that the front was open we looked in. Seated at a small table were two midgets, a man and a woman. Though fully grown, they were no bigger than I was then at five or six. They were folding leaflets, working steadily and silently. Neither of them looked up at us or showed any sign of being aware of our presence. They just carried on folding the leaflets. The sight was infinitely touching, and the image of the two midgets at their task haunted me for a long, long time.

… I was inside the Big Top. I do not remember how I got there, or who took me there, but I was inside the Big Top, eyes fixed on the arena below, oblivious to everything else. White horses trotted round the arena at the command of a man wearing a top hat and carrying a long whip; an elephant did ponderous tricks; red-nosed clowns in white made me laugh at their antics. But best of all were the Japanese acrobats. They ran nimbly up and down the high wire, a parasol helping them to keep their balance. From time to time one of them let out a tremendous shout in a language I did not understand. Another pretended to be about to fall off the wire but recovered himself in the nick of time with miraculous agility. Yet another ran up to the top of the wire then slid all the way down to the bottom holding his parasol triumphantly aloft as he did so. It was a glorious time I had, inside the Big Top that day.

Like other London children, Joan and I were taken to see the animals in the London Zoo. This was a family outing, in that it was both our parents who took us to the famous institution. We saw the Chimpanzees' Tea Party, had a ride on the back of an elephant with our father while our mother watched anxiously from below, and saw a polar bear stand on its hind legs to receive a stream of condensed milk which someone on the terrace above poured into its open mouth. These and a hundred other sights I shared not only with Joan and my parents but also with tens of thousands of other visitors to the London Zoo. Three of those sights made a stronger impression on me, perhaps, than they did on other people. The macaw is a gorgeous bird, but there was not just one of them. There were a dozen or more in a row, all on their individual perches, all preening themselves in the sunlight. It was the most brilliant display of colour I had ever seen. But if the gorgeous macaws impinged on my sense of sight, the occupants of the Big Cat House impinged less on my sight than on my sense of smell. It was not that I paid no attention to the lions, tigers and leopards, as that I was much less conscious of what they looked like than of how they smelt. Their combined stench was indeed overwhelming, and not easily forgotten. There was also Monkey Hill. It was surrounded by a moat and a parapet and inhabited by two or three dozen monkeys, all of the same species. The monkeys were always on the move. They ran up and down the hill, darted in and out of its caves, chased one another, and even sometimes fought. One monkey did not move about much. It was a female, and she sat there clasping a baby monkey in her thin arms. It did not take me long to realize that the baby was dead, had perhaps been dead for some time, and that the mother was refusing to part with the body. It was a pathetic sight, and must have moved me deeply, for forty years later, when I had long forgotten it, and when I was in a distant place and in a strange situation, the image of the mother monkey clasping her dead baby suddenly surfaced, as I have related elsewhere.[4]

Another family outing was the day trip we took from London Bridge to Clacton-on-Sea on a steamship of the Eagle Line. I spent much of the voyage leaning on the rail watching the Thames slowly widen as we moved downstream. It was the first time I had been on the water. On our arrival at Clacton-on-Sea I saw that the beach was jam-packed with people, which I suppose was the reason why we did not go there. At least I have no recollection of our going. All I remember is that we spent some time in the town, then boarded the ship for the return journey. When my grandmother gave me a model yacht on my seventh birthday I named it White Eagle, this being the name of the steamship that had taken us to Clacton-on-Sea. The yacht had adjustable sails and a polished wooden deck, and my father used to take me to Clapham Common so that I could sail it on the pond there. Once a dog swam out to it, seized it in its jaws, and returned with it to the shore. The yacht bore the mark of the dog's teeth on its deck for the rest of its days.

Not all my childhood outings were as exhilarating as my visits to the circus or the zoo. There were also outings of a quieter character. Most of them were with my father, who in those days was often out of work. I liked being with my father, for he always talked to me, and told me things. Several times he took me with him to the employment exchange (as I think it was) at Tooting Bec. There he always saw the same person. Her name was Mrs Cheeseman, and she always gave me a chocolate drop. There were also trips to Mitcham Common, where I fished for stickle-backs in the pond, and occasionally to the more distant Raynes Park. When he was in work he sometimes took me to his workplace on Satur-day mornings, from where we would go somewhere in the afternoon. Once he took me to Bennett's Yard, which was somewhere in the City. We climbed up a wooden outside staircase into a kind of loft where four or five men were at work. They must have been carpenters, for I remem-ber that the floor was ankle-deep in wood shavings. Another time he was working at Dean's Yard, Westminster, and one Saturday afternoon we visited the Abbey. I do not remember the monuments, but I well remem-ber seeing the very lifelike funeral effigy of Queen Elizabeth. I was no stranger to Good Queen Bess for I had already come across her in a story book, where she was depicted seated in a chair and wearing the familiar farthingale and ruff. My father bought me a picture postcard of her effigy, and I added it to my postcard collection. She has always been my favourite historical character. Another Saturday afternoon found us at the Natural History and Science Museums in South Kensington. I was tremendously impressed by the 100-foot long skeleton of a Brontosaurus and by

Leonardo da Vinci's winged flying-machines. We also saw the stuffed animals. Among them was the famous War Office Cat, an exceptionally large tabby. As a very small child he had ridden on its back, my father told me, for his father had worked in the War Office, and his mother had sometimes taken him there. I cannot vouch for the truth of what he said about his riding the War Office Cat, for my father was an inveterate teller of tall stories, which he always told with a perfectly straight face. When Joan and I were quite small, he once told us that when he first met our mother she was so thin that she could get through a keyhole. Naturally we believed him and spent the next half hour carefully studying the keyhole of the kitchen door and trying to work out how our mother had managed to get through.

## Shops and Shopping

My earliest memories of shopping are connected with my mother. We are walking along the street together, and she is carrying a shopping basket. Every few yards, as it seems to me, my mother meets someone she knows, and the two women stop to talk. They talk, and talk, and talk, and soon I am tugging at my mother's hand and saying impatiently, 'Oh, come *on*, Mum!' until finally she detaches herself and we continue our progress until she meets someone else or we enter a shop. It was one of the mysteries of my boyhood why women talked so much.

I remember some of the shops we entered by their smell. In one there was the cool, fresh smell of cheese and butter, in another the fusty smell of cloth, and in yet another the sickening smell of blood. This last was the smell that pervaded the butcher's shop, and so much did I dislike it that I insisted on waiting for her outside whenever my mother shopped there. There were also visits to Tooting Market. It was a covered market, with stalls on either side of a central aisle. One of the stalls sold rabbit meat, and skinned and unskinned rabbits hung upside down from hooks. Only later did I realize that there was a connection between them and the rabbit stew we occasionally had for lunch. One morning we learned that there had been a fire at Tooting Market and that much of it had been destroyed. The next time I went there with my mother only the first few stalls were open for business. The rest of the market was a tangle of charred and blackened beams.

My mother did not always take me with her when she went shopping. Sometimes she left me in the flat on my own, with the admonition that I was not to answer the door if anyone knocked or rang the bell. As soon as she was gone I would crawl under the kitchen table, for the tablecloth hung down on all four sides, thus making a tent in which I could hide. As I could not yet read, I amused myself by scribbling with crayons on the unpolished underside of the table. More often than not there would be no unexpected callers, but if the silence of the flat did happen to be suddenly broken by a knock or a ring, I would sit frozen with terror, imagining that someone or some*thing* horrible had managed to open the front door and was slowly creeping up the stairs. If the knock or the ring was not repeated I would gradually relax and the pounding of my heart would slow down. Only when I heard the front door open and my mother's familiar step on the stairs did I crawl out of my hiding place and sit on the floor, as if I had been there all the time. I never told my mother about the terror I had felt, probably because I did not have the words with which to describe my feelings.

Though my father disliked shops and shopping, there was at least one shop to which he did not mind going. This was the little toy shop in Tooting Bec, to which he took me from time to time. When quite young I had been given a wooden fort, complete with brightly-painted lead soldiers, but I was not particularly fond of soldiers and did little to add to their number. On the other hand, I was hardly less fond of lead animals than I was of their flesh and blood originals, and was always wanting to add to my collection. Hence the visits to the little shop in Tooting Bec with my father. By the time I was seven or eight I had a sizeable collection of lead animals of various kinds. My favourites among the wild animals were a giraffe, a kangaroo, and an elephant. The elephant came complete with a howdah, which could be placed on its back, and on which six tiny human figures could sit, three on each side – just like their real life counterparts at the Zoo. I also had a whole farmyard of domesticated animals, including a pig, piglets, a sheep, a bull, and a duck and ducklings. Sometimes I made a farmyard for these animals, with cardboard painted green for grass and a piece of mirror for a pond. I would then amuse myself arranging and rearranging them within the imaginary fences of the little farmyard until I was satisfied – or until the table had to be cleared for a meal.

Once I was taken shopping by my grandmother. Nana, as my sister and I called her, often came to see us on a Saturday afternoon, after she had been to Wandsworth Cemetery and placed fresh flowers on the grave of her second husband and their only daughter, who had died very young. It was in the course of one of these visits that she took me shopping with her. My sister wanted to have a black doll. She already had a white doll, called Muriel, but she very much wanted a black doll too and Nana had promised to buy her one. We did not have to go very far or search for long. At the entrance to one of the shops in Mitcham Road there was a large basket full of dolls of various kinds. Among the dolls there were several black ones, and one of these Nana bought. It cost her a shilling. Joan was delighted with the new doll, whom she christened Topsy. Thereafter she spent many happy hours playing with her two dolls, dressing and undressing them, putting them to bed when they were ill, and giving them medicine, and scolding them when they were naughty. In short, she loved both her dolls dearly and treated them equally without the least help from any Commission for Racial Equality.

There were two shops in the neighbourhood with which I was particularly well acquainted. One was the dairy at the top end of the street; the other the sweetshop that was just round the corner opposite the dairy. I was familiar with the dairy because my mother sometimes sent me there for an extra pint of milk, and old Mrs Marsden, who was usually behind the counter, knew me as well as I knew her. One day she gave me a pair of Oxo spectacles. They were an advertising gimmick on behalf of the well-known beverage, but I did not know this, and wore them proudly until they fell apart. At the dairy I naturally encountered other customers. One of them was a very old woman dressed from head to foot in rusty black. She had a yellow face and yellow, claw-like hands, and she emitted a horrible smell. I never learned who she was or where she came from and probably thought it better not to ask. The sweetshop was an Aladdin's Cave of multicoloured confectionery. Besides chocolate bars and other more expensive items, there were sherbet dabs, liquorice sticks, jelly babies, and scores of other sweets the names of which I have forgotten. The pleasure was not just in buying but in choosing, and I spent a lot of time deciding what I wanted. In those days, when there were two ha'pennies to a penny, or four farthings, one could get quite a lot of sweets for a penny, and like other boys I wanted to get as many sweets for my money as I could.

## Nana

Everyone has two parents, four grandparents, and eight great-grand-parents, but not everyone is brought up knowing them all. Apart from my parents, I knew only my father's mother and *her* mother, all the rest having died before I was born. I was my grandmother's first grandchild, and I was very much part of her life, as she was part of mine. In the family photo album there is a picture of her standing in the porch of her house in Southfields and holding me in her arms. I am still wearing long clothes, and she is smiling at me.

As a small child I sometimes stayed for a few days with Nana and Auntie Noni, Nana's unmarried daughter, who lived with her. A little bed was made up for me on the floor in the corner of the big downstairs bedroom they shared. When I was older I shared a bed with Uncle Charles, my father's much younger half-brother, who still lived at home, and who had a room upstairs. In the morning I watched him exercising with a pair of chest expanders, and once he gave me a blue and white school tie.

Nana lived not far from Wimbledon Park, and whenever I stayed with her she and Auntie Noni took me to feed the ducks who lived in the pond there. On the way we passed the local tennis courts, the entrance to which was flanked by enormous clumps of tall African grass, and where people in white could usually be seen playing. In the background, high up on the embankment, the red carriages of the District Line trains sped back and forth, their wheels going *clickety-click, clickety-click* as they passed. Among the ducks swimming on the pond, there floated a pair of swans, probably the first I ever saw.

It was Nana and Auntie Noni who took me on my first journey by train. I was then three or four years old. Our destination was Besthorpe, the Norfolk village where Nana had been born and where my father had spent several years of his childhood. At Attleborough we alighted and soon the three of us were walking along the road to Besthorpe. While Nana and Auntie Noni chatted, I ran on ahead, darting from one side of the road to the other excitedly plucking flowers from the hedgerows. We had not gone very far when from the opposite direction there came an old countryman on a bicycle, a sack of potatoes over one shoulder. Just then I happened to spot some flowers growing in the hedgerow opposite, and at once darted eagerly towards them. Unfortunately I did not look both ways first, as I had often been told I must do before crossing the road, and ran smack into the bicycle and its rider. The old countryman lost his balance and fell off his bicycle, and the sack burst open, spilling potatoes all over the road. As for me, I was knocked unconscious, and had to be carried to Besthorpe and my great-grandmother's cottage.

I did not know all this at the time, of course. I came to know it later because my father was fond of relating how he had seen Nana, Auntie Noni, and me off at Liverpool Street station, and how after the train's departure he had heaved a sigh of relief, thinking that whatever mischief I might get up to in the Norfolk countryside I was at least in no danger of being run over, as I certainly was in London owing to my habit of running out into the road without looking first to see if it was safe to do so. Evidently he had underestimated my capacity for getting into mischief, he would ruefully observe, after which he would recount the details of the accident as he had heard them from Nana and Auntie Noni.

The first thing I can remember after regaining consciousness was being given a boiled egg for my tea. The reason why I remember this is that the egg had two yolks, and as I had never seen such an egg before I thought it a wonderful thing.

In an upstairs room, probably the one in which I stayed, there hung an enormous crinoline. By some coincidence, I was given a children's book to look at in which ladies were depicted wearing just such crinolines over a pair of long frilly pantaloons. In an adjacent room lay Auntie Fanny, who was probably one of Nana's sisters. She was an invalid, I was told, and bed-ridden. The room was darkened, and all I could make out was a thin white face and the white bedclothes.

One morning I was taken to see Aunt Luke, who lived in the nearby row of almshouses. Whose aunt she was I do not know, but she was very old, said how pale I was, and gave me a glass of elderberry wine.

My only other recollection of my first visit to Nana's ancestral village, was of being told that I should on no account go near the well. This well was situated at the end of a lane behind the cottage, and apparently it was assumed that if I was allowed to go near it, I would somehow manage to fall in.

I have no recollection of my great-grandmother, but I remember my mother speaking of her, some years later, as a little woman and as 'a dear old soul', and no doubt the description would have held good at the time of my visit. She died not long afterwards, and my father travelled to Besthorpe for the funeral. He was very fond of his grandmother, and in after years I more than once heard him say that if ever he became rich he would put a headstone on her grave.

One of the things I looked forward to on my visits to Southfields was the Camp Coffee which Nana put into my hot milk. It was a mixture of coffee and chicory, which we did not have at home, and I was particularly fond of the taste of this famous beverage. A label on one side of the bottle depicted a kilted soldier seated in front of his tent as his turbaned Indian bearer brought him his Camp Coffee on a tray. I also looked forward to seeing Uncle Leonard, one of my father's Lingwood cousins, whose shoe repair shop was just round the corner from where Nana lived. The first time I went there it was with Nana, who wanted to have some shoes re-soled, but thereafter I went on my own. I always found Uncle Leonard working at his bench in the shop. He was about the same age as my father, had a lot of untidy brown hair, was invariably unshaven, and had a pair of very bright eyes. He always treated me in a very friendly fashion, and I never visited him without his giving me a few coppers from the till. Under the counter would often be a litter of puppies, for Uncle Leonard bred Sealyhams, and I looked forward to seeing the puppies too. Sometimes I went through into the living quarters behind the shop to see stout and hospitable Auntie Louie and the three boys, the youngest of whom was about my own age, and sometimes I stayed for a meal.

I do not know if Nana had a Norfolk accent, but her voice had a lilt, and she certainly always said *shootin'* instead of 'shooting', and *Tootin'* instead of 'Tooting'. Though she had spent the greater part of her life in London, she was a countrywoman at heart. Once I was in the kitchen with her, Auntie Noni, and my mother when a mouse ran across the room. Auntie Noni and my mother screamed, jumped onto chairs, and lifted up their skirts; but Nana, like a true countrywoman, seized a poker, chased the mouse, cornered it at the bottom of a cupboard, and killed it.

Both Nana and Auntie Noni believed that my sister and I were growing up rather spoilt, and since both were outspoken by nature they did not hesitate to tell my father so. But all he would ever say in response to this criticism was, "Let them enjoy themselves. They are only young once."

## Illness and Accidents

On the horizon, close together, there are two reddish-brown cones. They gradually grow larger, then disappear behind the rooftops.... Then I am in a large room. There are squares of glass on the walls of the room, and behind the glass something is moving. It looks like a spider.... I am lying on my back in another, much smaller room. I am lying in a kind of cradle, and faces are looking down at me.

These are among my very earliest memories. The facts behind the memories are that I was lying back in my pram, looking out on the world, that my mother was taking me to the post-natal centre at St George's

Hospital, Tooting, and that the reddish-brown cones were the cowls on the hospital's chimneys. The large room was probably the waiting room, and the squares of glass were either pictures or aquaria, but I have no idea what the 'spider' behind the glass may have been. In the smaller room I was evidently being weighed, and the faces looking down at me must have been the faces of the doctors or nurses. Walking beside my mother, and also pushing a pram with an infant in it, there would have been her friend Margaret, whose daughter Rita was almost exactly the same age as I was. The two women may well have met for the first time at the post-natal centre. Auntie Margaret, as I called her, lived in Bickersteth Road, which lay at the end of Selincourt Road, and formed a T-junction with it. I remember once being at Margaret's house when Margaret was suckling her baby, which probably was not Rita, but her second daughter, Mavis. I thought the big, brown dug was rather an ugly sight. I must have already forgotten my own breast-feeding days!

There were other things I had forgotten by this time, but about which I heard later from my parents, usually from my father. Several of the experiences I had forgotten were painful ones. There was my vaccination by our GP, Dr Bradlaugh, when I was a baby. Even if my parents had not told me about the vaccination, there on my upper left arm were the four tell-tale scars, each the size of a fingerprint, which testified to the fact until I was well into my teens. Then there was the time when I burned my left foot by touching a hot flat iron. I was then a baby, and was sitting on the kitchen table while my mother was ironing clothes. When she went into the scullery to get more clothes for ironing I crawled towards the flat iron, which she had stood up on the table, and happened to touch it with my foot. My piercing screams brought her hurrying back to the kitchen to see what was the matter. What happened next I do not know. What I do know is that for many years I had a small scar on my foot. Above all, there was the unremembered time when my parents, Joan, and I all went down with the flu. It must have been in 1927 or 1928, when Joan was still a baby. The four of us lay helpless in the big front bedroom together. Dr Bradlaugh came every day, and my father gave him the key to the front door, as neither he nor my mother had the strength to go downstairs and let him in when he called. Old Mrs Hartnell, who lived in the flat below, came and cooked for us, though I suspect none of us had much appetite.

Not long after we had all recovered from the flu my father was away for three weeks. He had been sent to a convalescent home for ex-service-men in St Leonards, near Hastings, for the injuries he sustained during the War had left him without the full use of his right arm and right hand. I do not remember missing him while he was away, but I must have missed him greatly, especially at bedtime, as he always came to my room and talked to me for a while before I went to sleep. Though I have no recollection of his going away, I well remember his return. This was due partly to the fact that he had a present for me from a relative called Aunt Dick, of whom I had not heard before, and of whom I never heard again. She lived in Hastings, and was probably my father's cousin or aunt. Her present to me was a toy telephone, which gave me many hours of innocent pleasure. I derived no less pleasure from my father's account of life at the convalescent home. Afternoon tea was served out in the garden, and I particularly enjoyed his description of the birds that came to the table and pecked fearlessly about his and the other men's feet. There were not only the ubiquitous sparrows, but robins and blue tits, as well as finches of various kinds and colours. So graphically did my father describe the birds that in my mind's eye I had a vivid picture of them as they hopped on his table and fluttered round his feet in all their diverse colours.

Though I have only one actual recollection of experiencing pain myself (when my finger was caught in the Hartnells' front door), I have several memories of my mother suffering pain. Like many other working-class women she had bad teeth, and when she was about thirty she had them all out and replaced by false teeth (c.f. the pub scene in T.S. Eliot's *The Waste Land*, first published in 1922). On her return from the hospital she told my father what had happened, and Little Pitcher that I was I could not but overhear what she said. While under the anaesthetic she could hear someone screaming in the distance and realized that it was she herself who was doing the screaming. The nurse had scolded her when she came round, saying, 'Oh Mrs Lingwood, you *did* make a fuss!' The removal of the teeth made a great difference to my mother's appearance. Without them, she looked like an old woman, as she did afterwards whenever she took her false teeth out, which it was her custom to do at night. There was also the occasion when my mother treated herself to a 'permanent wave', and as a result experienced severe headaches for several days. The flat, regular waves of the perm made her face look thinner and younger, but it did not improve her looks. My mother was never beautiful, or even very pretty, but old or young, pretty or not pretty, I loved her and could not bear even to think of her being hurt.

Fortunately for us both, only once during my early childhood did I actually see her hurt. Our back stairs were quite steep, and my mother was down them and up them twenty times a day. One day she lost her footing on the way down and fell headlong to the bottom. Though she was not injured, she was badly shaken and could not help crying. The sight of her flushed, tear-stained face affected me deeply and remained a painful memory for a long time afterwards.

There was another accident in the family around this time. One morning the door bell rang and my mother went downstairs to see who was there, and I trailed along after her. On opening the front door she found herself face to face with a member of the St John's Ambulance Brigade, across whose outstretched arms there lay a small body so completely swathed in bandages as to look like an Egyptian mummy. My mother let out a shriek, and without waiting for explanations turned and dashed up the stairs calling loudly for my father, who then happened to be at home. The 'mummy' was my sister Joan. She was not dead, only injured. It transpired that she had been playing outside with her friend Frances, a lively, adventurous little girl of about my age, and that Joan had been knocked down by a car as the two of them were crossing the main road, a thing which Joan, at least, was strictly forbidden to do. Frances was not hurt, but Joan sustained a few cuts and bruises, and for the next three weeks was confined to bed.

When I was six years old I underwent two minor operations. The first took place in hospital, the second at home. One was for the removal of my tonsils, the other for the lancing of a large swelling that had developed in my groin. About an experience I had at the hospital, and of how it aroused in me a sense of injustice (and therefore of justice), I have written elsewhere.[5]

The operation I had at home took place in my bedroom. While Dr Bradlaugh conferred with my parents in the kitchen, the anaesthetist was with me in my bedroom making his preparations. Inquisitive as ever, I wanted to know the name of the liquid with which he was soaking a wad of cotton wool. In fact I wanted to smell the liquid, but this he would not allow me to do. I soon found out what it smelt like! Afterwards I was told that when the time came for the anaesthetic mask to be placed over my face, I fought like a tiger and that it took the combined strength of Dr Bradlaugh, the anaesthetist, and my father, to hold me down. When the operation was over, and there stood beside my bed a basin half full of a yellow liquid, I complained vigorously. If I had been allowed to smell the liquid when I wanted to, I said, there would not have been all that fuss!

As a child, I knew that I had once had both measles and whooping cough, but I did not remember having them, probably because I was very young at the time. But I certainly remember having scarlet fever. I had it when I was eight, and I remember it mainly because it was the first of a series of events which, culminating in my being confined to bed for two years, affected the whole subsequent course of my life. Those two years draw a thick black line between my early childhood, on the one hand, and on the other my later childhood and my adolescence.

### Notes

1. Harmsworth's *Children's Encyclopedia* was published by the newspaper and publishing entrepreneur, Alfred Harmsworth, Lord Northcliffe (1865–1922). The Educational Book Company which brought out the *Encyclopedia* was a subsidiary of his Amalgamated Press. The writer and educator Arthur Mee (1875–1943) was the overall editor of the project. Appearing initially in fortnightly parts, in 1910 *The Children's Encyclopædia* was published as an eight-volume set that went through twelve editions – an indication of its popularity – before being extensively revised and brought out in ten volumes in 1922. At this point the digraph was dropped and it appeared under the title *The Children's Encyclopedia*. It was presumably the earlier version, *The Children's*

*Encyclopædia*, which the Hartnells gave to Dennis Lingwood in sixty-one, unbound parts. (*RR*, pp. 19–21).

2. The Rechabites were a non-conformist Christian sect that emerged in the mid-nineteenth century whose principal tenet was teetotalism. They were named after a clan commended by the prophet Jeremiah for following their ancestral customs faithfully (in contrast to some of the Israelites. See *The Bible*, Jeremiah 35). It seems this clan followed a ruling to abstain from all wine; and not to build houses but rather to continue following a nomadic lifestyle – a tenet *not* followed by their latter-day namesakes. Sangharakshita writes about attending a Rechabite meeting with his mother and his friend Gerald and Gerald's mother in *RR*, pp. 18–19.

3. From 'English Lullaby', by Alfred, Lord Tennyson in Archibald Watson Bain, *Poetry for Children*, Cambridge University Press, paperback edition 2011, p. 2 (first published 1927).

4. See *RR*, p. 306.

5. See *FGDS*, p. 101.

Reveries and Reminiscences

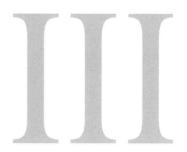

# A Room With a View

I shall soon be leaving Moseley, the quiet, leafy Birmingham suburb where I have lived for the last fourteen years, and I wonder what memories of my present residence I shall carry with me to my new home in the countryside and how long those memories will persist.[1] I shall certainly remember the garden, with its trees and shrubs, the flights of stone steps down to the lawn, the perimeter path round which I walked every morning, and the pond into which a small boy jumped thinking that the green algae with which it was covered was grass. The sounds of the place, too, I shall remember. I shall remember the hum of bees in the azaleas, the patter of rain on the roof of my study, and the dull drone of the low-flying passenger aircraft on its way to Birmingham Airport. Above all, I think, I shall remember the tremulous cry of the owls that lived in the neighbouring trees and called to one another in the late evening. I would remember the cry of the owls because my memories of the last two places in which I lived are inseparable from memories of the sound of birds. When I lived in Norfolk, on the outskirts of a village, I used to hear the sound of the wild geese flying overhead.[2] They flew very low, so low that I could distinctly hear the regular beating of their wings. I also used to hear the cuckoo. As in the old rhyme, he came in April, sang all day in May, in June changed his tune, prepared to fly in July, had to go in August, and in September was only a memory – until the following Spring.[3] When I lived in East London, as I did later on, I used to wake up every morning in summer to the sound of a blackbird's full-throated song.[4] He sang from the top of a neighbouring chimney pot, and he sang for an hour or more, after which he flew away, no doubt to go in search of his breakfast. I would have liked to celebrate the blackbird as magnificently as Shelley had celebrated the skylark[5] but this was a feat far beyond my limited poetic powers, and all I could produce was the following verse:

*Trill trill trill goes the blackbird*
*At the cold blue edge of day,*
*Trill trill trill goes Apollo's bird*
*From the chimney pot across the way.*

This became the first verse of 'The Birds and Their Gods', a series of six verses in each of which I describe a particular bird, its song, and the figure in Western mythology with which it is associated.[6]

The poem was written some time in 1992. During the last fourteen years I have written very little poetry, and I shall probably carry with me into my new home memories of only two of them, 'The Pilgrim' and 'Love and Duty'.[7] I shall carry them with me because I know them by heart, and I know them by heart not because I made an effort to memorize them but because they came spontaneously from somewhere deep in my psyche and have remained with me ever since. With me will go, also, all those poems and fragments of poems that I have memorized in the course of my life or which have clung to me almost in spite of myself, from 'Old King Cole' to 'Lycidas', and from 'Onward, Christian Soldiers' to 'Sister Helen'.[8] With them would be at least one line by a poet I 'discovered' only in the 1990s, though his name was familiar to me long before that. I was then corresponding regularly with an elderly Belgian Buddhist, a teacher of Zen, who was in the habit of sending me the typescripts of the talks he gave to members of his Zen group. The talks were interesting, and I enjoyed reading them. In the course of one of them he quoted the line 'Death is no different whined at than withstood'. It was a thunderbolt of a line and it struck me to the heart both as a Buddhist and as a lover of poetry. The line was by Philip Larkin, and came from his poem 'Aubade'. I was therefore soon deep in Larkin's *Collected Poems* and delighting in his highly individual style, which I found to be characterized by conciseness, lack of sentimentality, and a kind of controlled lyricism. His view of human existence was rather bleak, but I found it stimulating rather than depressing, and I found myself wanting to know about the man behind the poetry. I therefore read first Andrew Motion's biography of the poet, then Larkin's famous – or infamous – *Selected Letters*, and finally his *Required Writing: Miscellaneous Pieces 1955–1982*.[9]

Though I have written few poems during the last fourteen years, and will probably carry only two of them with me in my heart to my new home in the countryside, during the same period I wrote three books, besides editing – and to some extent revising – four seminars I had given some years earlier. I say I wrote the three books, but the fact is that I had to dictate them. I had to dictate them, for my eyesight had suddenly deteriorated. The trouble started when I was on a reunion retreat at Il Convento, the half-ruined monastery in Tuscany where, surrounded as we were by olive gardens and arbutus woods, I had led, for many a blue-roofed Italian summer, ordination retreats for men of several different nationalities.[10] One day I woke up to find my vision strangely distorted, and that I could neither read nor write. This did not disturb me unduly, as for the past week my eyes had been sore due to what I took to be eye-strain and they would, I thought, recover if I gave them a little rest from my constant reading and writing. My vision remained distorted, however, and it became obvious that it was time I saw a doctor. Someone therefore drove me to Grosseto, and to the town's new health centre. This was an imposing place, all white marble and huge, gilt-framed mirrors, and before long I was being seen by a young man in a white coat who may or may not have been a doctor. I told him what had happened, whereupon he wrote it all down, asked me a few questions, examined my eyes, and finally ushered me into the presence of a large, elderly man who may or may not have been a consultant. This gentleman read what the young man had written, grunted, wrote out a prescription for pills, assured me that my vision would be back to normal within ten days, and charged me the equivalent of sixty pounds for the consultation. Though I took the pills as directed there was no improvement in my vision, and it became obvious that despite my reluctance to leave the retreat I ought to return to England without delay and seek further medical advice. A few days later, therefore, I was back in Birmingham and my eyes were being examined and my vision tested by a cheerful, friendly ophthalmologist who stank of tobacco. Things were serious, he told me. I had 'wet' macular degeneration in both eyes (the 'wet' is the more rapidly developing form of the disease) and I ought to have seen him weeks ago. When I showed him the pills I had been taking he snorted contemptuously and tossed them into the wastepaper basket, saying 'they use a lot of these things in Europe'. But all was not lost. He would arrange for me to see a colleague of his, he said, and a week later I had my first appointment with her. There followed half a dozen sessions of laser treatment, a cataract operation on my right eye, a series of monthly Lucentis injections into my left eye, and a series of regular vision tests every few months that has continued down to the present day. Neither the laser treatment nor the Lucentis injections resulted in an improvement in my vision, but they prevented any further deterioration, and without them I would probably have become more than half blind by this time. The cataract operation, on the other hand, resulted in a marked change in my perception of colour. I saw the colour blue much more vividly than before. As I wandered round the garden, two days after the operation, the giant delphiniums, in particular, seemed almost to assault me with the intensity of their blueness, and I thought of D.H. Lawrence's blue gentians and their blazing torches of blueness.[11] Colour has always been important to me, which is why I love artists as different as Titian, Miro, and the Pre-Raphaelites,[12] as well as precious and semi-precious stones and birds like the peacock and macaw. People are also important to me, but that is quite another matter, and I shall return to it later.

The three books I dictated, either wholly or in part, are *Moving Against the Stream* (2003), *From Genesis to the Diamond Sutra* (2005), and *Precious Teachers* (2007). I worked on each of these books with a definite purpose in mind. In the case of *Moving Against the Stream*, only the last ten chapters of which were dictated, I sought to give a complete account of the events that led not only to my decision to return to England from India as I had promised, but also to the realization that a new Buddhist Movement was needed in the world. 'Do you know what this means?' I asked the friend who was with me at the time I received a certain letter. 'It means a new Buddhist Movement!' The letter in question was signed by one of the directors of the English Sangha Trust, under whose auspices I had been teaching in London, and in it he informed me, on behalf of the Trust, that they were dissatisfied with me and did not want me back. That was by no means all. He went on to suggest, in the blandest manner, that I should issue a statement saying that I had decided not to return to England after all, as I had changed my mind. But I had *promised* my friends and supporters that I would return to England, and I had *not* changed my mind, and I was deeply shocked that the representative of a Buddhist organization, writing to a Buddhist teacher, should suggest that he should not only break a promise but publicly lie about the reason for his doing so.[13] I also sought, in *Moving Against the Stream*, to give an account of my relationship with Terry Delamare, the friend who had been with me in India when I received the Trust's letter. In the epilogue to the book I tell the story of the last two years of Terry's life, a story of increasing depression that culminated in him taking his own life. He was my closest friend, and I felt his loss keenly.

Whereas *Moving Against the Stream* is wholly autobiographical, *From Genesis to the Diamond Sutra* is only partly so. The reason for this is that I wrote the book with a double purpose in mind. In the first place I wanted to describe how one Western Buddhist saw Christianity, especially in its Roman Catholic form, the form that for centuries had dominated the civilization and culture of Western Europe. In the second place, I wanted to make open acknowledgement of the nature of my sexual orientation, which I had not done in writing before. The two came together in my criticism of the Roman Catholic Church's attitude towards heresy and homosexuality, its attitude towards the latter case still being very much a live issue. *From Genesis to the Diamond Sutra* is thus a very personal book. Probably it is the most personal of all the books I have written. Though the process of dictating it was irksome and laborious, working on it gave me a deep satisfaction. I equally enjoyed giving expression to my rejection of the central doctrine of mainstream Christianity and expressing my admiration for some of the masterpieces of Christian art. Unfortunately, like a much more distinguished predecessor *From Genesis to the Diamond Sutra* fell stillborn from the press.[14] Indeed, it was lucky to fall from the press at all. The people at Windhorse Publications did not like the book and published it, as I thought, only grudgingly.[15]

*Precious Teachers* is almost wholly autobiographical, covering as it does my last seven years in Kalimpong, a small town in the foothills of the Eastern Himalayas. If I wrote *From Genesis to the Diamond Sutra* as the result of an inner urge, then I wrote *Precious Teachers* largely in response to requests from disciples and friends that I should write something about my eight main spiritual teachers, six of whom were from Tibet, while one was from India, and one from China. They were remarkable men. Besides being well versed in the traditions to which they belonged, they were men of deep spirituality, and I benefited greatly from their teaching and from the example they offered, in their different ways, of a life lived in accordance with the Dharma. Wherever I go I shall carry with me the memory of their great kindness to me and to all who came within the magic circle of their influence. Like visions of a divinized humanity, they soared above the horizon of our petty earthly concerns.[16]

*Precious Teachers* was the latest (and it probably will be the last) of a whole series of autobiographical works, a series which began with *The Rainbow Road* and included *Facing Mount Kanchenjunga* (1991) and *In the Sign of the Golden Wheel* (1996), as well as *Travel Letters* (1985), and *Through Buddhist Eyes* (2000). Although I call these works autobiographies, each of them covers only a certain period in my life, not the whole of it, and in the past I have spoken of them as memoirs rather than as autobiographies. Thus I have written no autobiography, and the 'memoirs' are just that. Their subject is my life at a particular period, as seen through my own eyes. They do not criticize, or evaluate, or compare; neither do they seek to contextualize my life with regard to the cultural and political happenings of the time. But whatever one may call them, I enjoyed writing *The Rainbow Road* and its successors. I enjoyed writing about my immediate surroundings, about my day-to-day activities, and about the various experiences that had befallen me. I enjoyed writing about the products of nature and about the creations of man. Above all, I enjoyed writing about people – the people with whom I had lived and worked, whom I had met in the course of my travels, and with whom I had enjoyed relationships of one kind or another. My descriptions of some of these people, such as the irascible Buddharakshita,[17] or the exigent French Nun,[18] could have come from the pages of a novel. Indeed, the relationship between the two genres seems to be closer than I had supposed. In *Experience*, Martin Amis speaks of 'high autobiography', by which he appears to mean something better than the ghost-written memoirs of a popular footballer or film star. He also suggests that autobiography is in process of replacing the novel as the dominant literary genre. This struck a chord. In the course of my life I had written *one* novel and *seven* volumes of autobiography, and it occurred to me that I might be an example of the general trend from novel to autobiography of which Martin Amis speaks. I wrote my novel when I was seventeen, after reading D.H. Lawrence's *The Rainbow*, an experience which I later described as being an emotional revelation. The typescript of the novel has long since disappeared, and I remember very little about it. There are two main characters, the young music master at a girls' school (I forget what name I gave him) and Bertha Aldobrandini, his sixteen-year-old pupil, who is of partly Italian descent. They fall in love, Bertha becomes pregnant and has a miscarriage, and the lovers move to Cornwall, my descriptions of which are based on my recollections of Devon. There is also a rather high-flown description of the interior of a Victorian Gothic railway station and a discussion of the art of El Greco, whose paintings I knew only from reproductions in a book by Sacheverell Sitwell.[19] The characters of Bertha and the young music master were not based on people I knew, neither did they have any literary progenitors. I created them, and I still have a strong sense of what they were like. The music master was tall, slim, and dark ('a pillar of darkness', as Lawrence might have said), whereas Bertha was of middle height, plump, and dark. He was serious, even melancholy, while she was carefree and impulsive. She may have been from Venus, but he was certainly not from Mars but Saturn. I had not intended that there should be a neat complementarity between the two main characters of my novel: it simply emerged as I wrote, and may have reflected a division within my own psyche. How good or how bad my novel was I cannot say. It must certainly have needed a lot of revision before it could be published, and Lawrence's influence on my style could not have been a good one. When I returned to *The Rainbow* some years ago, I found it unreadable. Nonetheless my admiration for Lawrence remained undiminished. Over the years I have read everything he wrote, and regard him as the outstanding creative force of his generation. The last time I was in the United States I spent a few days in hot, arid New Mexico, where I visited the isolated ranch where Lawrence had lived and worked, and saw the little chapel in which his ashes are enshrined.[20]

**Notes**

1. At the time of composing this piece, the plan to move to a larger, more rural setting was very much in the air although in the event it was only in September 2012 that a property was finally purchased. Sangharakshita himself moved to 'Adhisthana' in February 2013.

2. From 1976–1989 Sangharakshita was based at 'Padmaloka', a men's community and retreat centre in the village of Surlingham, Norfolk.

3. A traditional rhyme:
   *Cuckoo, cuckoo,*
   *Pray what do you do?*
   *In April I open my bill,*
   *In May I sing all the day,*
   *In June I change my tune,*
   *In July away I fly,*
   *In August, away I must,*
   *Cuckoo.*

4. From 1989 to 1994 Sangharakshita lived in a small flat attached to the London Buddhist Centre at 51 Roman Road, Bethnal Green.

5. Percy Bysshe Shelley (1792–1822) wrote his poem of 21 stanzas, 'To a Skylark' in 1820. It begins:
   *Hail to Thee, blithe Spirit!*
   *Bird thou never wert,*
   *Who from Heaven or near it,*

*Pourest thy full heart*
*In profuse strains of unpremeditated art.*
See e.g. *Shelley: Poems*, selected by Isabel Quigly, Penguin, London 1956, p.182.

6. *Complete Poems* 1941–1994, Windhorse Publications 1995, pp.373–6.

7. 'The Pilgrim', recounts Tannhäuser's legendary visit to Pope Urban IV. It is published in *The Call of the Forest*, Windhorse Publications 2000, p.37.

'Love and Duty', composed on 24 May 2001, is one of three 'Arthurian Poems'. Its theme is the illicit love of Queen Guinevere (wife of King Arthur) for 'gallant Lancelot'. See p.159.

8. 'Old King Cole' is a traditional nursery rhyme. 'Lycidas' is an elegy written in 1637 by John Milton (1608–1674) on the loss of his friend, Edward King. See *The Portable Milton*, ed. Douglas Bush, Penguin, 1977, pp.107–113. Sangharakshita first came across Milton's poetry at the age of twelve when he received *Paradise Lost* as a Christmas present, the reading of which gave him 'the greatest poetic experience' of his life. For many years Milton and Rossetti (see below) were his favourite poets. (*RR*, p.33).

'Onward Christian Soldiers' was a popular Victorian hymn whose music was composed by Arthur Sullivan in 1871. It was sung with gusto at the meetings of the Boys' Brigade group that the young Dennis Lingwood attended. (The group was affiliated to a Baptist church.)

'Sister Helen' is a long poem in the form of a ballad by Dante Gabriel Rossetti (1828–1882), a poet whose 'intensely fused sensuousness and mysticism ... went to my head like some subtle and dangerous perfume'. (*RR*, p.33).

9. English poet Philip Larkin (1922–1985) worked as librarian at the University of Hull for more than thirty years. Andrew Motion's biography, *Philip Larkin: A Writer's Life*, was published by Faber & Faber in 1993. Sangharakshita's poem, 'Revised Version', is headed, 'with apologies to Philip Larkin' – a play on Larkin's famous, 'This Be the Verse' which begins, 'They fuck you up, your Mum and Dad. / They may not mean to, but they do'. The opening lines of Sangharakshita's version runs, 'They bring you up, your mum and dad, / They don't know how to, but they do'. See *The Call of the Forest*, op. cit., p.38.

10. Il Convento di Santa Croce, near the Tuscan village of Batignano, was formerly an Augustinian monastery. From 1981 until 1985 it was the venue for the three-month ordination retreats for men entering the Western Buddhist Order. During these retreats Sangharakshita gave talks, notably including *The Journey to Il Convento* and

*St Jerome Revisited* (both given on the 1984 course, see *The Priceless Jewel*, Windhorse Publications 1993), led seminars, answered questions, wrote letters – and some poems – and, of course, performed ordinations.

11. 'Bavarian Gentians' was included in Lawrence's *Last Poems* published in 1932. (See *D.H. Lawrence: Selected Poetry*, selected by Keith Sagar, London, Penguin 1986, p.240.) Sangharakshita first came across Lawrence's poetry when he was a teenager. He wrote later (in 1997) that since that time 'rarely have I been without a copy of at least a selection from his poems' (*TBE*, p.278).

12. Titian or Tiziano Vecelli (c.1488–1576) was an Italian painter of the Venetian school; Juan Miro (1893–1983) a Spanish painter, sculptor and ceramicist. The Pre-Raphaelite painters include William Holman Hunt (1827–1910), John Everett Millais (1829–1896), and Dante Gabriel Rossetti (1828–1882). Sangharakshita's love of art began during his years confined to bed between the ages of eight and ten when he took especial pleasure in the art section of the *Children's Encyclopedia* (see p.41, note 1). He subsequently began drawing and painting himself so that for a while 'the feeling became general that I was going to be an artist'. (See *RR*, p.24.)

13. See *MAS*, p.330.

14. The empiricist philosopher David Hume (1711–1776) published *A Treatise of Human Nature* anonymously in 1739–40. Its reception was such that he wrote later that it had 'fallen dead-born from the press'. *An Enquiry Concerning Human Understanding*, was a much shorter revision of the treatise published in 1748 and went on to become a classic of the western philosophical tradition.

15. The Windhorse is a mythical creature who bears through the world the Three Flaming Jewels (see Sangharakshita's poem, 'The Song of the Windhorse', *Complete Poems*, pp. 301–3). Windhorse Publications was founded in 1976 by Nagabodhi with the purpose of making Sangharakshita's Dharma teachings available within the Movement he founded in 1967, and as widely as possible beyond. The first book to come out under the Windhorse imprint was *The Path of the Inner Life*. Over seventy titles by Sangharakshita followed, as well as books by members of the Western Buddhist Order (later Triratna Buddhist Order) and, more recently, by other Buddhists. Over the years the publishing house has been based in London, Glasgow, Sheffield, and Birmingham and is now run from Cambridge under the directorship of Priyananda.

16. Sangharakshita's eight main spiritual teachers – the Chinese Yogi C.M. Chen (1906–1987), the Indian bhikkhu Jagdish Kashyap (1908–1976); and the Tibetan teachers Dhardo Rimpoche (1917–1990), Chetrul Sangye Dorje (b.1913), Jamyang Khyentse Chökyi Lödro (1893–1959), Dudjom Rimpoche (1904–1987), and Dilgo Khyentse Rimpoche (1910–1991) are described in his memoir, *Precious Teachers*. Kulananda's *Teachers of Enlightenment*, (Windhorse Publications 2000) gives a brief synopsis of the lives of these remarkable figures as well as Sangharakshita's meetings with them.

17. Rabindra Kumar Banerjee was born in Manipur, India, in 1922. He and the future Sangharakshita met in Singapore in 1946. Banerjee came from a brahmin family but had renounced the caste system in favour of political activism – of the right-wing variety. Of very different temperament, the two became friends (see Sangharakshita's poem, 'To a Political Friend', *Complete Poems* 1941–1994, p.28) and through their discussions, Banerjee became interested in Buddhism. From 1947, for two years, they were constant companions, helping to rescue children from a Calcutta orphanage caught up in riots in the wake of Indian Partition, walking the roads of India, meeting great – and not so great – spiritual figures, and spending fifteen months in the haunted ashram of Muvattupuzha (see *RR*, chs.16–47). In May 1949 they received *samanera* ordination at Kusinara where Banerjee (or Satyapriya as by then he was calling himself) became Buddharakshita. Their paths diverged from 1949, Buddharakshita going on to study in Sri Lanka. He then went to Burma where he was the Indian bhikkhu representative to the 'Sixth Buddhist Council' organized by Prime Minister U Nu. He later based himself in Bangalore where he developed a branch of the Maha Bodhi Society (see Sangharakshita in question and answer session at Kuhhude 1991, www.youtube.com/watch?v=YX8Ihe5m2Hg.) Buddharakshita died in 2013.

18. When Sangharakshita first met 'the French nun' she was Dominique Delannoy, an alumna of the Sorbonne, studying in Calcutta. He was introduced to her again when she visited Kalimpong in early 1953 (*FMK*, p.482). Later that year, she took from him the Refuges and Precepts and received ordination from a Bengali monk, becoming Anagarika Dharmarakshita (*ISGW*, p.40). In 1954 she received ordination as a *getsulma* or novice nun from Dhardo Rimpoche, taking the name Thupten Chhokyi (ibid., p.174). 'Ani-la', as she was now addressed, was a frequent visitor to Sangharakshita's residence, where she would pour out her troubles, involve herself in activities, and was sometimes an embarrassment (op. cit., pp.181–3, 185–6). Both he and Dhardo Rimpoche sought ways to help her (op. cit., pp.207–11) but in the end her behaviour became so bad that Dhardo Rimpoche was forced to deprive her of her status as nun

(*PT*, pp.36–9). 'When next she was heard of she was in Calcutta, where she was seen with bobbed hair, in a short skirt, and smoking a cigarette.' (op. cit., p.39.)

19. Sacheverell Sitwell (1897–1988), brother of writers Edith and Osbert, wrote extensively on art and architecture, The book referred to here was probably either *Southern Baroque Art: a Study of Painting, Architecture and Music in Italy and Spain of the 17th & 18th Centuries* (1924) or *Spanish Baroque Art, with Buildings in Portugal, Mexico, and Other Colonies* (1931).

20. See *TBE*, pp.275–8 and *My Five Literary Heroes*, in this volume (p.117).

# Terra Incognita

Every language is unique, and for this reason a completely faithful translation from one language into another is hardly possible. To translate is to betray. This is especially the case with regard to poetry, in which language reaches the highest point of its development, and I have more than once noticed how a poem in one language can be translated into another language in half a dozen different ways. The best translations are not translations at all, in the literal sense of the term, but re-creations of the 'meaning' of the original in accordance with the genius of the language into which it is translated, a process of which Fitzgerald's rendition of the *Rubáiyát of Omar Khayyám* is probably the best example,[1] closely followed by some of Rossetti's translations from the Early Italian poets.[2] It would be too much to expect that poems of mine that have been translated into other languages should be re-creations of this kind, faithful though they might be in many ways to their English originals. Indeed, in one of the sixty-odd poems that have been translated into French (*Poèmes*, 2009)[3] there is one that perfectly illustrates the difficulty, even the impossibility, of translation from one language into another, particularly in the case of poetry. The line is 'Life is King', which also serves as the title of the poem, but the rules of French grammar do not permit a faithful translation. One has to say 'La Vie est Reine' (Life is *Queen*), which completely distorts my meaning. Similar difficulties arise in connection with the translation of a novel or other prose work of imagination from one language into another, but here there are probably more ways of getting round such difficulties than there are in the case of a lyric or other short poem, in which so much often hangs on so little. In the course of the last thirty or more years my books have been translated into some twenty European and Asian languages, and since I am far from being a polyglot I have been obliged to rely on the competence of my translators and the judgement of those who commissioned their work. At the same time I was always available for consultation and in this way I became more aware of the distinctive character, even the genius, of the particular language into which I was being translated. It has been said that to learn a new language is to acquire a new soul,[4] and perhaps one can acquire a little of that soul, or at least get a glimpse of it, on the strength of a very modest knowledge of the language in question. I remember that my old friend Lama Anagarika Govinda,[5] who was equally at home in German and English, once told me that in his opinion my newly published book *A Survey of Buddhism* (1957), would translate well into German, indeed would read better in German than in English, by which I understood him to mean that the two languages had very similar souls. Despite Lama Govinda's prognostications, the *Survey* has not yet been translated into German in its entirety.[6] Complete translations of the *Survey* have however appeared in two other languages, Spanish and Polish,[7] and I have had the satisfaction of knowing that what many regarded as my foundational work on Buddhism was now accessible to a wider circle of readers.

I have travelled in Spain with a friend,[8] have spent months together in a secluded valley high in the mountains near Alicante,[9] and on the shelves of my cottage there I have a small collection of books on Spain and its people. Even before my first visit to Spain, which took place in 1986, I had some knowledge of the country's history, and was acquainted with the literature and art of what has been called the golden age of Spain. Of Poland and its people I knew, until fairly recently, almost nothing. I knew that World War II had started with Germany's invasion of Poland in 1939, and that thousands of 'Free Poles' had fought on the side of Britain – and that was about all. In 1945 Poland disappeared behind the Iron Curtain, and it was only with the emergence of Solidarity in 1980[10] that I again became aware that there was a country called Poland and that it was part of Central Europe. Thus for many years Poland hardly existed for me, or existed as a *terra incognita* which it was unlikely I should ever visit. Then ten years ago, in 2001, there came from the heart of this *terra incognita* a letter informing me that *A Survey of Buddhism* had been translated into Polish and inviting me to visit Krakow and launch the publication of the book. The result was that in May 2002 I spent ten days in Krakow, the ancient capital of Poland, having flown there from Gatwick with two of my Polish friends. Those ten days in Krakow were the most delightful I had spent for a long time. In retrospect they were all the more delightful in that they preceded the upheavals and tribulations of 2003, my *annus horribilis*. I did not keep a diary while I was in Krakow, and I cannot recall all the things my friends and I did there in the order in which we did them. Not that this matters very much. As I now look back on the events of those ten days, they have 'the glory and the freshness of a dream'[11] and, as often is the case with dreams, it is difficult for me to remember what came first, what last, and what between. Certain experiences touched me deeply, simple though they were, and after returning to England I wrote three Krakow poems, as I called them.[12] In the first poem I am having breakfast on the balcony of the first floor apartment where I am staying. Sparrows are flying in and out of the eaves, chirruping loudly. There are a lot of them, and they make quite a noise, but I do not mind. I am glad to have the company of the little brown birds, for it is a long time since I saw so many of them together, the sparrow population of England having de-clined steeply in recent years. While having breakfast I watch the men working in the fields below. It is early morning, and spring has come to the Polish countryside (our apartment is in a house outside Krakow), and soon the sky will be a cloudless blue, as it would be for all ten days of my visit, except for a sudden heavy downpour late one afternoon. In the sec-ond poem it is evening, and I am sitting outside one of the restaurants in the great square of Krakow, said to be the second largest square in Europe. With me are the two Polish friends who flew with me from Gatwick, as well as six or seven other friends, mostly Polish, who have come from London, Brighton, and Paris. Some are staying with me at the apartment, others at hotels in the city. They are all here in Krakow for the launch of the Polish translation of *A Survey of Buddhism*. I drink tea, join in the conversation from time to time, and watch the passers-by. The young men are tall, and bear themselves well, as though they had spent time in the army. Nearby, there is a group of gypsy musicians, and I listen to them. Their ancestors came from India, many centuries ago, and the weird, wild music makes me think of the many years I spent in that country, eating its food, and sharing its culture. The third poem was addressed to my interpreter, Michal Balik. He was one of those staying with me at the apartment, and without him it would not have been possible for me to visit Krakow.

Between breakfast on the balcony in the morning and the evening cup of tea in the great square there was always much to see and much to do. There were occasions when all the members of our party kept together, and others when they split into little groups to explore different parts of the city or pursue particular interests. One of the things we did as a party was to attend a performance of a piano concerto by Chopin[13] (I forget which one) given by a young Polish pianist at the Philharmony Hall. It was a very bad performance; but the audience was in a forgiving mood, and applauded warmly. After all, they seemed to be saying, the pianist was a Pole, he was performing the music of Chopin, their national composer, and young talent ought to be encouraged. To this the young man responded by performing a short piece by Chopin by way of an encore. This time he played brilliantly and was rewarded with an outburst of spontaneous applause. After the concert those who had cameras took photographs of the rest of us as we stood in a row outside the Philharmony Hall.

I carried out my personal exploration of Krakow in the company of Michal and a few others. Much of the exploration took place within the old city, which was agreeably located within a circular park. If the park was the ring, then the stone in the ring was Wawel Castle, the seat of the old Polish kings, and it was only at this point that the circular park was interrupted. One morning Michal and I and a few others made our way up the steep, winding ramp that led to the Castle entrance, passing on our way the official residence of the archbishop of Krakow. Inside, the principal object of interest was the beautiful three-storeyed courtyard in Renaissance style. Open to the blue sky, and filled with sunshine, it had been built by, or for, an Italian princess who was married to the King. It was this princess who brought with her from Italy a painting that is the City Art Gallery's greatest treasure: Leonardo da Vinci's 'Portrait of a Lady with an Ermine'.[14] This was a favourite painting of mine, and I was overjoyed at having the opportunity of spending some time in front of it. Besides the Renaissance courtyard, we saw underneath the Castle, on the river, the cave from which the legendary Krakow dragon had terrorized the people of the surrounding countryside. One could not be long in Krakow before hearing of this celebrated monster. Indeed, at the airport I had been presented with a small statue of the dragon by my Polish publisher. The people of Krakow in fact seem rather proud of their dragon, especially now that it was dead and could not do any harm. According to one account it had been killed by a shoemaker's apprentice known as 'Little Twine' who had stuffed a dead sheep with gunpowder and left it outside the dragon's cave. The dragon naturally ate the sheep, but when the gunpowder reached its fiery entrails (for the dragon was a fire-breathing one) it exploded, blowing the unfortunate creature to pieces.

In the course of my travels in Italy, Germany, and Spain I had always been keen to visit their churches, mainly for the sake of seeing their art treasures; but in Krakow I felt no such inclination, even though the city was full of churches and monasteries and was the ecclesiastical capital of Poland. Even the cathedral was left unvisited. I did, however, see the inside of the Franciscan Church, which was situated not far from the great square. This was because Michal wanted to show me a beautiful mural in Art Nouveau style painted by a Krakow artist in the early twentieth century.[15] Though the friars had commissioned the mural, when they saw what the artist had done they were horrified and wanted to withdraw from the project. It was too bright and colourful for a church, they said. Nevertheless, in the end they had been obliged to accept the work. There were also big stained-glass windows by the same artist, one of which showed God the Father creating the world. Since the church was poorly lit, and I was partially sighted, I could hardly see the mural, though I could see the reds, blues and yellows of the stained glass windows. Though the cathedral might be unvisited, it could hardly be ignored, for it was an imposing structure and dominated part of the great square. Neither was it possible for one to ignore the bugle call which sounded from a window at the top of the cathedral tower. The first time I heard it Michal and I were sitting in the sunshine outside a café in the great square, and I looked up to see where the sound came from. It was the Krakow bugle-call signal, Michal told me, and it was played every day on the hour by a member of the fire brigade, as well as being played live on Polish radio every day at 12pm in full. It dated back to the Middle Ages, when it announced the opening and closing of the city gates. The bugler also sounded the alarm whenever he saw an outbreak of fire or an enemy army approaching the city. The Krakow bugle call was a long one, not unlike the Last Post, but it ended abruptly. This was said to commemorate the bugler who was shot through the throat by a Tatar archer when the Mongols besieged the city in 1241. The Mongol armies were then penetrating deep into Europe and the Middle East. Four centuries later, Eastern and Central Europe were threatened by the forces of the Ottoman Empire, and it was a Polish king, John Sobieski, who played a leading part in turning back the tide of advancing Islam.[16] The name of John Sobieski came up in the course of a conversation I had with Czarek Wozniak, the publisher of the Polish *Survey*. He wanted to know how many famous Poles I had heard of, apart from Chopin and the Pope.[17] I could think of only three: Paderewski, the pianist-president,[18] Górecki, whose 'Symphony of Sad Songs' was then very popular in England,[19] and John Sobieski. I failed to mention Copernicus, the famous astronomer, and Czarek reminded me that he, too, was a Pole, despite his name.[20]

My publisher was a cultured man who lectured on philosophy and had written a book on Heidegger. He was also a member of a Dzogchen group and in his capacity as a publisher he had brought out a number of books on Buddhism. Having read *A Survey of Buddhism* he had not only commissioned a translation but had invited me to come to Krakow to launch the book in its new garb and in that connection he had arranged for me to give three lectures. The first lecture was on 'Buddhism and Art', a favourite topic of mine, and I gave it at the Manggha Japanese Centre, a modern building overlooking the river. The subject of the second lecture was my own life and work as a Western Buddhist and the founder of a new Buddhist movement, and it was followed by a documentary film showing the various activities of that movement in different parts of the world. This time the venue was a gallery of modern art. The third and last lecture was on 'The Tension between the Academic and the Practical Approaches to Buddhism', the venue being the religious studies department of the Jagiellonian University, one of the oldest universities in Europe. All three lectures were fairly well attended, which was not the case with the formal launch of the Polish *Survey*, which took place at the Empik bookshop, next to the cathedral. Since I did not speak Polish, I had to use an interpreter, and for all three lectures my interpreter was Michal. I could not have had a better interpreter. He was fluent and confident, and only once or twice was momentarily at a loss for a word, and it was evident that he was communicating the spirit as well as the letter of what I had to say. Several members of our party commented that we seemed to be in complete harmony with each other, as though we were of one heart and one mind. In a way this was surprising, considering how different we were in age, in temperament and in personal history. Moreover, we had not known each other for very long, nor had we spent much time together. I had first met Michal a year or two earlier in Berlin. We met at a conference organized by the German Buddhist Union. He could not attend the talk I was about to give, as he had to go and cook a meal for me at the flat where I was staying with a German friend. Our next meeting also took place in Berlin, at a club[21] where I was giving a short series of talks. This time he was accompanied by four or five friends from Frankfurt University where he was then studying.[22] In 2000 he came to England and joined Friends Organic, a team-based Right Livelihood business based in Bethnal Green, East London.[23] He also moved into a residential men's community. In late January or early February he came to see me in Moseley, and we went for a walk in Cannon Hill Park.[24] He was then about to leave for Poland, where his mother was ill in hospital. She died in March. During the months that followed Michal continued to work at Friends Organic and live in a men's community. He also liaised with Czarek Wozniak regarding the publication of the Polish *Survey* and the arrangements for my visit to Krakow. Finally, he organized a meeting of the friends, mostly expatriate Poles, who were interested in being with me in Krakow for the launch. The meeting was held at the London Buddhist Centre and was attended by eight or nine people, including me.

The result was that early in May we were all in Krakow, and Michal was staying with me at the rented apartment, translating my lectures, and accompanying me wherever I wanted to go. In the course of one of our explorations we came across a tablet commemorating the Katyn Massacre.[25] It was a reminder that terrible things had happened during the War, and that Auschwitz was only 60 miles away.[26] Horrors of a very different kind were to be found nearer home – architectural ones. An acquaintance of Michal's had invited our party to eat at the pizza restaurant he had recently opened in Nowa Huta, a sort of satellite town that the Communist government had built in an effort to lure the inhabitants of Krakow from their ancient city, away from the influence of its 'uncooperative' civic authorities. They had even built a church there! On our arrival at Nowa Huta, which was more like a sleazy suburb of Krakow than a separate town, I saw row upon featureless row of multi-storey apartment blocks, all grey and dingy, and separated by what seemed to be waste ground. As for the new restaurant, the food was remarkable for quantity rather than quality, and I soon realized that we had been invited not as guests but as customers and would have to pay for our meal. The host-proprietor nonetheless sat and ate with us. He was more than half drunk, and had evidently been reading books on Zen Buddhism, for he kept firing 'Zen-like' questions at me from the opposite end of the table. I amused myself by responding in similar fashion, often monosyllabically and forcibly, which puzzled and confused him, so that in the end he subsided into silence. After the meal it was a relief to feel the cool night air and look up at the stars.

Another exploration took Michal and me to the Arcade, a huge building situated almost in the middle of the great square. On our entering at one end, I saw that for its entire length it was lined on either side with brightly lit shops. We were there because we would soon be leaving Krakow and I wanted to take back with me a few presents for friends. I could not have come to a better place. The shops specialized in traditional Polish handicrafts, of which there was an amazing variety on display on open counters or under glass. I bought an amber egg for Paramartha, with whom I had travelled in Spain and elsewhere, an onyx chess set for

Prasannasiddhi, with whom I had travelled in Italy and elsewhere, and little painted wooden boxes and T-shirts for various other friends. On my last day in Krakow the members of our little party met for a farewell meal at an Indian vegetarian restaurant where Michal and I ate more than once in the course of our stay. I ordered a *masala dosai*, which was one of my favourite Indian dishes; but no sooner was it set before me, and I had raised the first morsel to my lips, than I experienced an utter revulsion to the very idea of food and started retching violently. So violent was the retching that I thought I was about to vomit and made a dash for the toilet. The intense revulsion I felt was probably akin to the kind of insight known to Buddhists as 'the perception of the loathsomeness of food'.[27] Be that as it might, I soon recovered, the uneaten *masala dosai* was distributed among our friends, and a few hours later, with Michal[28] and another friend, I was flying back to England, ten wonderful days in Krakow now behind me.[29]

## Notes

1. Omar Khayyám (1048–1131) was a Persian polymath. Famous as mathematician and astronomer, he wrote on many other subjects from music to mineralogy. He became known in the English-speaking West chiefly as a literary figure when the poet and writer Edward Fitzgerald (1809–1883) published a translation of his poetry: *The Rubáiyát of Omar Khayyám* (first edition 1859), a collection of quatrains (ruba'i). (During the mid-1950s Sangharakshita, perhaps influenced by Khayyám, wrote a number of quatrains on a variety of themes. See *Complete Poems 1941–1994*).

2. Dante Gabriel Rossetti (1828–1882) (see also note 2, p.97) was both painter and poet. His *The Early Italian Poets*, which included a translation of Dante Alighieri's *La Vita Nuova*, was first published in 1861.

3. *Poèmes* is a bilingual edition of sixty-three of Sangharakshita's poems, translated by Barbara-Laure Desplats, Christian Richard, Varadakini, and Vassika, and published by Amis de l'Ordre Bouddhiste Occidental, Paris, in 2009. The poems were chosen to give as complete a picture of the author as possible: the mystic, the friend, the philosopher, his life in India and in Britain, and his founding of a new Buddhist movement.

4. Attributed to the King and Emperor Charlemagne (c.747–814).

5. Lama Anagarika Govinda (1898–1985), was born in Germany and given the name Ernst Lothar Hoffman. He became a Buddhist while in his teens. His early interests included philosophy and archaeology, and he was an accomplished painter. For a while he lived in a painters' colony on the island of Capri before taking the orange robe as Anagarika Govinda and immersing himself in Theravadin Buddhism in Ceylon and Burma. In an unexpected development, he became a disciple of the Tibetan Tomo Geshe Rimpoche and in 1933 founded the Arya Maitreya Mandala, one of the very first Buddhist movements active in the West. Lama Govinda was an early contributor to *Stepping-Stones*, the Himalayan monthly journal of Religion and Culture which Sangharakshita founded and edited in Kalimpong in the early 1950s. They met when the Lama and his wife, Li, visited Kalimpong in June 1951 (*FMK*, ch. 13) and from then on their friendship blossomed. In Lama Govinda Sangharakshita found a kindred spirit, someone who, like him, was not only dedicated to the Buddhist spiritual path, but who saw that path in all forms of Buddhism. The two maintained their contact until the Lama's death in California, where he and Li had taken up residence: a letter written just a few days before he died, was addressed to Sangharakshita.

6. The introduction and first chapter of the *Survey* was published in German in 1999 by Do Evolution with the title *Buddha-Dharma — Einheit und Vielfalt des Buddhismus, Band I*.

7. A Spanish translation was brought out in 2008 under the title *Una panorámica del budismo* by Ediciones Dharma, Alicante. The Polish version, *Wprowadzenie do buddyzmu*, was published by Wydawnictwo A, Krakow, in 2002.

8. The friend was Paramartha, and their travels are recounted in Sangharakshita's 'Fourth Letter From London' written in November 1990. See *TBE*.

9. Guhyaloka, or the 'secret realm', is a valley in the Sierra Aitana mountains of southern Spain. Here, since 1987, men's ordination retreats have been held. At the top of the valley is the retreat centre; a house for the resident community is at the bottom — while midway between the two is a bungalow where Sangharakshita has stayed whenever he visited the valley.

10. Solidarity or *Solidarnosc* is a Polish trade union founded in 1980 at the Gdansk shipyard. It became widely known as the first trade union of any Warsaw pact country not under the control of the communist party and it quickly grew in power. After the fall of the communist regime, its first leader, Lech Walesa, took up office as President of Poland in 1990.

11. From William Wordsworth's 'Ode: Intimations of Immortality from Recollections of Early Childhood', first published in 1807, first stanza.

12. 'In Krakow', three poems written on 20 May 2002, see pp. 161–2.

13. Frederic Chopin (1810–1849) grew up in Warsaw, though he lived as an adult in Paris where he was renowned both as a virtuoso pianist and as a composer of works for piano. He wrote two piano concertos.

14. Leonardo da Vinci (1452–1519) painted the *Lady with an Ermine* in c. 1490.

15. The painter of the murals was Stanislaw Wyspianski (1869–1907) who was also an architect, writer, and musician.

16. John Sobieski (1629–1696) was king of Poland from 1674. He is famous for his military victory over the Turks in 1683.

17. Karol Jozef Wojtyla (1920–2005) became Pope John Paul II in 1978. He was not only the first Polish pope, but the first non-Italian pope since 1523. He was canonized in 2014 and is now known as Saint Pope John Paul II.

18. Ignacy Jan Paderewski (1860–1941) was an internationally acclaimed pianist and composer, as well as a politician, who was briefly prime minister of independent Poland in 1919.

19. Henryk Gorecki (1933–2010) was first a composer of *avant garde* classical music. His third symphony, *Symphony of Sorrowful Songs*, composed in 1976, is in a more tonal vein. Its theme is the separation of mother and child through war. After the fall of communism, the symphony was played widely on the radio in western Europe and the USA.

20. Nicolaus Copernicus (1473–1543), mathematician and astronomer, was widely read in many other fields. He published his *De revolutionibus orbium coelestium* (*On the Revolutions of the Celestial Spheres*) just before his death, putting into motion a revolution of ideas with his model of the sun, and not the earth, at the centre of the (known) universe.

21. This was the Kalkscheune, a venue for events of all kinds. Amogharatna, now chairman of the Triratna Centre in Berlin (Buddhistsches Tor), who attended one of the talks, recalls there was a bar serving drinks even during the talk!

22. Frankfurt-an-der-Oder is a town on the German-Polish border, 100 kilometres south-east of Berlin. Michal was a student here from 1993 to 2000 when he studied Law and Humanities.

23. Friends Organic (originally Friends Foods) was founded by Ratnaguna in c.1976. It first ran from London market stalls in Brick Lane (Bethnal Green), Hampstead, and Swiss Cottage, and was the first team-based Right Livelihood enterprise of the FWBO. It moved into premises at the new London Buddhist Centre just before the Centre opened in 1978, and in 1990 to larger premises at 83 Roman Road. In 2000 it became Friends Organic. The shop stocked a whole range of wholefoods and other products, initially all packed by the team of workers. It continued trading until 2009 when, owing to on-going financial losses, it had to close.

24. Cannon Hill Park has 80 acres of formal parkland and 120 acres of conservation and woodland through which runs Birmingham's tiny River Rea. The first 57 acres were donated to the citizens of Birmingham by Miss Louisa Ryland (1814–1889) that it might be 'a source of healthful recreation'. It was opened to visitors in 1873. Cannon Hill Park was just ten minutes walk from 'Madhyamaloka'. It is well used by local people including the local Buddhists for taking walks or tea at the MAC (Midlands Arts Centre), situated in the park's grounds.

25. The Katyn Massacre refers to a series of mass executions of Polish nationals, in particular officers of the Polish army, politicians, members of the intelligentsia, and clergy of the Roman Catholic church, by the Soviet secret police in April and May 1940. The largest number of executions took place in the Katyn Forest in Russia. It is estimated that some 22,000 people were killed.

26. The Auschwitz concentration camp (in fact a series of connected camps), created by the Nazis, took its first prisoners in May 1940. It went on to become one of the main camps for the extermination of Jews and other unwanted peoples. Over a million people were killed, 90% of whom were Jews, mostly Hungarian or Polish. Others who lost their lives were Roma, Sinti, homosexuals, or Russian prisoners-of-war. There were also many non-Jewish Poles who died in Auschwitz. The camp was liberated on 27 January 1945, now commemorated as Holocaust Remembrance Day.

27. The Perception of the Loathsomeness of Food (*ahare patikula-sanna*) is one of the forty *kammatthanas* cited by the fifth-century Theravadin commentator, Buddhaghosa, as a support for the development of meditative concentration (see Sangharakshita, *A Survey of Buddhism*, 9th edition, Windhorse Publications 2009, pp.179–80, 186.)

28. Michal Balik (b. 1973), who went on to play a crucial part in Sangharakshita's life, was ordained in 2004. The private ordination ceremony, in which he received the name Nityabandhu, was conducted by Sangharakshita during a long weekend at Tyddyn Rhydderch, a cottage in a remote part of North Wales belonging to Order members Hridaya and Vajrapushpa. The public ordination ceremony took place during a ten-day retreat at Padmaloka retreat centre and was conducted by Sona, a long-standing member of the College of Public Preceptors. Nityabandhu means 'eternal friend'.

29. A delightful and informative record of this trip was made for Clear Vision's News-reel 23. It can be viewed at vimeo.com/24211675.

# A Season in Hell

The liner had left port a few days before. She was a new ship, though some of her timbers had been salvaged from an ancient craft that had come to the end of its seafaring days. On board there were more than a thousand passengers. The majority of the passengers were middle-aged, but there were old people and young people too, and a few children. Manning the liner there was a crew of thirty, headed by the captain, an experienced officer who had been associated with the ship since the laying down of its keel. Besides having a strong sense of duty, he loved his beautiful ship, with its clean lines; he loved his well-trained crew, and he loved his passengers and was concerned for their safety and comfort. During the voyage the passengers occupied themselves in various ways. Some of them spent much of their time in the ship's gym, others sat on deck watching the rising and falling of the waves, while a few simply counted the hours to the next meal and slept a lot. As might have been expected, disagreement sometimes broke out among the passengers, and occasionally these were so serious that the captain had to intervene personally to restore peace and harmony. Thus life went on more or less smoothly from day to day. The sky was generally clear, the sea generally calm. Only once did the ship encounter a storm, when it pitched and rolled dreadfully and a number of passengers were seasick.

One morning some of the passengers noticed that the captain was not on the bridge as usual. They thought nothing of it, however, and life on the ship went on much as before. But another morning came, and yet another, and still the captain was not seen on the bridge. Nor was that all. Other figures appeared on the bridge from time to time. First it was one of the ship's officers, then a small group of crew members, all talking loudly and apparently disagreeing with one another. But still there was no sign of the captain, and before long a rumour went round the ship that he was seriously ill and was confined to his cabin. This was later confirmed and the passengers were informed that the captain was seeing no one except his personal steward. By this time it was clear that the ship was no longer steaming straight ahead but was veering now to the right, now to the left, in a highly erratic and even dangerous manner. Some of the passengers welcomed the change. They were tired of always travelling in the same direction, they said. Most of the passengers wished the captain well, and hoped he would soon be better; but a minority criticized him, saying that he was not properly qualified, that he wore his cap at the wrong angle, and so on. A few were of the opinion that the passengers should take over the ship and elect their captain. A few others declared that they had never trusted the captain, and they wished they were travelling on another liner. As if in answer to their wish a vessel suddenly appeared out of the early morning mist. So many passengers rushed to get a better view that the ship listed dangerously and the crew had to remonstrate with them. The strange ship flew a variety of flags, and from bow to stern was so swathed in colourful bunting that it was difficult to make out its outline or even whether it actually was a ship. The passengers who wished they were travelling in another liner at once lowered one of the lifeboats, rowed themselves over to the strange ship, and were welcomed on board. A few of the other ship's passengers then jumped into the now empty lifeboat, rowed back to the ship it came from, climbed up over the side, and joined the passengers. All this time the captain remained in his cabin, cared for by his personal steward and, occasionally, by a couple of crew members. It was rumoured that he was very ill, even dying, though no one knew what was the cause of his illness. Some thought it was a bug he had picked up in the tropics, others that it was bad karma catching up with him. But the captain did not die, and eventually appeared on the bridge again, though less frequently than before, and looking paler and thinner. The liner was set on its old direct course, the crew was reorganized, the passengers reassured. Having seen to this, the captain then sat down in his cabin and wrote his report.

The liner in the parable is the good ship FWBO (since refurbished, and renamed Triratna Buddhist Order and Community),[1] and the captain is the present writer. Given this key, even those who were not around in 2003 will have little difficulty interpreting the parable and understanding something of what happened to me and to the FWBO in that year. They should, however, bear in mind that not every detail of the parable corresponds to something that actually happened, while not everything that happened to me in 2003 has its parabolic counterpart.

From the beginning of May 2002, when I returned from Krakow, to the beginning of January 2003, when the events shadowed forth in the parable began, I continued to lead quite an active life, despite my age.[2] After my return from Krakow I spent the rest of May first at Madhyamaloka,[3] dictating the epilogue to *Moving Against the Stream*, then at Guhyaloka, the men's retreat centre in Spain, where I dedicated the stupa that had been built to enshrine a portion of the ashes of Dhardo Rimpoche.[4] Guhyaloka was a favourite place of mine. Over the years I had spent many a month in the high valley in the mountains, usually in the summer, drinking in the silence and inhaling the pine-scented air. Later on in the year I spent time at Padmaloka, another favourite place, where I lived in the eighties,[5] besides visiting Sheffield, where I 'cut the ribbon' at the opening of the new Sheffield Buddhist Centre,[6] and London, where I lived in the nineties. Despite being busy in these and other ways, I kept in touch with Michal, who was still living and working in East London. Both he and I were keen to develop the friendship that had sprung up between us in Krakow, and which was to be such an important part of both of our lives in the years ahead. When I was in London, staying in my old flat above the London Buddhist Centre, we spent as much time together as we could, and one evening I had dinner with him and the other members of the Amritakula community.[7] In August Michal came to see me. It was my 77th birthday, and he gave me a silver spoon with a bear handle. I was much moved by the gift, especially as the spoon had been given to Michal by his brother, and soon afterwards I wrote a poem entitled 'The Silver Spoon'.[8] One of my friends thought the poem sentimental, but it was a true expression of my feeling for Michal. It was at about this time, I think, that Michal started coming up to Madhyamaloka every other weekend in order to study with me. But black clouds were already gathering on the horizon, and a storm was brewing. In October I had to pull out of a study retreat I was leading at Madhyamaloka, as owing to insomnia I was too tired to continue. As I wrote at the time to Padmadaka[9] at Padmaloka, I was 'half dead from sleeplessness'. In all the years that I had lectured and led retreats and seminars, this was the first time I had been forced to let people down in this way, and I was much mortified. But insomnia was only part of the problem. Writing to Vidyadevi[10] in Herefordshire a few weeks later, I confided, 'At the moment I am enjoying a relative respite from my sleeplessness but the underlying problem is still there and will no doubt shortly be confronting me again. It is a combination of high blood pressure, insomnia, and palpitation, which appear to reinforce one another and between them to create a cycle which is difficult to break through.' The underlying problem was indeed still there and a week later I was writing to the same friend that I had 'experienced a few ups and downs with my health, including an alarm on Christmas Eve that took me to the primary care unit of Selly Oak Hospital[11] for a consultation, and I am not sure what the future holds.' The alarm in question was the sudden acceleration of my pulse rate to a dangerously high level, and for this the doctor at the primary care centre prescribed beta blockers, which together with other prescription drugs I am still taking ten years later. Though my pulse rate had been stabilized, at least for the time being, as regards my insomnia there were still ups and downs. In fact there were now more downs than ups, and I was fast moving into a period of chronic sleep deprivation that would last for a year or more. Michal was aware of these developments, and at the beginning of January 2003 he moved into Madhyamaloka. I had already asked him, some time in the autumn, if he would like to keep me company and study with me, and he was thinking about it. The reason he did not say yes immediately was that he quite liked his life in London, where he attended classes at the London Buddhist Centre, and where he had a girlfriend, and in any case he was debating whether to spend half the week in London and half at Madhyamaloka. Before he could make up his mind, however, my insomnia became much worse, and I told him that I needed him. He hesitated no longer, and moved to Madhyamaloka as soon as he could leave Friends Organic.

By this time I had been living at Madhyamaloka for six years. Paramartha[12] and I had moved there straight after returning from a seven-month tour of the United States, Australia, and New Zealand, in the course of which we had visited all the FWBO centres in those countries.[13] Though I did not then know it, this was the last time I, at least, would travel outside Europe. The house to which we moved was a large, late Victorian property, and it stood halfway down a winding, tree-lined street of properties of a similar size and similar design. The house had a garage, and above the garage there was a flat consisting of three small rooms, together with a kitchen and a bathroom. There was also a small guest-room downstairs. During our absence abroad the flat had been thoroughly renovated, not to say redesigned, and it was into this flat that Paramartha and I moved. My books, manuscripts, archives and images had been brought from Padmaloka, so that for the first time for many years I had them all under the same roof as myself. I did not have Paramartha's company for long. Three or four months after our arrival at Madhyamaloka he went to live with his girlfriend in Beaconsfield. We remained in regular contact until he rejoined me in 2008. In the meantime I turned his room into a private office, where I kept my dozens of box files and my scores of ring binders on improvised shelving. Despite Paramartha's departure I was not alone. Next door to me, occupying the four-storey Victorian house, there was the Madhyamaloka men's community, the members of which were senior members of the Western Buddhist Order. I had brought them together at Madhyamaloka in the hope that as a result of living and working in harmony under one roof for a few years they would be better prepared for the time when I handed on to them, and to their counterpart in the women's community nearby, the leadership of the new Buddhist movement I had founded. My hope was fulfilled only to a limited extent, but that is another story, a story that does not belong here. My insomnia was naturally a cause of much concern to the community, as it was to many friends both far and near, and they were greatly relieved when Michal arrived and moved into Paramartha's old room, the box files and ring binders having been distributed round the rest of the flat and a bed installed in their place.

I had started trying some of the traditional remedies for insomnia towards the end of 2002, and I carried on taking them well into the following year. First I tried Camomile tea, drinking a cup of it before I went to bed, and sometimes getting up to make a second cup in the course of the night. Next I tried Valerian tea, which disagreed with me, so I experimented with some of the Bach flower remedies, which reminded me of Bishop Berkeley's belief[14] in the efficacy of tar-water, and seemed to be based on a similar understanding of the natural world, the world of trees and flowers. Lastly, I tried drinking brandy and hot water last thing at night. Dr Johnson[15] had extolled brandy as the drink of heroes; but I could not have been much of a hero, for I found both the smell and the taste repugnant, and soon stopped taking it. With the exception of Valerian, all these remedies had a slightly relaxing effect, but they made not the least difference so far as the insomnia was concerned. In the end, I went to see my GP,[16] whom I was already seeing in connection with my high blood pressure and palpitation. She prescribed Temazepam, a popular sleeping pill, which at best gave me a couple of hours of something that was not really sleep, and which I took much longer than I should have done. At the suggestion of a doctor friend, I also started taking acupuncture treatment. Eight years later I am still taking it, and from the same practitioner, Rosi Roper, now a good friend. The first time she saw me, Rosi afterwards related, my face was green. As a result of the insomnia, which by then amounted to chronic sleep deprivation, I was extremely debilitated, had very little energy, and was on the verge of collapse. Though I have spoken of 2003 as my *annus horribilis*, the latter did not exactly correspond with the calendar year. The period of my chronic insomnia in fact lasted for more than a year, and though I know roughly when it began I find it difficult to say when it ended. During the whole of this period I carried on more or less as usual, except that early in 2003 I told Subhuti, Sona, and Mahamati,[17] and the rest of the community, that I did not want to hear anything of a disturbing or controversial nature, with the result that for about a year I did not know about the upheaval that was going on within the community and within the FWBO.[18] I dictated letters to Khemavira, my secretary, who was a member of the community, worked on *Living with Awareness*[19] with Cittapala, also a member of the community, continued to have laser treatment at the hands of Miss Tsaloumas, my consultant ophthalmologist, walked in the garden, and went through a number of Buddhist texts with Michal. I did all this while living, at the same time, in a kind of hell, the hell of chronic insomnia. The insomnia was cumulative in its effect. Tiredness was piled on tiredness, suffering on suffering, torture on torture. I more than once declared, to whoever would listen, that prolonged insomnia was in fact torture, and that I could well understand how a prisoner who had been deprived of sleep for four or five days might well be prepared to confess to anything, sign anything, in order to end the torture and get some sleep. Even when, on a 'good' night, I had three or four hours sleep, I did not have it *en bloc*, so to speak, but in anything up to eight or nine bits, each separated from the other by a period of wakefulness. Thus the clouds were very black, but they had, from time to time, a lining not of silver but of gold.

That lining was made up of the dreams and visions that came to me during my *annus horribilis*, whenever I was able to enjoy a little sleep. In the earlier part of that period I used to find myself sitting in the midst of a group of monks. Sometimes the group was yellow-robed, sometimes red-robed, but it was always either the one or the other. The monks I saw in my dreams were not monks I had known in real life, but I always knew the monks very well, in those dreams of mine, and I felt quite at home with them. I did not always find myself with the other monks in the same kind of place. Sometimes it was a temple, sometimes the forecourt of a monastery cut out of the rock. In front of us there would be a shrine, and we were all chanting. I do not know in what tongue of men or angels we chanted, but there was a sense of our worshipping the Buddha and chanting his praises. Reflecting on these dreams, I concluded that they were not just a reminiscence of my days as a monk, even though such reminiscences may have provided those dreams with their 'language'. What the dreams really expressed, I believe, was the upward thrust of my being, a thrust which showed itself in my lifelong devotion to the Buddha and his teaching, in my enjoyment of poetry, music, and the visual arts, and in my love of noble friendship. These 'monastic' dreams were succeeded but not entirely eclipsed by dreams in which I saw glittering displays of precious stones, mostly diamonds. Some displays took the shape of many-petalled flowers, others that of necklaces and tiaras, and yet others that of complex geometrical designs. All these displays were constantly changing, so that they were more like clouds than solid objects. There were also occasions when I saw diamonds strewn across a dark background like stars across the midnight sky. Once I found myself walking down a broad tunnel that led into the depths of the earth. The tunnel was not dark but filled with a soft golden radiance, while the walls of the tunnel were lined at every turn with diamonds which flashed and glittered. My dreams also assumed a variety of architectural forms. Many times did I find myself, for example, alone in a dark, empty, cathedral-like structure which I seemed, in successive dreams, to take over. Once there was carried into the vast building, in a little procession, the dead body of an ecclesiastical dignitary of some kind. The atmosphere of these dreams was one of solemnity and awe. At other times I was walking in the mountains, amid the most beautiful scenery, each turn of the road revealing a prospect more glorious than the last. Far below me there was a river, while away in the distance, on the horizon, was a strip of dark blue that was the sea. In more than one dream did I make my way down from the mountain to the scattering of sunlit, white villas lying at their foot, walk through them to the beach and the sea, or up and down the promenade, mingling with the holiday crowd. These 'mountaineering' dreams were accompanied by feelings of expansion, exhilaration, and joy. In another dream I found myself not beside the sea but high above it, looking down on a small white cruise liner far below. There was nothing but the blue sky above, nothing but the blue sky all around. I think I intended to drop straight down onto the deck of the liner, but before I could do so the dream ended and I awoke. Most of my dreams during this period were not so much dreams as visions, but there were a few in which I heard music. On one or two occasions the music came from a hall, outside which I was standing, and once it simply came from above. It was not orchestral music, but the music of a thousand human voices. The music from above, in particular, was of an indescribable beauty and sublimity, far surpassing any music I had ever heard, and it threw me into an ecstasy. What was strange, it progressed, but at the same time it stood still. Paradoxically it was static music. It united time and eternity. At the time I did not know Thomas Tallis's *Spem in Alium*,[20] but when I did happen to hear it, years later, I was at once reminded of the heavenly music I had heard in my dream, of which it seemed a distant echo.

I was about half way through my *annus horribilis*, in which dreams went some way towards redressing the imbalance between pain and pleasure in my life, when there occurred an incident that gave everyone cause for concern. Michal and I often spent the morning in Cannon Hill Park, where after walking round the bigger of its two ponds we would settle down in the courtyard in front of the tea house over a cup of tea and get on with Dharma study. After finishing Sogyal's *The Tibetan Book of Living and Dying*,[21] on which we had made a start during my visits to London, we passed on to select portions of the Pali scriptures, and, I think, some of my own writings. The road from Madhyamaloka to Cannon Hill Park was partly downhill, which meant that on the way back it was partly uphill. One day I took the acclivity more quickly than I should have done, and arrived at the top hot and a little out of breath; there was a cold wind blowing. Ten or fifteen minutes later, when Michal and I were back at the flat, I suddenly felt sick and dizzy. Michal sat me down on a chair, and I fainted. The next thing I knew was that two burly paramedics were bending over me, and administering oxygen, Michal having telephoned for an ambulance. I was chairlifted down the stairs and taken by ambulance to Selly Oak Hospital, where I was given a number of tests and told that I had suffered neither a heart attack nor a stroke and that there was nothing wrong with me. Nonetheless, during the time that I was unconscious my pulse had been barely discernible for three or four minutes, and Michal and other friends urged me to have a proper health check. After all, I was now seventy-seven! I therefore went to see my GP, who gave me a referral to Dr Sandler, a 'general specialist', who after giving me a thorough physical examination gave me referrals in his turn, first to a radiologist, then to a psychiatrist. The radiologist looked at my heart and other internal organs (I looked with him), while the psychiatrist, with whom I had an interesting conversation, assured me that Freudian psychoanalysis was out of date, having been superseded by cognitive behavioural therapy, which was much more effective. The next time I saw Dr Sandler his opening words to me were that he had only good news for me. As I wrote to Paramartha the following week, 'he went on to say that my heart was quite sound organically and was functioning well, as were my other internal organs, and I therefore had no cause for concern. In fact he said that I was in robust physical health and that there was no reason why I should not be good for another ten or fifteen years.' This was good news indeed, especially as my sleep seemed to be gradually improving and my energy returning, though there were frequent blips and though the end of my period of chronic sleep deprivation was not yet in sight. The improvement was due principally to the acupuncture treatment I was receiving from Rosi, whom I now saw only once a week, instead of twice a week as before. More than once, when I was not well enough to go to her for treatment, she came and treated me at the flat, and I well remember the smile with which she manoeuvred herself round my bed on her knees so that she did not risk straining her back by having to bend over me. But although it certainly did seem that acupuncture worked, I had no idea how it worked. In particular, I was not sure whether it worked, in my case, by attacking the insomnia directly, so to speak, or whether it worked by building up my energy so that I was better able to tolerate the insomnia.

Be that as it might, I soon noticed that the improvement in my sleep was being accompanied by a change in the nature of my dreams, which were now less visionary and more mundane. Not that the more visionary dreams entirely disappeared, especially those in which I was surrounded by magnificent mountain scenery, which I continued to have for some time. In these more mundane dreams I often found myself walking through darkening streets, occasionally going into a shop, usually a second-hand book shop. Before long I would happen to meet two or three friends (friends in the dream, not in real life), and together we would go to a café or a tea shop, where I would have a cup of tea and a cake. Strange to relate, I never consumed more than a cup of tea and a cake, even though the food and drink of the dream seemed to stand for food, and I was as hungry for sleep as a starving man is for food. In the early days of my acupuncture treatment with Rosi I had once dreamed of a fierce black bull, a bull that I was trying to stop escaping into another field. Rosi thought the bull represented my natural energy, of which the insomnia had deprived me and which I was now trying to 'capture' or regain. Much later on, when I was beginning to get a little more sleep, I started having dreams of very young animals, usually puppies or kittens. Both puppies and kittens were very playful, and sometimes I played with them. Rosi saw these dreams as a sign that my energies were returning, and I was inclined to agree with her. They were like the green shoots which show that spring is on its way. But although I may not have survived without Michal's unfailing care and support and the regular sessions of acupuncture with Rosi, there were other friends who in various ways also helped me to get through my *annus horribilis*. One of these was Saraha, a member of the Madhyamaloka community,[22] who on many an afternoon sat and meditated beside me as I had my siesta, in the hope that the positive atmosphere thus created would help me to sleep. It *did* seem to help! On two or three occasions I was suddenly plunged into a deep sleep which lasted for twenty or thirty minutes, from which I woke feeling refreshed. Another friend who helped me was Mahamati.[23] Once, when I was getting even less sleep than usual, and Michal was in London visiting his girlfriend, Jenny, and other friends, he remained at my bedside all night, holding my hand and talking to me in a way that made the time pass more quickly. Other members of the community must have helped me from time to time, but it is Saraha and Mahamati whom I remember in this regard. 'Get well' cards came from friends both old and new, and around the time of my 78th birthday there arrived at Madhyamaloka hundreds of birthday cards, some of them very large and colourful and signed by scores of people. There was also a small group of friends who helped me in a special way, and to whom I am particularly grateful. These were Bodhaniya in Birmingham, Karunamati in East London, Kularatna in Stroud, and Santacitta in Brighton – four doctor friends, whom I felt free to telephone for information and advice, since my own GP was not easily available. There were times when I telephoned at an unreasonable hour, but they never minded, and were invariably sympathetic and helpful. So far as I remember, I needed to consult them not about the insomnia but about the alarming vagaries of my blood pressure and my pulse.

In October 2003 I left Birmingham for the first time in more than a year. For the first time in many months I was separated from my usual environment and all my customary supports, except for Michal and the cocktail of prescription drugs I was now having to swallow every day. The cottage Michal had found for us was situated in the depths of rural Shropshire. Completely isolated, with no sign of other human habitation in any direction, it was surrounded on all sides by hills, including the Stiperstones, which legend associated with the Devil. During our three days at the comfortable, well-appointed cottage we did not do very much. We went for walks (I now had to use a walking stick), talked, and took photographs, and in the evening sat back with legs stretched out towards the warmth of a blazing fire, which Michal kept well supplied with logs. So far as I remember, we did not do any study. My most vivid recollection of the place, and of the time we spent there, is of its intense silence. At night, when I stepped outside to look up at the sky, there was not a sound to be heard – not even the bark of a dog. All was utter stillness and silence.

It was also in October that I issued a report on my *annus horribilis*, which I termed 'the most difficult year of my life'.[24] In the report I traced the rise and progress of my insomnia, acknowledged how much I had been helped by acupuncture treatment, and insisted that any attempt to diagnose the cause or causes of my insomnia was purely speculative and that nobody, myself included, really knew why it had been visited upon me. I also confided that the sleep deprivation had made me even more sensitive than usual, so that I had 'shed many more tears than usual, sometimes to relieve tension and sometimes because I was touched by hearing of some noble or inspiring action or experience.' Some of these actions and experiences belonged to well known figures of the past; others to men and women of our own day. What touched me most often, however, and most often brought tears to my eyes, was seeing how day in and day out, week after week, in small matters and in great, Michal (later to become Nityabandhu) regularly put my needs before his own. It therefore was not surprising that in these circumstances the friendship between us should have deepened.[25]

I concluded my report with the hope that I would eventually be able to return to something like normal health for one of my age.

## Notes

1. Sangharakshita founded the Friends of the Western Buddhist Order (FWBO) in 1967 and the Western Buddhist Order a year later. In the decades that followed the movement spread to many parts of the globe. In India in particular its growth was rapid as followers of the great Buddhist convert Dr Ambedkar became involved. There the movement was known as the Trailokya Bauddha Mahasangha Sahayaka Gana (TBMSG). In 2010 the order and movement were given a new name, one suitable for both the Indian and 'western' wings, becoming the Triratna Buddhist Order and Community. (The Triratna are the Three Jewels that represent what to a Buddhist are the most precious of all values.)

2. Sangharakshita had celebrated his 77th birthday on 26 August 2002.

3. See Introduction, p. 2.

4. Dhardo Rimpoche (1917–1990) was one of Sangharakshita's eight main teachers (see note 16, p. 55). The story of his life is recorded in Suvajra's *The Wheel and the Diamond*, Windhorse Publications 1991. Sangharakshita first met Dhardo Rimpoche in 1952 in the Himalayan town of Kalimpong, where they were then both living. There are many references to the Rimpoche in Sangharakshita's memoirs (see especially *PT*, ch.4). Particularly memorable perhaps is an account of a tour of the Buddhist Holy Places which they took, together with other 'Eminent Buddhists of the Border Areas', as guests of the government of India in the Buddha Jayanti year 1956 (*ISGW*, ch.22). In October 1962 Sangharakshita received the Bodhisattva ordination from Dhardo Rimpoche whom he had 'come to revere as a living Bodhisattva' (*PT*, p. 122). In Kalimpong, Dhardo Rimpoche responded to the plight of the Tibetan refugees then fleeing from Chinese occupation by founding the Indo-Tibetan Buddhist Cultural Institute School which members of the Triratna Buddhist Order and community have continued to support down to the present day. During his life, Order members visited Dhardo Rimpoche 'inspired by gratitude for his teaching and respect for his practice'

and because, as he said, 'he made no distinction between his own disciples and those of Sangharakshita' (*Dhardo Rimpoche: A Celebration*, ed. Sara Hagel, Windhorse Publications 2000, p. 2). After his cremation (described in *The Wheel and the Diamond*, op.cit., ch. 15) a portion of his ashes was sent to Sangharakshita. Portions of these ashes have been enshrined at a number of retreat centres around the world: Padmaloka and Tiratanaloka retreat centres in the UK (centres of training for ordination for men and women); at Guhyaloka, the men's retreat centre in Spain; at Aryaloka, New Hampshire, USA; at Sudarshanaloka in New Zealand; and at Vimaladhatu in Germany.

5. See note 2, p. 52.

6. FWBO (now Triratna) activities started in Sheffield in 1990 and the first Centre was opened in 1997. In 2001 the local sangha purchased a former Catholic church which was converted into the present Buddhist Centre. The opening ceremony took place on 15 September 2002 when Sangharakshita cut the ribbon in the presence of the Lord Mayor of Sheffield and local and visiting members of the sangha. See: www.youtube.com/watch?v=LltnG4u-1lM.

7. Amritakula – which could be rendered 'the brotherhood of the nectar of the deathless' – was a men's community in East London which at this time had some seven or so members, including Order members and men training for ordination.

8. 'The Silver Spoon': see p. 171.

9. Padmadaka was at this time the chairman of Padmaloka Retreat Centre.

10. Vidyadevi (b. 1962) was ordained within the Triratna Buddhist Order in 1993. She has worked closely with Sangharakshita on the Spoken Word Project, producing books based on teachings given in the form of lectures, or in the context of study seminars on a wide range of Buddhist texts and topics – books such as *Who is the Buddha?*, *The Bodhisattva Ideal*, and *Transforming Self and World*. Vidyadevi also compiled the encyclopedic *The Essential Sangharakshita* (Wisdom Publications 2009), and Sangharakshita's *The Purpose and Practice of Buddhist Meditation* (Ibis Publications 2012). She lives in rural Herefordshire where she is involved in various literary projects and from where she organized the setting up of the new Sangharakshita Library at Adhisthana.

11. Selly Oak, a suburb of Birmingham, was about three miles from Madhyamaloka.

12. Paramartha (b. 1960) grew up in the remote town of Invercargill in New Zealand. He first met the FWBO in 1982 and moved to England in 1987 before his ordination retreat at Guhyaloka the following year. From 1989 to 1996 he lived with Sangharakshita in the small flat above the London Buddhist Centre in Bethnal Green during which time he trained as an osteopath. Paramartha was companion on several of Sangharakshita's tours (see *TBE*). For a brief period in 1997, and then from 2008 onwards he lived with Sangharakshita in the flat in Moseley, moving with him in February 2013 to Adhisthana in Herefordshire where he is now based, and from where, as well as some work as an osteopathic consultant, he continues to provide companionship to Sangharakshita.

13. For an account of these travels see the last three letters in *TBE*.

14. Bishop George Berkeley (1685–1753), the Anglo-Irish philosopher whose chief work, *A Treatise Concerning Human Knowledge*, was published in 1710. His last major work, *Siris*, (1744) begins by advocating the medicinal use of tar-water.

15. Samuel Johnson (1709–1784), one of Sangharakshita's 'literary heroes' (see My Five Literary Heroes, pp. 111–12), according to his biographer, Boswell, once spoke of a glass of claret thus: 'No, Sir, claret is the liquor for boys; port, for men; but he who aspires to be a hero (smiling), must drink brandy.' James Boswell, *The Life of Samuel Johnson*, Penguin Books 1986, p. 264.

16. A GP is a general practitioner or family doctor usually, as in this case, working with a team of other doctors and nurses caring for a very large number of local patients.

17. Subhuti, Sona, and Mahamati were three of the most senior Order members living at Madhyamaloka at this time.

18. Vajragupta writes about this period in *The Triratna Story: Behind the Scenes of a New Buddhist Movement*, Windhorse Publications 2010.

19. *Living with Awareness: A Guide to the Satipatthana Sutta* was published by Windhorse Publications in 2003.

20. Thomas Tallis (c. 1505–1585), the great organist and composer of choral music who served four English monarchs, composed his *Spem in Alium* around 1570. It is a unique work, being a motet written for five choirs of eight voices, i.e. there are forty parts.

21. *The Tibetan Book of Living and Dying* was published by HarperCollins in 1992. Its author, Sogyal Rimpoche (b.1947) is a Tibetan lama of the Nyingma school, founder and spiritual director of Rigpa, a Buddhist organization with centres all over the world. Sangharakshita met Sogyal Rimpoche when the latter was still a small boy (*PT*, p. 18). As a teenager the Rimpoche came to visit Sangharakshita at his Kalimpong vihara during his farewell tour of India in 1966 (*MAS*, p. 337). The two met again many years later in Berlin at the European Buddhist Forum in 1992 when they shared a platform with other leading Buddhist teachers including Thich Nhat Hanh and Ayya Khema (see note 1, p. 283).

22. Saraha (b.1968) came across the FWBO during a building project in Manchester in 1995. He was ordained in 2001. He spent some years living at Padmaloka retreat centre before moving to Madhyamaloka in early 2003 in response to a request from Sangharakshita to whom he was able to offer some companionship during this crucial time and afterwards. Since 2005 Saraha has worked full-time for the Birmingham Buddhist Centre introducing many people to the Dharma and encouraging them to 'go deeper'. His love of meditation has taken him on two occasions to spend three months living in a remote cave in the Pyrenees in the tradition of the hermits and siddhas of old. (Saraha is the name of one of the early Indian siddhas or yogis.)

23. Mahamati (b.1955) was ordained in 1977. He was manager of Friends Foods (see note 23, p. 68) from 1980 to 1982 and Director of the Karuna Trust charity from 1983 to 1992. He went on to become the charity's Overseas Director, spending seven years living and working in India, during which period he was also involved with TBMSG (the Indian Order and movement). He returned to the UK at the end of 1999 and lived at Madhyamaloka for the remainder of the time Sangharakshita was based there. He became a member of the College of Public Preceptors and from 2006–2014 was an International Order Convenor, visiting Triratna centres and bringing together Order members from all over the world. He now lives in Malvern, not far from Adhisthana, from where he continues to make himself available to Sangharakshita, including from time to time standing in as his secretary.

24. This report was published in the October 2003 issue of *Shabda*, the monthly newsletter that goes out to all Order members.

25. Nityabandhu continued living with Sangharakshita until 2008 when he returned to Poland, along with Santaka, another Polish Order member, and Jenny, who was by now ordained and known as Sassirika. Together they inaugurated the Triratna Buddhist Order and Community in a country where over 94% of the population

consider themselves Roman Catholic. That same year Sangharakshita cut the ribbon to mark the opening of Sanghaloka, the new Triratna (then FWBO) centre in Krakow. Since then the sangha has grown with activities in Krakow and in Warsaw, and several men and women training for ordination. The friendship between Sangharakshita and Nityabandhu has continued across the miles, Nityabandhu visiting regularly at Sangha-rakshita's headquarters at Adhisthana.

# Thoth, Hermes, and Sanatkumara

Above the mantelpiece of my study in East London, long ago, there hung a reproduction of Holman Hunt's *The Scapegoat*.[1] It hung there for quite a few years. Visitors sometimes looked askance at the evil-eyed goat who was the subject of the painting, evidently wondering how it had come to occupy the place of honour in the study of a Buddhist writer and teacher. There was a reason for its being there. I had always liked and admired the Pre-Raphaelites,[2] of whom Holman Hunt was one, and *The Scapegoat* (of which there are two versions) is one of his finest works. I also wrote two poems entitled, respectively, 'Scapegoat' and 'The Scapegoat',[3] the second poem being a sonnet in which I describe the version of the painting in which the goat is white-haired and there is a background of dayglow yellow sky and a line of mauve-pink hills. Both poems were written a few years before I hung Holman Hunt's painting on my study wall, and several of my friends speculated that my fascination with the subject was due to my having been made a scapegoat by the then British Buddhist establishment. Yet although I had indeed been cast out by that body, I did not feel in the least like a scapegoat and was quite happy to live in the wilderness, where instead of dying like the poor goat, as my critics had expected, I became the founder of a new Buddhist movement.[4] However, scapegoat or not, my mood must have changed, for eventually Holman Hunt's *The Scapegoat* was taken down and replaced by Turner's *The Bridge of Sighs, Ducal Palace and Custom-House, Venice*.[5] I had paid my first visit to Venice thirty-three years earlier, in 1966,[6] and Turner's well-known painting, where the pink and white facade of the Doge's Palazzo gleamed from across the olive green water and the pink and white finger of the Campanile points into the blue Italian sky, reminded me of the days I had spent in the great and glorious city, which for centuries was Europe's gateway to the mysterious East.

In 1997 I moved from East London into a different city and a different flat.[7] My study in the new flat had no mantelpiece, and there was very little wall space, two walls being lined with bookshelves, while a third was taken up by a picture window. Any picture I favoured had to be hung or pinned on the inside of the door, so that seated at the opposite side of the room in my red armchair, with the picture window behind me, I could have it directly in view. Over the years many a picture had taken its turn on the door, as my mood or interest dictated, but there is one picture that has lasted longer than any other and which, for the last five or six years, has confronted my gaze whenever I looked across the room. It is a small picture of the Egyptian god Thoth, the ibis-headed inventor of writing, author of the sacred texts, and patron of the arts and sciences. He wears a short kilt, the whiteness of which contrasts strongly with the reddish brown of his body. He is depicted in profile; his left hand holds up a tablet, his right a brush or stylus, as if in readiness to take down a message from the gods. He is the very embodiment of Ancient Egypt, with its pyramids, its temples, and its priestly lore. I came across that Egypt, as I came across so many other things, in the pages of the *Children's Encyclopaedia*. I marvelled at the strange yet comprehensible art, the colours which were still fresh after more than three thousand years, at the bewigged men in their still white garments, and at the beds of tall papyrus reeds from which there protruded the mild head of a cow. Above all, I marvelled at the colossal temples, which seemed built not for men but for giants. Nor, indeed, had they been built for men but for the gods, whose houses they were, from which through the semi-divine pharaohs and priests they ruled, dynasty after dynasty, over a humble, happy, and hard-working people who, if they had honoured the gods and lived rightly, could look forward to an even happier life hereafter. In many ways it was an attractive picture.

It was a picture that formed the backdrop of Joan Grant's evocation of Ancient Egypt in *Winged Pharaoh*,[8] which was the first book I borrowed when, after three years of invalidism, I rejoined the children's section of the Tooting Public Library. A *winged* was an *initiated* pharaoh, and according to the author the pyramids of Egypt were not tombs, as was commonly believed, but places of initiation, in whose central chamber a pharaoh underwent, alone, the spiritual trials that would transform him from a human being into a semi-divine personage. What was more wonderful still, Joan Grant claimed that *Winged Pharaoh* was a work not of imagination but of recollection, that she had once lived in Ancient Egypt, and that she was simply recording what she remembered of her life in that particular existence. I cannot remember how literally I took that claim, but I could have offered little resistance to the idea of reincarnation, which from then on came to be entwined with my thinking. Even so, the effect that *Winged Pharaoh* had on me was less philosophical than literary, for not long afterwards I started writing a short story set in Ancient Egypt. The story began, and perhaps ended, with a detailed description of a lotus pond. (I am by nature fond of detail.) The pond was situated in the garden of a white marble palace or temple surrounded by cypresses, and it was here beneath an eternally blue sky that the hero of my story lived. Unlike the author of *Winged Pharaoh* I had no memories of a previous life in Ancient Egypt on which to draw, but it was not difficult for me to imagine – or to dream – that I had lived beside the Nile in the days when Stonehenge was new or perhaps not yet built. Probably I would have been a priest, shaven-headed and clad in stiff white garments, and had spent my life in the service of one or other of the gods, whether Ra, or Thoth, or Ptah, or the dead and resurrected Osiris; and perhaps, when I was old, I would have spent the cool of the evening in the temple garden, beside the lotus pond, and perhaps, when the moon rose, the young priest would come and ask me about my life, and I would say: 'I was born into a baker's family, and as a boy I used to take a basket of fresh loaves to the temple every morning. The pillars and walls of the temple were decorated with pictures of men and beasts, and with strange signs. I was fascinated by the pictures, and used to stop and look at them. One of the priests noticed this, and one day he asked me if I would like to know the meaning of the pictures. I said I would, so a few days later, with the consent of my parents, I entered the temple as a novice. For the next few years I swept the temple floor, served the priests, learned how to arrange the tray of offerings to the gods, and eventually learned to read the sacred texts. Soon afterwards I became a priest, and from that time onward I spent my days performing the sacred rituals, studying the sacred texts, and exploring the mysteries of our religion. Now I am old. I have passed on what I know to the younger priests. Soon I shall die. My body will be embalmed, Thoth will conduct me to the Hall of Truth, my heart will be weighed, and I trust I shall be found worthy to enjoy the company of the blessed gods for all eternity.' No, it was not difficult for me to imagine all this, and I could almost hear the sound of the old priest's voice as he told the story of his life to his young auditor. Nor did I find it difficult to imagine myself living in Ancient Egypt centuries later, during the time of the Ptolemies[9] and the Roman occupation.[10] Then, too, I would probably have been a priest, and perhaps, when a visitor asked me about myself, I would say: 'All my life I have lived here in Hermopolis,[11] serving the great god Thoth, whom the Greeks call Hermes. In my younger days we had few Greek visitors. Now there are many. They are a young upstart people. They think they know everything. But a few of them have begun to realize that we, the priests of old Egypt, far surpass them in wisdom, and that they have much to learn from us.'

Thoth and Hermes each possessed a number of different attributes and functions, and since they possessed some of these in common it was not difficult for the Greeks to see in Thoth an Egyptian version of their own god Hermes. Both Thoth and Hermes were originally moon gods, we are told, for the moon has no light of its own and simply reflects the light of the sun. Thus Thoth is called 'ray of Ra', the Egyptian sun god. Similarly, when Hermes, the divine messenger, delivers a message from Zeus, the words he speaks are not his own but 'reflect' the words of Zeus, as when he tells the nymph Calypso, in the *Odyssey*, that she is to allow Odysseus to leave her island, where she has detained him the last seven years.[12] Thoth and Hermes have two important functions in common. Both are communicators or messengers, and both are psychopomps, guides or conductors of the souls of the dead from this world to the next. Thoth is the scribe of the gods, as well as being the inventor of writing and author of the *Book of the Dead*[13] and other sacred texts, so that it is not difficult for us to see him as the revealer or communicator of divine wisdom to mankind. Hermes, similarly, communicates the will of Zeus to the lesser gods and to mortal men. Both Thoth and Hermes are channels of communication between heaven and earth, the divine and the human, even the transcendental and the mundane. Moreover, just as Thoth conducts the deceased person to the Hall of Justice, in the same way Hermes drives the ghosts down to the River Styx. As Virgil says of Hermes in the *Aeneid* (Dryden's translation):

> But first he grasps within his awful hand
> The mark of sovereign power, his magic wand;
> With this he draws the ghosts from hollow graves,
> With this he drives them down the Stygian waves;
> With this he seals in sleep the wakeful sight;
> And eyes, though closed in death, restores to light.[14]

I had first learned about Hermes and the other Greek gods, as I had learned about the gods of Ancient Egypt, from the lavishly illustrated pages of the *Children's Encyclopedia*. Later I became better acquainted with them through the *Iliad* and the *Odyssey*. From then onwards they were no less real to me than were the characters in a play by Shakespeare or a novel by Dickens. In a way they were more real, for the greatest of them had, considered as archetypes, a numinous quality that characters in a novel and the drama did not possess. At the same time they all had a distinct individuality that was evident in everything they said and did. Reading the *Iliad*, in particular, in Chapman's translation,[15] I found Hera and Pallas Athena at least as believable as Agamemnon and Achilles, and I followed debates among the gods with the same eagerness that I followed the skirmishes between the Greeks and the Trojans. I sided with the Greeks, though I was sorry for the Trojans, for I was well acquainted with the events that led to the armies of the Greeks being encamped before the walls of Troy. The story began with a secret. The secret concerned Thetis, one of the sea nymphs, and was to the effect that she was destined to bear a son who would be greater than his father. Now Zeus wanted to marry Thetis, but when he learned the secret he changed his mind and Thetis was married to Peleus, a mortal. All the Olympian gods took part in the wedding feast, in the course of which a golden apple was thrown onto the festive board. It was thrown by Atë, or Discord, and it was inscribed 'For the Fairest'. Hera, Pallas Athena, and Aphrodite each laid claim to the apple, and in the end Zeus decided that the case should be judged by Paris, one of the sons of Priam, the King of Troy. Each of the three goddesses showed herself naked to Paris and at the same time offered him a bribe. Hera offered him power, and Pallas Athena knowledge, but Aphrodite offered him the love of the most beautiful woman in the world. It was therefore to Aphrodite that Paris awarded the golden apple. The most beautiful woman in the world happened to be Helen, the wife of Menelaus, the brother of Agamemnon, King of Argos. Paris therefore sailed for Argos, in the Peloponnese, with Aphrodite's help abducted Helen and sailed away with her, and Helen of Argos became Helen of Troy. Soon Agamemnon and Menelaus had gathered an army and a fleet and set off in pursuit of the fugitives. Thus began the Trojan War, in which Hera and Pallas Athena sided with the Greeks, and Aphrodite and Ares with the Trojans, and which resulted in the utter destruction of Troy and the death or enslavement of her people. The real subject of the *Iliad*, however, is not the Trojan War but the 'wrath of Achilles', the son of Peleus and Thetis, who was the handsomest of the Greeks and their greatest warrior – the baneful wrath that 'imposed infinite sorrows on the Greeks and many brave souls loosed from breasts heroic',[16] due to Achilles' quarrel with Agamemnon. But that is another story.

Not many years after I first 'heard Chapman speak out loud and bold'[17] I paid my first visit to the British Museum and, in particular, to the galleries of Greek and Egyptian antiquities. Almost the first thing I noticed was that the gods of Greece and the gods of Ancient Egypt were represented in very different ways. With few exceptions, the former were represented in human form, whereas the latter were theriomorphic, having human bodies but the heads of animals, including reptiles and birds. There were male divinities with the head of a ram or a hawk and female divinities with the head of a hippopotamus or a cow. Whether because of the skill of the sculptor or for some other reason, these hybrid deities were artistically and spiritually credible, and I did not find it difficult to imagine them being objects of worship. I was especially fascinated by the figure of the lioness-headed goddess Sekhmet, the personification of the hot wind that blows in from the desert bringing with it clouds of dust. There were several representations of her in the museum's collection, all hewn from black stone and all of full human size. The finest of these showed her seated, upright, as though on a chair. Dignified and composed she sat there, her hands on her knees, and her leonine face had what I thought was a grandmotherly look. By contrast, the gods in the adjacent Greek and Roman galleries were represented in human form, indeed in *idealized* human form. Hermes, the divine messenger and intermediary between gods and men, was represented as a beautiful young man, naked except for his winged sandals and winged hat, and carrying the caduceus, a rod round which two snakes were twined, one male and one female. The image of the divinely beautiful, slightly androgynous young man is not confined to Ancient Greece or to the figure of Hermes. In the Christian art of the Middle Ages and the Renaissance angels are often represented as beautiful young men, albeit decently clad in flowing robes and equipped with a pair of multicoloured wings. In this connection it is noteworthy that when, in *Paradise Lost*, Milton describes the archangel Raphael, whom God has sent to warn Adam and Eve to be on their guard against Satan, who has just escaped from hell, he can think of no one better with whom to compare the beautiful archangel than Hermes, the son of the mountain nymph Maia and Zeus.

> *Like Maia's son he stood,*
> *And shook his plumes, that heavenly fragrance filled*
> *The circuit wide.*[18]

In Christianity the angels have no feminine equivalent, though the Virgin Mary may be seen as an equivalent to some extent. She is invariably depicted fully clothed, so that her youthful beauty has to be expressed, even concentrated, entirely in her face. In the Buddhist art of the East the beautiful young man appears in the form of the Mahayana bodhisattva, the wise and compassionate being who, in the popular imagination, gives up his own salvation in order to work for the salvation of others. He is depicted neither naked nor fully clothed but wearing the armlets and jewelled headdress of an Indian prince. There are also the devas and brahmas of pre-Mahayana Buddhist cosmology who when they appear to human beings do so in the form of a beautiful young man radiating brilliant light in all directions.

The story goes that Govinda, the learned brahmin, has heard that any-one who remains in solitude for the four months of the rainy season and cultivates the absorption in universal compassion, sees Brahma face to face and converses with him. Having so heard he decides to practise that discipline, and informs the king, his brahmin students, and his wives ac-cordingly, and has a new rest-house built to the east of the city. There he wholeheartedly cultivates the absorption in universal compassion for the four months of the rainy season, pervading each of the four quarters in turn with thoughts of compassion for suffering living beings. Despite all his efforts, however, at the end of the fourth month Govinda does not see Brahma, nor does he converse with him, and he experiences anguish and distress. Becoming aware of Govinda's thoughts, Brahma Sanatkumara, the Eternal Youth, vanishes from his own heaven and appears before Govinda in the form of a beautiful young man radiating brilliant light in all directions. Govinda is struck with fear and trembling at the sight, so that his hair stands on end, and he exclaims, 'Oh Glorious vision, tell me who you are.' To which the vision replies, 'in the highest heaven I am known as Brahma Sanatkumara, the Eternal Youth. Know me as such.' Govinda asks his divine visitor what offerings he requires, and Sanatkumara replies that he takes the offerings as already given, and says that Govinda should ask him for whatever he desires, whether it pertains to this world or the next. After reflecting Govinda puts a question that will be not only for his own benefit but for the benefit of others. He wants to know what mortals have to do in order to reach the deathless world of Brahma. Sanatkumara's reply goes to the heart of the matter:

He among men, O Brahmin, who eschews
All claims of 'me' and 'mine'; he in whom thought

*Rises in lonely calm, compassion-filled,*
*Aloof from 'stench', from lust exempt and free –*
*Established thus, and training thus, I say,*
*Can mortals reach the deathless Brahma world.*[19]

Govinda then says that he understands, in detail, what Sanatkumara has told him. The one thing he does not understand is what he means by 'stench'. Sanatkumara therefore goes on to explain what he meant, giving a long list of negative mental states, from anger and lying down to dullness and delusion, all of which prevent a man from reaching the world of Brahma. Govinda realizes that these negative mental states are not to be overcome if one lives the household life and resolves to go forth as a homeless wanderer, a decision that Sanatkumara approves.

It seems that the story of the brahmin Govinda and the brahma Sanatkumara was a popular one among the Early Buddhists, and several versions of it have survived in various Buddhist scriptures. My own telling of the story is a free adaptation of the *Mahagovinda Suttanta* (*Digha Nikaya* 19), as translated by Rhys Davids and by Walshe,[20] though in the case of the story's central event, the exchange between Govinda and Sanatkumara regarding the way to the deathless world of Brahma, I have produced a composite version of the work of the two translators. The fact that the story of Govinda and Sanatkumara was popular with the Early Buddhists, and indeed came to be incorporated in a text regarded as *buddhavacana* or 'word of the Buddha' suggests that it is worthy of serious attention. To begin with, it would appear that the deathless brahma world (*amatambrahmalokam*) of which both Govinda and Sanatkumara speak is none other than the 'Deathless State' (*amatapadam*) of the *Dhammapada*[21] and other Pali texts, the Deathless State being synonymous with Nirvana. Sanatkumara is thus a hypostasis of this deathless world or deathless state, as his name, the *Eternal* Youth, clearly suggests. Moreover, when Govinda asks Sanatkumara how a man may reach the immortal (or deathless) world he is using much the same language as the Buddha uses in the *Ariya Pariyesana Sutta* (*Majjhima Nikaya* 26) when, speaking of his early struggles, prior to his attainment of Supreme

Enlightenment, he relates how, having formerly sought that which was subject to birth and death he decided to seek what was *not* subject to birth and death. The brahmin Govinda is in fact Everyman. When he asks Sanatkumara how mortals can reach the immortal world of Brahma he is humanity becoming aware of its contingent nature and aspiring to go beyond all contingency. At the beginning of the story Govinda has political power, social position, and domestic happiness, but he wants to find out for himself if, as he has heard, one who practises the meditation on universal compassion for the four months of the rainy season really does, at the end of that period, see Brahma and converse with him. Govinda practises the discipline faithfully, but despite all his efforts Brahma does not appear and he is overwhelmed by anguish. Here two points are worthy of comment. Govinda practises the meditation on universal compassion, but not universal love. However, it is universal loving kindness (*metta*) itself that becomes universal compassion (*karuna*) when confronted by the suffering of living beings. Secondly, and more importantly, Sanatkumara appears to Govinda not because he has completed the discipline but in response to his anguish, for his anguish reveals how deep and how sincere was his longing to see Brahma and converse with him. An intense feeling of spiritual failure, or remorse for unethical behaviour, or of one's own utter contingency – all may serve to precipitate a spiritual experience, or even a liberating insight.

In my view the story of Govinda and Sanatkumara is an example of what may be called pre-Buddhist Buddhism. After his attainment of Supreme Enlightenment the Buddha had no alternative, at first, but to communicate his radical message through the medium of the existing religious language. He was obliged to put his new wine into the old bottles. Later he devised a religious and philosophical language of his own, and for a while the two 'languages', the old and the new, appear to have existed side by side within his community. Later still, however, when the Buddha's new wine was increasingly being stored in bottles of his own design, the old bottles came to be regarded as containing the old brahminical brew. Thus when the compilers of the *Majjhima Nikaya* came to include the story of Govinda and Sanatkumara in their collection a sequel was added in which the Buddha is represented as declaring not only that he himself was Govinda in a former life, but that the path he had then taught, the path to union with Brahma, did *not* lead to Nirvana: it led only to rebirth in the brahma world, that is, to the brahma world in the sense of a heaven within the sphere of mundane existence. Here for 'former life' we must surely understand – reading between the lines – 'early stage in the Buddha's teaching career'. Elsewhere in the *Mahagovinda Suttanta* Sanatkumara assumes the form of a minor divinity called Panchasikha or Five-Crest, and with this we pass from early Buddhism to the Mahayana, in which the 'archetypal' bodhisattva Manjughosha or Manjushri is depicted wearing on his head a wreath of five blue lotuses. Like Hermes, he appears in the form of a beautiful young man, radiating light, and indeed his full name is Manjushri-kumarabhuta, or Manjushri-'who became a youth'. Like Thoth, he is the patron of the arts and sciences and is associated with writing. One of my own precious teachers, the incomparable Jamyang Khyentse Chökyi Lodrö,[22] was widely revered as a manifestation of Manjughosha, and it was from him that I received initiation into the *sadhana* of Manjughosha, whom I have come to regard as a hypostasis of the Buddha's transcendental wisdom.

## Notes

1. William Holman Hunt (1827–1910) painted the Scapegoat during the years 1854–6. For part of that time he lived in the desert around the Dead Sea in Palestine. The subject is from the Old Testament and refers to the Jewish ritual of purification in which a goat, who was supposed to bear all the sins of the nation with him, was sent out into the desert. Two versions exist, one now in the Manchester City Art Gallery, the other at the Lady Lever Art Gallery, Port Sunlight.

2. The Pre-Raphaelites were a group of young men, primarily painters but including poets and critics, formed in 1848 by William Holman Hunt, John Everett Millais and Dante Gabriel Rossetti with the intention of transforming British art, reintroducing a spiritual dimension that they felt had been lost since the time of Raphael. They emphasized keen observation of nature, and drew on medieval and, especially in the case of Holman Hunt, biblical themes.

3. 'Scapegoat' was written around 1970 (see *Complete Poems* 1941–1994, op. cit., p. 287); 'The Scapegoat' around a decade later (ibid., p. 321).

4. As recounted in *MAS*.

5. J.M.W. Turner (1775–1851) completed his *The Bridge of Sighs, Ducal Palace and Custom-House, Venice* in 1833. Today it is on display at the Tate Gallery, London.

6. There is a brief account of this visit in *MAS*, pp. 224–5.

7. i.e. to Birmingham and the flat at Madhyamaloka.

8. Joan Grant (1907–1989) went on to write many other books but *Winged Pharaoh* (published 1937) was her most famous.

9. The Ptolemies were a dynastic family of Greek Macedonian extraction who succeeded the pharaohs in ruling over Egypt, establishing an empire that lasted 275 yeas (305–30 BCE).

10. In 30 BCE the Roman ruler Octavius (later emperor Augustus) defeated his rival, Mark Antony, and deposed Mark Antony's lover, the Ptolemaic queen Cleopatra, annexing the kingdom of Egypt to the Roman empire. Egypt remained under Roman rule, later becoming part of the Byzantine Eastern Roman empire, until the Muslim invasion of 639 CE.

11. Hermopolis, 'city of Hermes', was the name given by the Greeks to the ancient Egyptian city of Khmun. It was a main centre of the cult of Thoth whom the Greeks identified with Hermes. (Today the town is known as El Ashmunein.)

12. Homer, *Odyssey*, Book V.

13. *The Book of the Dead* was the name given to a collection of ancient Egyptian funerary texts meant as a guide to one who has died, and, with its spells, as a protection. An alternative rendering of the title is given as 'Book of Emerging Forth into Light'.

14. Virgil, *Aeneid*, Book IV, lines 330–6.

15. George Chapman (c.1559–1634) was a dramatist and poet who is most widely famed for his translations of Homer's *Odyssey* and *Iliad*. A copy of Chapman's *Iliad* was

one of the first purchases made by the young evacuee, Dennis Lingwood, when he arrived in Barnstaple, Devon in the summer of 1940. "Though the poem had long been familiar to me in prose translation, and though I knew all the episodes, it was a new poem that burst upon me that afternoon..." (*RR*, p. 47).

16. The Chapman version of the *Iliad* begins:
>   Achilles baneful wrath resound, O Goddess, that imposed
>   Infinite sorrows on the Greeks, and many brave souls los'd
>   From breasts heroic...

c.f. a modern – prose – translation: 'The Wrath of Achilles is my theme, that fatal wrath which, in fulfilment of the will of Zeus, brought the Achaeans so much suffering and sent the gallant souls of many noblemen to Hades....' (E.V. Rieu, first published 1950)

17. From the sonnet by John Keats (1795–1821), 'On First Looking into Chapman's *Homer*' written in 1816.

18. *Paradise Lost*, Book V, lines 285–7.

19. *Mahagovinda Sutta, Digha Nikaya* 19 (D.ii.245). In Walshe, *The Long Discourses of the Buddha: A Translation of the Digha Nikaya*, Wisdom 1995, p. 308.

20. For Walshe's translation see note 19 above. The Rhys Davids translation was by Thomas (T.W.) and his wife Caroline (C.A.F.), published as *The Long Discourses of the Buddha*. The *Mahagovinda Sutta* is in volume III, published by Oxford University Press in 1910.

21. *Dhammapada* 21.

22. An account of this initiation which took place in October 1957 is given in *PT*, pp. 13–15. Jamyang Khyentse Rimpoche (1893–1959), also known as Dzongsar Khyentse Chökyi Lodrö, was born in the eastern Tibetan province of Kham. At the age of seven he was officially recognized as the 'action emanation' of Jamyang Khyentse Wangpo, the great founder of the Rime tradition. His training meant studying the teachings and performing practices from all four Tibetan schools of Buddhism, in line with the Rime tradition of his predecessor. In due course he became himself highly renowned as a teacher. His last years were spent in the Eastern Himalayas, both in India and Sikkim. It was in Kalimpong that Sangharakshita first met him at the home of a mutual friend, Burma Raja.

# The Big and the Great: Vandalism and Iconoclasm

'How big is God?' This was a question that perplexed me when I was a child and I thought about it from time to time. I had probably been told about the greatness of God at Sunday school, and thinking that 'great' meant 'big' I tried hard to imagine how big he was. From the way this greatness was described I concluded that God was not only very big but that he possessed, moreover, a giant human form. I therefore tried to imagine an enormously big foot, no doubt thinking that with this as a starting point I could work my way up to an idea of just how big God really was. The foot I imagined was a hundred miles long from heel to toe, and in my mind's eye I saw it stretching from where I stood into the far distance. To visualize a foot of such enormous dimensions was diffi-cult enough, but when I tried to visualize the leg to which that foot belonged I failed entirely. I could not get even as far as God's ankle. Most human beings tend to identify great with big, so that it is not surprising that as a child I should have tried to work out how big was God. This very natural tendency finds expression in the field of the visual arts. In Michelangelo's *Last Judgement*[1] his Hercules-like Christ is of superhuman dimensions, while colossal images of the Buddha are to be found through-out the East. I think in particular of the twin Standing Buddhas of Bamiyan in central Afghanistan, both of which were carved out of the side of the cliff in the sixth century CE. One was 180 feet high, the other 121 feet. For fifteen-hundred years they looked out over the fields of the peaceful Bamiyan Valley. They looked out over them until March 2001, when on the orders of Mullah Mohammed Omar, the Taliban leader, they were blown up with dynamite, the government having declared the two Buddhas to be 'idols'.

The destruction of the Buddhas was widely condemned, though it should not have come as a surprise to anyone familiar with the history of

Islam. It was no coincidence that the second name of the mullah who ordered the destruction should be Omar, that being also the name of the Muslim general who was responsible for the burning of the great Library of Alexandria, with its 700,000 volumes, in 640 CE. There were commentators who characterized the Taliban's action as pure vandalism, or vandalism for the sake of vandalism. But I do not think it was that. There are in fact two kinds of vandalism: pure vandalism, such as the wanton vandalism of boys defacing a poster or Napoleon's soldiers using the Sphinx for target practice, and what may be termed *principled vandalism*, or vandalism which is the practical corollary of a philosophical or theological principle. The Taliban's vandalism was of the second kind. They demolished the Twin Buddhas because they saw them as idols and because they hated idolatry as the greatest of sins. When I first heard that the Bamiyan Buddhas had been reduced to a heap of rubble I felt shocked and dismayed, both as a Buddhist and as a lover of art. At the same time, I reminded myself that images, and the worship of images (if indeed it is the image itself that is being worshipped), had not always been part of Buddhism. Was it not well known that for at least two centuries after his *parinirvana* the Buddha's presence was indicated by such symbols as a tree, a wheel, and a pair of footprints? Indeed, it is not difficult to imagine a Buddhism that is without images, and therefore without image-worship, and even without religious art of any kind, and a Buddhism of this stripped down kind may well exist somewhere in the Buddhist world. What I, for one, cannot imagine is a Buddhism that did not include among its spiritual practices *puja* or worship, in the sense of the inward and outward expression of a heartfelt devotion to the Buddha, whether as represented by a material image, a painting, or a mental image. I also reminded myself that what I have called principled vandalism was by no means unknown in England and other countries to which the Reformation had spread. In the seventeenth century, under Oliver Cromwell,[2] English Puritans destroyed an enormous quantity of religious art on the grounds that statues and paintings of Christ and the saints were idols and that their worship constituted idolatry. Even today there are Protestants for whom the Roman Catholic Church, which continues to worship what

Milton in a celebrated sonnet derisively calls 'stocks and stones',[3] is idolatrous and hence not truly Christian. The Eastern Orthodox Church, after a good deal of internal conflict, decided to allow the worship of two-dimensional paintings (commonly known as 'icons') but not that of their three-dimensional counterparts.

Principled vandalism is fuelled by hate, an emotion which in Buddhism is regarded as a highly unskilful mental state. When its object is a material image it may be termed iconophobia. Iconophobia had its origins in Ancient Judaism, from which it passed to some forms of Christianity and to Islam. It appears in conjunction with monotheism, but seems to be unknown to polytheism and pantheism. Perhaps the most characteristic feature of iconophobia is its conviction of its own absolute rightness, a conviction that enables it to override all other considerations. The Taliban soldiers who dynamited the Twin Buddhas of Bamiyan did not care that they were hurting the religious feelings of millions of Buddhists throughout the world. They may even have been glad to hurt them, for in their eyes were not the Buddhists idolators and therefore deserving of punishment and even death? Neither did the Taliban soldiers care that in demolishing the Buddhas they were destroying *works of art*, or, at the very least, works of archaeological importance that were part of the cultural heritage of the people of Afghanistan and of mankind. For the Taliban, the need to destroy idols trumped all other values. Principled vandalism also has its more secular forms. Besides being responsible for a great deal of human suffering, Communist China's 'Cultural Revolution' of 1966–1969 saw the wholesale destruction of works of art of every kind. Acts of principled vandalism may be committed not only by governments but also by individuals, whether as a form of political protest or as a means of drawing attention to a personal grievance. I remember Leonardo da Vinci's drawing of the Virgin Mary and St Anne, in the National Gallery. The painting was fired at with a sawn-off shotgun, splinters from the shattered protective glass piercing the painting. (The damage was afterwards invisibly mended.)[4] A few years later a student set fire to the Music Room at the Brighton Pavilion, destroying the ornate, gilded interior almost entirely. The cost of restoration ran to tens of thousands of pounds, but so far as I remember the culprit was not even fined.[5] In my view such principled – or rather unprincipled – vandalism should be treated as a crime, and punished regardless of the merits of the cause for whose sake it was committed. I am aware, however, that it would be difficult to arrive at a legally satisfactory definition of vandalism, and still more difficult to decide how an object the destruction of which constitutes vandalism is to be defined. Were the two visitors to Tate Britain who jumped up and down on Tracey Emin's unmade 'Bed',[6] thus disturbing its carefully arranged disarray, guilty of vandalism? Or was Lady Churchill guilty of it when, after her husband's death, she destroyed a portrait of the former prime minister by Graham Sutherland that others thought a masterpiece, but which she detested?[7]

In his *Novum Organum* Francis Bacon[8] speaks of the idols of the tribe, the idols of the cave, the idols of the market place, and the idols of the theatre, which represent the false ideas that prevail in the four principal areas of human life and activity. Thus the word 'idol' can not only be used literally, as referring to figures of wood, stone, or metal considered to be objects of worship; it can also be used metaphorically, as when it refers to ideas, as in the *Novum Organum*, or to a book, a nation, or a person. But where there are idols there will be iconoclasts, or breakers of idols, regardless of whether the idols in question be of the literal or the metaphorical variety. And behind the iconoclasm fuelling it, there will be at least a degree of iconophobia. This means that iconoclasm is of various kinds according to the nature of the object against which it happens to be directed. In apophatic theology or mysticism, for example, whatever concept that can possibly be predicated of God, the Absolute, or Ultimate Reality, however abstract or rarefied it may be, is rejected as inadequate. Similarly, in the *animitta* or 'signless' *samadhi*, which is achieved through deep contemplative insight into the transitoriness of conditioned existence, the Buddhist meditator realizes that the Unconditioned is altogether beyond words. This 'apophatic' trend within Buddhist thought and spiritual practice finds its fullest expression in the Prajnaparamita or Perfection of Wisdom scriptures, the best known of which is the *Heart Sutra*, in which the most cherished doctrinal categories of Buddhism, from the five *skandhas* or 'heaps' to Nirvana, are one by one negated. The *Heart Sutra* might therefore be described as the manifesto of transcendental iconoclasm. As Buddhaghosa observed long ago, "As on the unwholesome plane hatred does not cling, does not stick to its object, so wisdom on the wholesome plane. As hate seeks for faults, even though they do not exist, so wisdom seeks for the faults that do exist. As hate leads to the rejection of beings, so wisdom to that of all conditioned things".[9] The radically iconoclastic nature of wisdom is symbolized in the Vajrayana by the figure of the wrathful Vajrapani. Dark blue in colour, and surrounded by flames, he holds in his right hand the vajra with which he annihilates all mental constructions. Perhaps Nietzsche's 'philosophizing with a hammer'[10] may be seen as a distant reflection of Vajrapani's vajra.

But let me return to the Twin Buddhas of Bamiyan. Many years ago I saw, in a book or magazine, a photograph of them as they loomed up out of their cliff, the pleats of their robes accentuating their extreme verticality. At their foot was a scattering of black dots that I took to be human beings but so tiny that I was unable to tell whether they were local people, or travellers, or Buddhist pilgrims. Whatever they were, they were utterly dwarfed by the figures of the two Buddhas. Had they been pilgrims, they would have had an overwhelming sense of the spiritual greatness of Vairochana and Shakyamuni (as the two Buddhas are said to have been called); for although bigness and greatness are not synonymous, it is certainly possible for the former to suggest, or symbolize, or shadow forth the latter, so that I was not entirely on the wrong track when, as a child, I tried to ascertain how big was God. I was not on the wrong track because I had, even at that age, an obscure sense of something not merely greater than me but immeasurably *higher* in the scale of existence. This sense has always been strong in me, and as I grew up it became increasingly focused on the person of the human, historical Shakyamuni, the Buddha or Enlightened One. Between the Buddha and the ordinary, unenlightened human being there is an immense gulf. The Buddha attained Nirvana, a state utterly free from greed, hatred, and delusion. The ordinary, unenlightened human being is dominated by these three 'poisons', which in depictions of the Wheel of Life are represented by a cock, a snake, and a pig. This is not to say that human beings are not potentially enlightened, or that they may not from time to time give evidence of generosity, compassion, and wisdom, but the path to the actualization of that potential has to pass through many steps and stages. Scratching the surface of one's being with a little meditation will not be sufficient to reveal the Buddha within. If one thinks one is near Enlightenment, one is far from it; and if one thinks one is far from it, one is near.

I began writing these pages around the tenth anniversary of 9/11, the day when hijacked passenger aircraft were deliberately flown into the twin towers of the World Trade Center in New York and into one wing of the Pentagon, the US government's military complex in Washington DC.[11] I do not remember precisely where I was when I first heard of the attack, or what I was doing at the time, but I must have been in my study and heard about it on the radio not long after it took place. Being partially sighted I neither saw what had happened on television nor read about it in the newspapers; but so graphic were the radio reports of the atrocity that I could see it all in my mind's eye. I could see the twin towers, see the hijacked aircraft approaching their target, see one of the towers blazing, see scores of people jumping, some of them hand in hand, to their deaths hundreds of feet below. The picture of all those bodies falling through space, as in a Magritte painting,[12] haunts me still. Some years after the attack I wrote a poem on 9/11. More than three thousand people had lost their lives on that fateful day; but I did not write about this, for it was a subject beyond poetry – beyond any poetry that I could write, at least.

> Proudly they stood, those towers, a monument
> To money, and the power that money brings.
> But hate was stronger. Now they lie in dust,
> And impotent hands a mighty nation wrings.[13]

On second thoughts, I decided that the inversion in the last line was clumsy, and therefore changed the line to 'And a mighty nation wrings its impotent hands', albeit at the cost of two hypermetric syllables. Thus from being a rhymed quatrain the poem became four lines of blank verse. But if the terrorists were motivated by hatred, those who had built the World Trade Center were surely motivated by greed and worshipped what Francis Bacon called the 'idols of the market place'. These idols are of two kinds, the first of them being words which are names of things that do not exist. Some years ago I had a long discussion with a friend who had co-authored a book on money, and the conclusion to which we came was that there was no such thing as money: money did not exist. [14] At the same time, although money does not really exist those who possess or control this non-existing thing have tremendous power, as we have been reminded by the economic events of the last few years. However, this is not a suitable topic for a reverie or reminiscence, at least not at present. [15]

**Notes**

1. Michelangelo (1475–1564) painted the huge fresco of the Last Judgement on the wall of the Vatican's Sistine Chapel in the years 1536–1541.

2. Oliver Cromwell (1599–1658), who became a convinced Puritan after a religious conversion in 1630, was one of those who led the parliamentarian armies to victory in the English Civil War (1642–51). After the execution of King Charles I in 1649 he became for nearly five years Lord Protector of England, Scotland, and Ireland.

3. From John Milton's Sonnet 18, 'On the Late Massacre in Piedmont' written after the brutal massacre in northern Italy in April 1655 by troops belonging to the Duke of Savoy of more than 1,500 peaceful Waldensians who refused to convert to Roman Catholicism:

> Avenge, O Lord, thy slaughter'd Saints, whose bones
> Lie scatter'd on the Alpine mountains cold,
> Ev'n them who kept thy truth so pure of old
> When all our Fathers worshipped stocks and stones…

4. Leonardo da Vinci's cartoon, *The Virgin and Child with St Anne and St John the Baptist* is a charcoal and chalk drawing dating to around 1500. It was acquired by the National Gallery in London in 1962. In July 1987 a visitor to the gallery pulled out a gun he had concealed beneath his coat and fired at the drawing, shattering the protective glass and causing significant damage. Richard Cambridge, the perpetrator of this deed, told the

police that he wanted to express his disgust with 'political, social and economic conditions in Britain'. The restoration took more than a year to complete.

5. The Royal Pavilion in Brighton was built between 1787 and 1823 as a residence for the Prince of Wales, later King George IV. Its architects included John Nash who was responsible for the introduction of its characteristic Indo-Islamic architecture. The arson attack took place in 1975. It was carried out by a 23-year-old art student because it was 'the sort of place people looked up to'. The attack led to the Music Room being closed for 11 years. In fact the arsonist, who suffered serious burns, was later sentenced to six years imprisonment.

6. Tracey Emin (b. 1963). 'My Bed' – an installation consisting of her unmade bed with used condoms and blood-stained underwear and other paraphernalia – was exhibited at the Tate Gallery in London in 1999 and shortlisted for the Turner prize. In October 1999 two half naked men jumped on to the bed with the intention of adding to the art experience. They called their act *Two Naked Men Jump into Tracey's Bed*. 'My Bed' recently sold at Christie's for over £2.5 million.

7. Graham Sutherland (1903–1980) was an English artist who not only painted but worked with glass and fabric (he designed the tapestry for the rebuilt Coventry cathedral). He was commissioned to paint a full-length portrait of Churchill towards the end of the great war-time leader's second period as prime minister. It was presented to him at a public ceremony celebrating his 80th birthday. Churchill hated the portrait.

8. Francis Bacon (1561–1626) was an English philosopher and statesman, scientist and essayist who has been called the father of the empirical scientific method. His *Novum Organum* or *Novum Organum Scientiarum* ('new instrument of science') was published in 1620. *Organum* is a reference to Aristotle's treatise of that name on logic and syllogism. Bacon's work puts forward a new system of logic. This includes an exploration of the four *idola* or idols that impede the mind's capacity for objective reasoning.

9. Buddhaghosa's *Visuddhimagga*, iii.76, quoted in *Buddhist Scriptures*, selected and translated Edward Conze, Penguin 1959, pp. 116–7.

10. Friedrich Nietzsche (1844–1900) wrote his *Twilight of the Idols or How to Philosophize with a Hammer* (*Götzen-Dämmerung, oder, Wie man mit dem Hammer philosophirt*) in 1888. *Götzen-Dämmerung* is a pun on Wagner's *Götterdämmerung*, the Twilight of the Gods. Götze means false god or idol and may be a reference to Francis Bacon's *Novum*

*Organum.* It is a devastating critique of those aspects of contemporary culture that Nietzsche saw as nihilistic and life-denying.

11. The attack took place on 11 September 2001.

12. René Magritte (1898–1967) was a Belgian painter whose early impressionist style was succeeded by his sometimes shocking surrealism where unexpected images were juxtaposed to make the observer question the nature of reality. The reference here is to his 'Golconda' (1953) which depicts businessmen in suits falling like raindrops from the sky.

13. See p. 293.

14. This friend was Kulananda, author of *Principles of Buddhism* (2003) who, with Dominic Houlder (Mahaprabha), (now Adjunct Professor in Strategic and Entrepreneurial Management at the London Business School) co-authored *Mindfulness and Money: the Buddhist Path to Abundance*, published by Broadway Books in 2002.

15. Sangharakshita did refer to this topic a few months later at the launch of *Dear Dinoo: Letters to a Friend* in a talk given at the Birmingham Buddhist Centre on 10 December 2011. See www.freebuddhistaudio.com/audio/details?num=BH18.

# My Five Literary Heroes

In the beginning there were the gods. Later there came the heroes, who were part god and part man. The Babylonian *Epic of Gilgamesh* (third millennium BCE) says of its eponymous hero 'When the gods created Gilgamesh they gave him a perfect body. Shamash the glorious sun endowed him with beauty, Adad the god of the storm endowed him with courage, the great gods made his beauty perfect, surpassing all others, terrifying like a great wild bull. Two thirds they made him god and one third man.' The Greeks were not so exact. They were content to say of their heroes that they were part human and part divine, since they were either the offspring of a god by a mortal woman or of a goddess by a mortal man. Heracles (or Hercules) was the son of Zeus, the king of the gods, by Alcmene, with whom he had contrived to sleep by assuming the form of her husband Amphitryon. Alone among the heroes, after his death Heracles was taken up into heaven and received into the company of the gods. Zeus was also the father of Perseus, the slayer of Medusa the Gorgon, by princess Danaë, upon whom he descended in a shower of gold, after her father had shut her up in a brazen tower on being told that she would give birth to a son who would supplant him. Achilles, whose 'baneful wrath' brought infinite sorrows on the Greek forces besieging Troy, was the son of the sea goddess Thetis by Peleus, a mortal man. When he was born his mother dipped him in the black waters of the river Styx, one of the rivers of the Underworld, which made him invulnerable – except for the heel by which she had held him. It was by an arrow through this heel that he was eventually slain, which is why we still speak of a person's weak spot as his 'Achilles' heel'. Although only Achilles was vulnerable in this kind of way, the other heroes were not without their weak spots, any more than are their modern secular counterparts. Aeneas, the eponymous hero of the *Aeneid*, who was the son of Venus (or

Aphrodite) by the Trojan prince Anchises, had to be reminded of his duty as the founder of the future Roman Empire.[1] All these names and stories were familiar to me almost from my earliest days, along with the narratives of the Old Testament and the parables of the New. Besides the *Children's Encyclopaedia*, my only sources of information were Charles Kingsley's *The Heroes*[2] and a little book entitled *The Story of the Iliad*,[3] yet Hercules and the other heroes were very alive for me and it was not difficult for me to believe in their historical existence. Or rather, the question of their historical existence did not arise for me at that time.

Years later I read Thomas Carlyle's *On Heroes and Hero Worship*.[4] According to Carlyle, world history is at bottom the history of great men. It is the story of heroes, as well as of hero-worship and the heroic in human affairs. Great men were indeed 'the modellers, patterns, and in a wide sense creators of whatsoever the general mass of men contrived to do or to attain.'[5] Heroism could manifest itself in any field of human ability, and Carlyle describes the different forms taken by the hero in different phases of human history. There are six such forms. The hero can appear as Divinity, as Prophet, as Poet, as Priest, as Man of Letters, and as King. One of Carlyle's heroes was one of my heroes too. This was Samuel Johnson, who along with Rousseau[6] and Burns[7] was for Carlyle an example of the Hero as Man of Letters. Samuel Johnson was one of my literary heroes, not one of my spiritual heroes, though in his case, at least, there was a degree of overlap between the two.

There are five men of letters who, throughout my life, have been my literary heroes. It was not simply that I admired the writings of these men – and I admired them immensely. Their lives and their personalities were also of great interest to me, and it was this combination that made them my literary heroes. Over the years I not only bought and read their works but read books about them by their friends, their admirers, and their critics. Thus I came to be the owner of a small library of books about each of them. From time to time I would immerse myself in one or another of these libraries, in this way renewing my acquaintance with this or that literary hero and deepening my understanding of his life and work. I was so fortunate as to meet with all five heroes quite early in life, so that I have now had the benefit of their companionship for more than seventy years. I met Dr Johnson, as I have always called him, before I met any of the others. I met him at the Tooting Public Library, when I borrowed, two at a time, the six volumes of his *Lives of the Poets*, edited by Birkbeck Hill.[8] What led me to him I do not know, though the *Children's Encyclopaedia* may have had something to do with it. Months later, when living in Barnstaple, I was able to borrow from the local public library most volumes of an early edition of *The Works of Samuel Johnson, LL.D.*, and during a visit to Ilfracombe I obtained for a shilling a second-hand copy of Boswell's *Life of Johnson*. By the time I was fifteen I was an ardent Johnsonian and have remained one down to the present day, when a portrait of the great lexicographer looks down at me from the wall of my study. I greatly admired the precision of my hero's language and loved the beautiful literary style of *The Rambler*[9] and its successors. I also admired his poetry, especially the long, sombre *The Vanity of Human Wishes*,[10] and the much shorter, tender and pathetic *On the Death of Dr Robert Levet*.[11] The theme of the long poem is the inconstancy of such objects of human ambitions as wealth, political power, literary fame, and military glory, a theme the poet illustrates by graphic descriptions of the dramatic rise and fall of men like Cardinal Wolsey[12] and Charles XII of Sweden.[13] I found the lines describing the fall of the latter particularly moving, and I soon knew them by heart.

> *His Fall was destin'd to a barren Strand,*
> *A petty Fortress, and a dubious Hand;*
> *He left the Name, at which the World grew pale*
> *To point a Moral, or adorn a Tale.*

I particularly relished the cumulative effect of the adjectives in the first two lines. Towards the end of the poem, when he has sufficiently enlarged upon his theme, the poet abruptly asks a question:

> *Where then shall Hope and Fear their Objects find?*
> *Must dull Suspense corrupt the stagnant Mind?*
> *Shall helpless Man, in Ignorance sedate,*
> *Roll darkling down the Torrent of his fate?*

It is a good question, for it is an existential question, and one which every reflecting human being must ask himself at some time. Johnson proceeds to answer his own question, and with this the poem concludes. His answer is the traditional Christian one. Man must trust in God; for God in his infinite wisdom knows what is best for us, and we must accept his decisions. Though I was far from sharing my hero's religious beliefs, I could appreciate the sincerity with which he held them, besides appreciating the language in which he gave expression to them. A practising Christian as well as a believing one, he examined his conscience at regular intervals, and bitterly reproached himself for his shortcomings. One shortcoming, which perhaps was his 'weak spot', was Sloth, one of the Seven Deadly Sins. But though he was a Christian he was not a happy one. Melancholic by nature, and with a Calvinistic streak in his sober Anglicanism, he tormented himself with the thought that he was damned and would suffer in hell everlastingly. It pained me to think that so good and great a man should be afflicted in this way, and when I came to the end of Boswell's biography I was relieved to find that Johnson's life had ended peacefully.[14] Dr Johnson was a good man, as well as a great one. Compassionate and truly philanthropic, he was the sworn foe of cant and humbug, a moralist in the best sense of the term, and a passionate believer in the importance of friendship.[15] Throughout my life he has been to me much more than just a literary hero.

William Blake, my next literary hero, was born in 1757, and the first twenty-seven years of his life overlapped with the last twenty-seven of Dr Johnson's. Whereas Johnson was conservative in politics and religion, Blake was decidedly radical in both. Although the two men lived in the same city they moved in different social circles – indeed inhabited different worlds. My first acquaintance with Blake and his work was through Swinburne's *William Blake: A Critical Essay*, published in 1868 and available to me per courtesy of the Tooting Public Library, an institution to which I shall be ever grateful. In this pioneer study Swinburne[16] quotes extensively from Blake's literary output, from the early lyrics to the last of the so-called Prophetic Books, thus giving me an idea of his extraordinary originality as both a poet and as a thinker. As I realized later, Blake was quite aware that he was original, but he did not seek to be original. He was 'original' because he was true to his own experience and his own spiritual vision. At that time I was greatly struck by *The Marriage of Heaven and Hell,*[17] a short work which includes what Blake called 'The Proverbs of Hell'. I was fascinated by its bizarre imagery and by its bold reversal of conventional values, a reversal that reminded me of certain of the old Gnostics and which seemed to anticipate Friedrich Nietzsche. I know how impressed I was by *The Marriage of Heaven and Hell*, for I remember copying out the whole work, or as much of it as Swinburne gives, into one of my notebooks. I also greatly enjoyed some of Blake's shorter poems, especially the beautiful *Thel*, a minor Prophetic Book, and the much earlier 'To the Muses', a youthful lament for the disappearance of true poetry. Later, I became acquainted with Blake's graphic output, for he was that *rara avis*, a poet who is as much a painter (or a painter who is as much a poet as one might also say), the only other example known to me being that of Dante Gabriel Rossetti, who was born a year after Blake died, and who was to acquire important Blake manuscripts. I was particularly fond of Blake's illustrations to the Book of Job, my favourite book of the Bible. In fact I came to own an edition of the authorized version of the Book of Job in which the text was printed as poetry, and which was illustrated, moreover, by Blake's sublime engravings. I spent many a happy hour poring over the precious volume, which I lost in the summer of 1943 when our house was destroyed by a German v-1 or 'flying bomb'.[18] In the years – or decades – which followed my love for Blake steadily grew, and I had the satisfaction of seeing him become a popular figure with the poets and writers of the Beat Generation on both sides of the Atlantic, but especially with Allen Ginsberg.[19] When Ginsberg came to see me in 1979, or 1980, in London, he changed one of Blake's poems for my benefit, chanting in a hoarse, unmusical voice to the accompaniment of his finger cymbals. I was then still struggling to understand Blake's major Prophetic books, *The Four Zoas, Jerusalem* and *Milton.*[20] In these extraordinary works, written in a kind of loose hexameter, scores of strange, non-human beings with outlandish names act and interact with one another in ways that run the whole gamut of human emotions. At intervals, there are descriptive passages of astonishing beauty, as well as spiritual insights such as are hardly to be met with elsewhere in English poetry. In *Milton*, the eponymous hero of the poem declares:

> *I go to Eternal Death! The Nations still*
> *Follow after the detestable Gods of Priam, in pomp*
> *Of warlike Selfhood, contradicting and blaspheming....*
>
> *I will go down to self-annihilation and Eternal Death;*
> *Lest the Last Judgement come and find me unannihilate,*
> *And I be seiz'd and giv'n into the hands of my own Selfhood.*[21]

Blake's bodily death took place in 1827, when he was 69. He died happily, even joyfully, singing songs of his own composition, and leaving to the world a rich spiritual legacy. The complex myth he created in the Prophetic Books is not really part of that legacy, for a myth is the creation of a whole people, not of any individual, however gifted. Perhaps the most valuable and influential part of his legacy is his emphasis on the importance of the imagination. It is not just a human faculty but the man himself, in the deepest and truest sense, and without it there can be no true art and no true religion. It is the Divine Vision or Divine Humanity, in which all things have their existence.

In his insistence on the importance of the imagination Blake resembles Samuel Taylor Coleridge, my third literary hero, who was the first to distinguish between fancy and imagination. For me there is no first meeting with Coleridge that I can remember. It is as though I have always known him, or at least have always known *The Rime of the Ancient Mariner*, *Christabel*, and *Kubla Khan*.[22] *The Rime of the Ancient Mariner*, especially, has always formed a part of my imaginative landscape. I delighted in its subtle rhythms, its vivid and precise images, its nightmarish apparitions, its glimpses of heavenly beauty. Underlying all this there are the deeper, darker themes of sin and guilt. With his crossbow the Mariner has shot a friendly albatross, as a result of which the body of the innocent bird is hung round his neck instead of a cross as a sign of his guilt. It is only when he marvels at the beauty of the water-snakes and blesses them that a 'spring of love' gushes from his heart, whereupon his burden falls from his neck and sinks 'like lead into the sea.' Love and guilt were important themes in Coleridge's life and in his work. Though he craved for love, he did not always find it. His marriage was not a happy one (unlike Blake's), and he was desperately in love with Wordsworth's sister-in-law, whom he was hardly ever able to meet. He also felt guilty on account of his failings as a husband and a father and his failure to fulfil his brilliant early promise. These feelings of being unloved and a failure were among the factors contributing to that fatal dependence on opium for which he is best known to the general public. Now although *The Rime of the Ancient Mariner* has always been part of my imaginative landscape, Coleridge's prose writings have not. My first acquaintance with them was when I read his *Biographia Literaria* in the Everyman edition.[23] I read it while living in the foothills of the Eastern Himalayas, and it at once became one of my favourite books. Whereas Blake speaks of the imagination in a bewildering number of ways (though his general drift is clear), Coleridge attempts a formal definition which owes much to the German idealist philosopher Friedrich Schelling.[24] In chapter 13 of the *Biographia*, after delays and hesitations, Coleridge at last says:

> The Imagination then I consider either as primary, or secondary. The primary Imagination I hold to be the living power and prime agent of all human perception, and as a repetition in the finite mind of the eternal act of creation in the infinite I AM. The secondary Imagination I consider as an echo of the former, co-existing with the conscious will, yet still as identical with the primary in the kind of its agency, and differing only in degree, and in the mode of its operation. It dissolves, diffuses, dissipates, in order to recreate: or where this process is rendered impossible, yet still at all events it struggles to idealize and to unify.[25]

Coleridge's account of the imagination has given rise to a lot of discussion, a discussion that continues down to the present day.

Between the death of Coleridge in 1834 and the birth of Oscar Wilde, my fourth literary hero, there is a gap of twenty years.[26] The Industrial Revolution was at its height, and both Wilde and D.H. Lawrence, my fifth literary hero, were in their different ways out of sympathy with the age in which they lived. Wilde was an aesthete, a lover of beauty, and a leading representative of that cult of 'Art for Art's sake' of which the high priest was Walter Pater.[27] As such Wilde is akin to Tennyson's 'Glorious Devil, large in heart and brain, That did love beauty only', and who eventually tires of his solitary, selfish enjoyment of the arts and seeks to purge his guilt through renunciation.[28] For several years I have had on my shelves the three stout volumes of the beautiful Folio edition of Wilde's complete works, and looking into them I can see that at one time or another I have read – or seen on stage – almost everything he wrote. It so happened that of all Wilde's writings I first read the early poems and some of the Fairy Tales, and I read them in the green pocket volumes of the uniform edition. While the poems may not be among the jewels in the crown of English literature, they are of interest as revealing both Wilde's innate Hellenism and his taste for the cultural trappings of Roman Catholicism. Among the shorter poems I particularly liked 'Requiescat', which shares its title with a similar poem by Matthew Arnold.[29] and 'The Harlot's House', with its concluding image of the dawn creeping down the long, silent street 'like a frightened girl'.[30] My favourite among the longer poems was 'The Sphinx'. I greatly admired its clever internal rhymes, its exotic imagery, and its rich vocabulary. Next there came *An Ideal Husband*,[31] which I saw in a war-time production, and *The Picture of Dorian Gray*[32] I have always regarded the latter as a highly moral work, illustrating as it does the truth that conduct affects character, and that a morally ugly life creates a morally ugly soul and *vice versa*. Wilde nonetheless prefaces *The Picture of Dorian Gray* with a series of aphorisms some of which appear to subvert morality. Among them are 'All art is quite useless' and the no less provocative 'There is no such thing as a moral or an immoral book. Books are well written, or badly written. That is all.' In all Wilde's work there is, in fact, an element of 'reversal of values' that makes him, in this respect at least, a link between Blake and Nietzsche.

Later in life I read and re-read Wilde's essays, especially *The Soul of Man under Socialism* (a very Wildean Socialism), *The Importance of Masks*, and *The Decay of Lying.*[33] They were of importance to me at a time when I was giving such lectures as 'The Individual, the Group, and the Spiritual Community',[34] and coining aphorisms like 'Better a live sinner than a dead saint', 'One should not waste time helping the weak. Nowadays it is the strong who need help', and 'I am much worse than people think I am, and also much better.'[35] Around this time I also read Wilde's *De Profundis*[36] an incomplete edition of which I had read in my teens without being able to understand what it was all about. It is a long, bitter, and recriminatory letter to Lord Alfred Douglas, his lover, and he wrote it while in prison serving a two-year sentence, with hard labour, for what was then the crime of homosexuality.

In 1895, the year of Wilde's trial, David Herbert Lawrence was ten years old. He died in 1930 at the age of 44. And though his life was a comparatively short one it was a life packed with creative activity in a variety of genres. Besides the famous novels, from *The White Peacock* to the three versions of *Lady Chatterley's Lover,*[37] there poured from him a stream of short stories, novellas, essays and articles, plays, travelogues, critical studies, book reviews, and letters, not to mention the colourful paintings. In the latter part of his life Lawrence was a great traveller, despite his poor health moving from country to country and eventually travelling round the world. He wanted not only to get away from England, which he both loved and hated, but hoped to find, or found, a community of like-minded people dedicated to fostering new shoots of life within themselves. His nomadic lifestyle did not interfere with his writing, and often provided him with fresh material. He seems never to have suffered from writer's block, and provided he had paper and pen (or pencil) he could settle down and write wherever he found himself. One of the places in which he found himself was Taos, in New Mexico, and it was in Taos that I first met Lawrence, so to speak. The book that brought us together was Mabel Dodge Luhan's *Lorenzo in Taos*[38] (borrowed, inevitably, from the Tooting Public Library). It was not the best introduction to Lawrence the man, any more than *The Rainbow* was the best introduction to Lawrence's own writings. But be that as it may, as I have testified elsewhere, *The Rainbow* struck me with the force of an emotional revelation,[39] and I at once started work on a novel of my own.[40] I completed it in the autumn of 1943, shortly before receiving my call-up papers. Thereafter I returned to books by Lawrence, as well as about him, whenever I had an opportunity, especially in the 1970s and 1980s, when I read or reread everything he had written. Among the novels, *Kangaroo* and *The Plumed Serpent* in particular chimed with me, as did *The Woman Who Rode Away* and *The Man Who Died* among the short stories, while 'The Ship of Death' has long been one of my favourite poems.[41] I always enjoyed Lawrence's lively and sensitive style, whatever the genre in which he wrote. If it could be said of Oliver Goldsmith that he touched nothing that he did not adorn,[42] it could be said of Lawrence that he touched nothing that he did not bring to life.

I am conscious that I have not done justice to the genius of my five literary heroes. I have not even done justice to my feeling for them or to the influence they have had upon me. I would have liked to write a full-length study on each of them, but other activities, perhaps more important ones, have left no room for this. All I have been able to do in this connection is to write a poem in which I briefly describe each of the major works of Dr Johnson,[43] an article on 'Buddhism and William Blake',[44] and an article on 'D.H. Lawrence and the Spiritual Community'[45] I am also aware that my literary heroes are all men and that I do not have a single literary heroine. This certainly does not mean that I do not admire and enjoy the poetry of Christina Rossetti or the novels of Jane Austen, the Brontë sisters, Mrs Gaskell, and George Eliot. It only means that they are not literary heroes in the sense in which I am using the term. I do, however, have three heroines of another kind. The first of these is Elizabeth I (1533–1603), celebrated by the poets of her time as 'Gloriana' and the 'Faerie Queen', who has always been my favourite historical character. The second is Florence Nightingale (1820–1910), the legendary 'Lady with the Lamp', the foundress of nursing as a profession, whose biography by Cecil Woodham-Smith I read in my teens.[46] The third is Edith Cavell (1865–1915), who was matron, or head nurse, at a hospital in occupied Belgium during World War I. She secretly helped wounded Allied soldiers to escape, and for this she was court-martialled by the Germans and executed by firing squad. There is a statue of her in the heart of London, opposite the entrance to the National Portrait Gallery. On the base of the statue are words which while they may not have been her last, were certainly among her last: 'Patriotism is not enough. I must have no hatred or bitterness towards anyone.' Edith Cavell was eventually buried in the grounds of Norwich Cathedral, and I remember being taken to see her grave as a boy.

**Notes**

1. Publius Vergilius Maro (70–19BCE), the great Roman poet and friend of the emperor Augustus, composed his epic poem, the *Aeneid*, from 29BCE until his death, when it was left unfinished. Modelled on the earlier Greek epics by Homer, the poem tells the story of the founding of the Roman empire, with its themes of love versus duty, and the role of destiny in human life.

2. Charles Kingsley (1819–1875) was a clergyman (at one time chaplain to Queen Victoria and in later life canon of Westminster Abbey), as well as academic, historian, and novelist. *The Heroes* (1856) was a book for children about Greek mythology. Among his historical novels are the well-known *Westward Ho!* (1855), set in the reign of Queen Elizabeth I; and *Hypatia* (1853), a fictionalized account of the Alexandrian Neoplatonic philosopher of that name – a book that gave Sangharakshita, who it read as a boy, his first acquaintance with mystical religion 'never to be forgotten' (*RR*, pp. 17–18).

3. This was probably by Alfred Church (1829–1912), a classical scholar who brought out various editions retelling the stories of Homer and Virgil for children. His *The Story of the Iliad* was first published in 1881 with 'illustrations after Flaxman'.

4. Thomas Carlyle (1795–1881), the Scottish philosopher, historian, and satirist whose influence was widely felt in Victorian England through his social commentary. *On Heroes, Hero-Worship and the Heroic in History* was published in 1841, based on six lectures given the previous year.

5. Thomas Carlyle, *On Heroes, Hero-Worship and the Heroic in History*, Chapman and Hall, London 1872, lecture 1, p. 1.

6. Jean-Jacques Rousseau (1712–1778), the Genevan political philosopher, writer, educationalist – and composer – whose writings were so influential on thinkers and various movements from the French Revolution onwards.

7. Robert Burns (1759–1796), the most famous of Scottish poets, and collector of Scottish ballads.

8. Samuel Johnson (1709–1784) is known for his essays, poetry, literary criticism and his *Dictionary of the English Language* (1755). His *Lives of the Most Eminent English Poets* was published 1779–1781, comprising short biographies and critical appraisals of no fewer than 52 English poets of the seventeenth and eighteenth centuries. Birkbeck Hill's edition was published in three volumes in 1905.

9. *The Rambler* was a periodical published on Tuesdays and Saturdays from 1750 to 1752 in the tradition of Richard Steele's *The Tatler* (1709–1711) and Joseph Addison and Richard Steele's *The Spectator* (1711 and 1712). This regular publication gave Johnson the opportunity to write on a wide variety of themes – morality, literature, society, politics, and religion.

10. *The Vanity of Human Wishes* (1749), a poem in heroic couplets, is in style an imitation of the Latin poet Juvenal.

11. Dr Johnson's friend and apothecary, Robert Levet, who had a room in the great man's house, died in 1782 (Johnson was 72). They had been friends for some 36 years. The poem has nine stanzas of which the fourth runs:
    *When fainting nature call'd for aid,*
    *And hov'ring death prepar'd the blow,*
    *His vig'rous remedy display'd,*
    *The power of art without the show.*

12. Thomas Wolsey (1473–1530) became cardinal of the Roman Catholic church in 1515. Favoured by King Henry VIII, he became his chief adviser with huge powers as Lord Chancellor, but he fell from favour when he was unable to negotiate an annulment of the king's first marriage. He died while travelling to London to face charges of treason.

13. Charles XII of Sweden (1682–1718) led his armies to military defeat in the Great Northern War.

14. James Boswell (1740–1795) met Dr Johnson in 1763 and they remained life-long friends. His *Life of Dr Johnson* was published in 1791 to an acclaim that has accompanied it ever since. The account of Dr Johnson's death is given in Boswell's *Life of Samuel Johnson*, Penguin Books 1986, p. 341.

15. In 1983 Sangharakshita led a study seminar at Padmaloka on Johnson's poem 'Ode to Friendship'. This was the first occasion on which he led study for his western disciples not on a Buddhist text but on a text from the Western tradition that expresses Dharmic values.

16. Algernon Charles Swinburne (1837–1909), poet, playwright, novelist and critic, whose critical essay on Blake appeared in 1868.

17. William Blake (1757–1827) composed *The Marriage of Heaven and Hell* between 1790 and 1793 in the aftermath of the French Revolution. The title is a reference – an ironic one – to Swedish theologian Emanuel Swedenborg's *Heaven and Hell* (1758).

18. See *RR*, p. 99.

19. Allen Ginsberg (1926–1997), the American poet and social activist, best known for his poems 'Howl' (1956) and 'Kaddish' (1961). Along with William S. Burroughs and Jack Kerouac he was a central figure of the 1950s Beat Generation of poets. In later life he was drawn to Eastern religion, both to Buddhism (through meeting Tibetan teacher Chögyam Trungpa) and the Hare Krishna movement. He first met Sangharakshita in Kalimpong in June 1962 when he was eager to discuss Tantric initiation. Sangharakshita took him to meet his teacher, Yogi Chen (see 'With Allen Ginsberg in Kalimpong (1962)' in *The Priceless Jewel*, op. cit.). Three years later Ginsberg visited Sangharakshita at the Hampstead Buddhist Vihara and recounted some of the Indian adventures that had befallen him since they last met. Shortly afterwards the American poet organized for Sangharakshita to give a Buddhist poetry reading. A decade later Ginsberg visited Sangharakshita at his flat above the London Buddhist Centre. On this occasion he sang a version of Blake's 'The Tyger' while accompanying himself on finger cymbals. (*MAS*, pp. 106–7).

20. *Vala, or the Four Zoas* (subtitled 'The Death and Judgement of Albion, the Fallen Man') was written from 1797 to 1807, but left unfinished. Albion was originally four-

fold but 'self divided'. The four zoas are Urthona, Urizen, Luvah, and Tharmas. The nine books that make up the work show the interactions of the zoas, their fallen forms, and their emanations.

*Jerusalem: the Emanation of the Giant Albion* was written from 1804 to 1820, another telling of the story of the fall of Albion.

*Milton* was written 1804–1810. (Its preface includes the verses, 'And did those feet in ancient time …' – subsequently famous as a hymn). It is the visionary account of a journey by poet John Milton who returns to earth to correct his former errors. ending with a vision of the complete transformation of human perception.

21. William Blake, *Milton*, ed. Kay Parkhurst Easson and Roger R. Easson, Shambhala 1978, Book the First, p. 81.

22. Samuel Taylor Coleridge (1772–1834), poet, philosopher, and literary critic wrote *The Rime of the Ancient Mariner* in 1797–8. It was published in *Lyrical Ballads* (1798), a collection of work by Wordsworth and Coleridge.

*Christabel*, a poem in two parts, with its haunting atmosphere and theme of innocence and corruption, was composed in 1797 and 1800 but never completed. It was first published in 1816 alongside *Kubla Khan*, to which Coleridge gave the subtitle, 'A Vision in a Dream: A Fragment'. The lines of *Kubla Khan* came to him in an opium-induced sleep after reading a description of the wonders of 'Xandu', the summer capital of Mongol emperor Kublai Khan. On awaking, he set to recording the lines that had come to him but was famously interrupted by 'a person from Porlock'. By the time the visitor had left, the lines had faded and only the fragment remained.

23. *Biographia Literaria* (subtitled, 'Biographical Sketches of my Literary Life and Opinions') was first published in two volumes in 1817. The Everyman edition was published in 1956.

24. Friedrich Schelling (1775–1854), the German philosopher, was a student of Fichte and a contemporary of Hegel – from whose philosophy he diverged. Coleridge travelled to Germany in 1798, staying in university towns, learning German, and studying German philosophy, especially idealist philosophy, and literature.

25. *Biographia Literaria or Biographical Sketches of my Literary Life and Opinions and Two Lay Sermons*, George Bell & Sons 1891, p. 145.

26. Oscar Wilde (1854–1900), Irish writer, poet, and playwright.

27. Walter Pater (1839–1894) was an Oxford don. (Among his students was Gerard Manley Hopkins.) In the course of his life he wrote both fiction and non-fiction. Of the latter, his writings on art and artists, literature, and writers influenced literary and artistic life both during his life and after. Most controversial during his life (and of particular interest now to Buddhists) was the conclusion to his *Studies in the History of the Renaissance* (1873). In his unfinished novel, *Gaston*, Pater engaged with some of the figures of the 'Yellow Nineties' including Oscar Wilde whose *Picture of Dorian Gray* he reviewed in 1891 in the *Bookman* magazine.

28. Alfred, Lord Tennyson (1809–1892), the great Victorian Poet Laureate. These lines are from an early work, 'a kind of allegory' entitled 'To— with the following poem' (see *Tennyson's Poetry*, ed. Robert W. Hill Jr., W.W. Norton 1971, p.26). The lines are dedicated to Richard Trench who, like Tennyson, belonged to the Cambridge University 'Apostles' (a secret society founded in 1820). Tennyson's poetry was well-known to Sangharakshita from an early age (see his humorous account of the attempt of his junior school teacher to verse her class in *The Lady of Shalott*. *RR*, pp. 26–7). When he left school at the age of fifteen, a gift from the English mistress was Tennyson's *Complete Poems* (*RR*, p. 52).

29. Wilde's 'Requiescat' (a prayer for the dead) is in five short verses. It was first published in a collection of *Poems* (1881). It begins:
> *Tread lightly, she is near*
> *Under the snow,*
> *Speak gently, she can hear*
> *The daisies grow.*

The poem of the same name by Matthew Arnold (1822–1888) was first published in 1853. In four verses, it begins:
> *Strew on her roses, roses,*
> *And never a spray of yew!*
> *In quiet she reposes;*
> *Ah, would that I did too!*

30. 'The Harlot's House', composed probably in Paris in 1883, was published only once during Wilde's lifetime in 1885. The last of the twelve verses runs:
> *And down the long and silent street,*
> *The dawn with silver-sandalled feet,*
> *Crept like a frightened girl.*

31. *An Ideal Husband* was first staged early in 1895 at the Haymarket Theatre, London, when it had 124 continuous performances. Despite his arrest in April, his conviction for 'gross indecency', and subsequent incarceration, the play continued to be performed, without the author's name being advertised. It continues to be one of Wilde's most popular plays.

32. *The Picture of Dorian Gray* was first published as a serial in *Lippincott's Monthly Magazine* in 1890. It was revised and brought out as a book edition in 1891.

33. *Oscar Wilde: Letters and Essays*, ed. Merlin Holland, Folio Society 1993.

34. This lecture was given in 1971, four years after the founding of the FWBO. It can be found at www.freebuddhistaudio.com/audio/details?num=91. See also Sangharakshita's *What is the Sangha?*, ch. 5.

35. See *Peace is a Fire*, 2nd edition, Windhorse Publications 1995, pp. 82, 85, and 83.

36. Written in the first months of 1897 towards the end of his imprisonment in Reading Gaol. The early published editions were expurgated. The full text appeared only in 1962 in *The Letters of Oscar Wilde*, edited by Rupert Hart-Davis.

37. *The White Peacock* was Lawrence's first novel, published in 1911. The story is set in the Eastwood of his own childhood. *Lady Chatterley's Lover*, his last novel, was printed privately in Italy in 1928. The first unexpurgated version to be published in England was not until 1960.

38. Mabel Evans Dodge Sterne Luhan (1879–1962) – she was married four times – was a patron of the arts. From 1919 she lived in Taos, and with her then husband, started a literary colony. D. H. Lawrence and his wife Frieda were invited to visit in 1922. They returned in 1924 for eighteen months, living on land given to them by Mabel. *Lorenzo in Taos*, published in 1932, is a memoir of Lawrence's visit.

39. In *TBE*, Sangharakshita writes, 'It was also as a teenager that I first read *The Rainbow*, which affected me like an emotional depth charge....' (p. 278). See also *FMK*, p. 283.

40. See *A Room with a View* in this volume, p. 51, and *RR*, p. 84.

41. *Kangaroo*, set in Australia, was published in 1923 after Lawrence's visit there with his wife Frieda. The story is of an English writer and his German wife and their visit to New South Wales. *The Plumed Serpent* is set in Mexico. The plumed serpent of the title is Quetzalcoatl, an indigenous deity. Lawrence began writing it during his stay in New Mexico on the ranch at Taos. It was published in 1926.

*The Woman Who Rode Away* was written in Taos in 1924 and published the following year. *The Man Who Died* was first published in 1929 as *The Escaped Cock* (Lawrence's preferred title). Its protagonist is Christ, who survives his crucifixion, returns to the world, and goes in search of the meaning of life, a search which takes him to a temple of Isis.

'The Ship of Death' was written not long before Lawrence's own death and published posthumously in 1933.

42. Dr Johnson's epitaph for Oliver Goldsmith (1728–1774) translates from the Latin: "Oliver Goldsmith: A Poet, Naturalist, and Historian, who left scarcely any style of writing untouched, and touched nothing that he did not adorn…"

43. 'Lines Composed on Acquiring "The Works of Samuel Johnson, LL.D.", in Eleven Volumes, MDCCLXXXVII', written in 1983. See *Complete Poems*, pp. 345–50.

44. 'Buddhism and William Blake' in *Alternative Traditions*, Windhorse Publications 1986, pp. 185–97.

45. 'D.H. Lawrence and the Spiritual Community', ibid., pp. 171–84.

46. Cecil Blanche Woodham-Smith (1896–1977) whose first historical work, *Florence Nightingale*, was published in 1950. She went on to write on other historical themes including the Irish famine of the 1840s and the life of Queen Victoria.

# The Language of Scents

On returning from church on Sunday mornings I would go straight to the kitchen, where I would usually find my mother putting the finishing touches to the Sunday lunch. More often than not, there would be a batch of cakes fresh from the oven. Sometimes it was rock cakes, sometimes coconut pyramids. When it was rock cakes my mother would burn two or three of them, for I was particularly fond of the taste of burnt cake, a predilection which continues down to the present day. I was also fond of the smell of coal, and from time to time I would open the door of the coal bunker, put my head inside, and stand inhaling the dusty fragrance with deep breaths. Another favourite smell was that of roasting coffee beans. As we did not have coffee at home, I experienced this pleasure only when I happened to pass a certain shop in the Tooting Bec High Street. My nostrils would respond to the rich, warm aroma long before I came abreast of the shop, in whose window a coffee mill would be perpetually grinding the roasted beans. I was then twelve or thirteen. Even now, though I am not a coffee drinker, I can enjoy the smell of freshly ground coffee. Whether suddenly caught in a crowded restaurant, or slowly inhaled after sharing a meal with coffee drinking friends, that unique aroma can give rise to all kinds of associations, just as the scent of the famous madeleine was responsible for Proust's 'remembrance of things past'.[1] More often than not, I would float on cloud upon cloud of recollection to South India, where I spent 1947 and 1948, and where I used to hear just before dawn the *clunk clunk* of stone on stone as the housewife pounded roasted beans for the morning coffee. During much of my time there I stayed at the Haunted Ashram in Muvattapuzha with my Bengali friend Buddharakshita (then known as Satyapriya), whom I had first met in Singapore, with whom I had teamed up in Calcutta, and with whom I had 'gone forth' from home into the homeless life in Kasauli in 1947.

Buddharakshita had many sterling qualities, but as readers of *The Rainbow Road* will know he was possessed of a vile temper, or rather there were times when a vile temper possessed him. This demon of ungovernable rage would possess him whenever he thought – often mistakenly – that he was being slighted, or looked down on, or treated as an inferior. His fury would then know no bounds and might even lead to an act of violence, an act of which he would afterwards feel deeply ashamed and for which he would apologize profusely. Over the years I have often wondered why my old friend was cursed with such a temper, and what it was that made him so quick to take offence. Perhaps there was a clue in the way he had been brought up. I knew that he came from a Brahmin family, and that even as a very small child he had been – according to his own gleeful admission – unruly and disobedient in the extreme. I also knew that as a boy he had been highly competitive, for he had more than once regaled me with stories of how he had always come first at this or that sport or taken the lead in this or that activity. Evidently the young Buddharakshita, like the Buddharakshita I knew, always had to be on top. Thus when he went to see his family in rural Bengal after being ordained as a bhikkhu in Ceylon (now Sri Lanka) he had given them an ultimatum. Either all his elder brothers and his mother (his father was long dead) must bow down before him in the traditional Buddhist manner or they would never see him again. They had all bowed down, he told me triumphantly. I was not surprised to hear this. It had so happened that I had been ordained as a bhikkhu before him,[2] which meant that according to monastic custom he was junior to me and therefore had to bow down before me. When we met for the first time after our respective ordinations, however, he told me, with an embarrassed laugh, that he would not be bowing down before me as we were friends. I said nothing, but I knew quite well that if he had been the senior his attitude would have been very different. But the smell of coffee – to return to my original theme – was not the only smell for which I remembered South India. There was also the smell of coconut oil. The housewife cooked with coconut oil, young men drenched their hair in it just as I had once plastered mine with Brylcreem, and it filled the lamps in the temples and in homes that were without electricity.

From coffee-drinking South India the clouds of recollection carry me to *cha*-drinking North India. There the cooking medium was not coconut oil but mustard oil. This was certainly the case in crowded, insanitary Calcutta, to which in the 1950s and 1960s I was a fairly regular visitor.[3] As darkness fell, smoke arose from innumerable cooking fires, and the air would be filled with the acrid smell of mustard oil as the Calcutta house-wife fried not only vegetables but fish, of which the Bengalis were passionately fond. Not that all the smells of North India were unpleasant. In the foothills of the Eastern Himalayas, 300 miles north of Calcutta, was the little town of Kalimpong, where I lived for fourteen years. There I became familiar with the fresh, purifying smell of the juniper, masses of which were burned by the town's Tibetan Buddhists in connection with their religious observances. Juniper also entered into the composition of Tibetan incense, along with a variety of Himalayan herbs. I liked to burn a stick of Tibetan incense in the morning and a stick of the much sweeter Indian incense in the evening. The effect of the one was stimulating, I found; that of the other, calming. In Kalimpong I also became familiar with the seductive fragrance of the gardenia. I had no gardenias in my own garden, but on the day of the Vaisakha full moon, when I celebrated the anniversary of the Buddha's attainment of supreme perfect Enlighten-ment, Princess Irene of Greece, who lived further up the hillside, would send down to me a huge wicker basket filled to the brim with the velvety white blossoms for the decorating of the shrine-room.[4] Not that I was always in Kalimpong, which was perhaps more my headquarters than my home. During the winter months I usually travelled in the plains, criss-crossing the northern and central parts of India by train, bus, and bullock cart. The clouds of recollection now bring to me the intensely sweet per-fume of a tiny red rose. I first inhaled this perfume in Rajasthan, when I saw small baskets of the flowers being offered at the shrine of a *pir* or Muslim saint. Later I breathed in the same perfume in Maharashtra, where Buddhist friends would offer me a posy of the little red flowers when I gave a lecture or officiated at a ceremony. The clouds of recollection also bring to me, from that time, the scent of the thin sticks of incense that burned in the houses I visited, or to which I was invited for lunch. Sometimes the scent was that of white sandalwood, delicate and purifying; but more often it was the strong, sickly sweetness of the cheaper kind of incense, which owed its sweetness to chemicals rather than herbs. The lighting of a stick of incense was one of the ways in which the Indian householder traditionally received an honoured guest. On his arrival the guest would be given water with which to wash his feet, then water to drink, and a garland of sweet-smelling flowers would be placed round his neck. He would then be conducted to the seat of honour, an oil lamp lit and a stick of incense burned to drive away the flies and mosquitoes. Finally, the guest would be served a meal, after which he would be sprinkled with rosewater and entertained with song and instrumental music by the daughters of the house, all dressed in their best. In the Mahayana these simple acts of hospitality were transformed into a set of seven (or eight) ritual offerings to the Buddha, the guest of all guests, who appears to us as it were from another dimension – the dimension of the Transcendental. On Tibetan Buddhist shrines these offerings are represented by a row of small bowls. Normally the bowls are filled with water, the water being changed each day. On special occasions one bowl is replaced by a lighted lamp, another filled with scented water, the remaining three (or four) being filled with rice. The bowls of rice are topped, respectively, by a flower, a stick of incense, a ripe fruit, and a pair of finger cymbals, though when there are seven bowls the cymbals are placed beside the last bowl. Incense of one kind or another has in fact been used in religious worship since the earliest times, and by faiths widely separated in time and space. It was certainly used by the ancient Egyptians. According to Plutarch (46–120 CE), in the temples of Egypt frankincense was burned in the morning, myrrh at noon, and *kifr* (also spelled *kyphir*), a compound of various herbs and resins, in the evening. Moreover, certain gods were associated with specific types of incense. For example, Hathor, who was the goddess of Love as well as of War, was strongly associated with myrrh. The ancient Greeks, too, associated certain gods with specific types of incense. Thus in the 'Orphic' hymns the chanting of the hymn to Zeus is to be accompanied by 'the fumigation from borax' (Thomas Taylor's translation), that to Hermes by 'the fumigation from frankincense', and that to the Muses by 'the fumigation from myrrh'. To the modern ear the word 'fumigation' is suggestive of the sickroom and the beehive, but to the Egyptians and Greeks, and the other peoples of antiquity, it meant something very different. It meant the cleansing and purifying not just of the atmosphere we breathe but the 'psychic' atmosphere in which we live as spiritual beings. If *this* atmosphere is sufficiently pure the gods would be more likely to come near and the worshipper be more likely to feel their presence. The burning of incense was thus an essential part of religious worship.

In 1964 I returned to England, where for the next five or six years I lived in London.[5] The smells that the clouds of recollection now bring to me from this juncture are not of the pleasantest kind. The predominant smell is that of petrol, a smell occasionally overpowered by the stronger smell of frying fish and chips. I did not then reacquaint myself with the smells of English flowers, though I had arrived at the height of summer and the little front gardens were bright with flowers of every hue. Later, when I once more had a shrine, my nostrils were again pleasantly tickled by the smell of incense, usually of the Indian sandalwood variety. Later still, when I was living on Highgate West Hill, not far from where the much diminished Coleridge had spent his last days,[6] I used to hold what I called incense-burning parties. By this time I was familiar with many different types of incense. There was the sweet Indian incense of both the inferior and superior kind. It came in thin black sticks, which sometimes were so flexible that they would bend. This was the first kind of incense I ever bought. When I was about eleven or twelve years old I bought a few sticks of it (at a penny a stick) from a little shop in Brighton, along with a small glass Buddha of Japanese manufacture.[7] Then there was Tibetan incense. This, too, came in sticks, though the sticks were not only reddish brown in colour but longer and thicker than their Indian counterparts. Wherever they had been made, whether in a monastery in Tibet or at a Tibetan refugee settlement in India, when lit they gave off the same healthful, invigorating scent as the incense I was accustomed to use in

Kalimpong. Chinese incense was less interesting than either the Indian or the Tibetan variety. The sticks came in bright red packets, and were sand-coloured, and they gave off a smell rather like that of burning sawdust. Chinese incense was in fact of an austere, 'Confucian' character, and unlike its Indian cousin it made no concessions to sensuous enjoyment. Thai incense, too, had a woody smell, but the smell was mixed with a touch of sweetness. The sticks in which it came were remarkable in that each of them broadened at the top end into an inverted cone. Finally, there was Japanese incense, which came in short thin sticks of different colours and had a fragrance like that of women's face powder, so that it was redolent more of the boudoir than the shrine. If Tibetan incense was masculine, then Japanese incense was decidedly feminine. Thus we had many types of incense with which to experiment at our incense-burning parties. These gatherings started at about seven in the evening and generally went on until midnight. The eight or nine people who came to them were friends I had made since my arrival in England a few years earlier. They were all young people, nearly half of them being students at a well known art school. Sessions began with the burning of a single type of incense, and we all sat around inhaling the aroma and chatting quietly. At the very centre of things was blonde, beautiful Louie in her long green dress who officiated as priestess, so to speak, and who remained in contact with me much longer than any other member of the group.[8] Every now and then a different type of incense was burned, so that smoke mingled with smoke and scent with scent. At one time we burned different types of incense together, at another we burned them in a certain order, in each case noting the particular way in which we were affected. As the evening progressed, the atmosphere in the room changed, there would be a kind of quiver in the air, and we would feel less and less inclined to talk. Whether because of the order in which the different types of incense had been burned, or because of the cumulative effect of the various odours of the various aromas we had inhaled, by the end of the evening we would find ourselves in a state of altered consciousness that was both individual and collective. In the hippie jargon of those days we were 'stoned'.

It was at about this time that I had my first experience of LSD. I have written elsewhere about the second time I took it,[9] and perhaps the time has now come for me to record the little that I remember of that first occasion. I took LSD together with my young American friend and flatmate Carter, whom I had befriended when he was in deep disgrace with some of my other friends. He had taken LSD some seven or eight times, but the trips had all been bad ones, and he was convinced that if he and I dropped 'acid' together he would at last have a good trip. I agreed that we should do this, whereupon he obtained from a contact in California (by post!) a few tablets of what was guaranteed, he said, to be one hundred percent pure LSD. The trip lasted for about twelve hours. I had intended to record the effects of the LSD as it took hold, but this proved not to be feasible. All I could write was 'feel as though little fish were nibbling at my brain', followed by the single word 'laughter'. I was, in fact, laughing uncontrollably, and the laughter was releasing huge quantities of energy. After that, there were only squiggles on the paper. The entire trip is virtually a blank to me. All that I could remember of it, even immediately afterwards, was of my being present at the dawn of creation. 'First light on first water' were the words that came to me, accompanied by the visual image of a vast expanse of water upon which a light was shining. The experience was not a spiritual one, strictly speaking, but neither was it psychological in the narrow sense of the term. Perhaps it is best described as 'cosmic'. Whatever it was that had happened during those twelve hours, I was well satisfied with my first experience of LSD, though it left me feeling physically and mentally tired. Carter, for his part, was greatly relieved at having had a good trip, even though nothing remarkable had happened.

It was about this time, too, that Carter and I were in the habit of smoking cannabis in a secluded corner of Parliament Hill Fields, which lay only a stone's throw from my flat on the way to Kenwood House.[10] It was high summer, and we lay on our backs in the long grass feeling the warmth of the sun on our bodies. The cannabis gave me a delightful, floating sensation. I was floating through the air, floating with the white clouds – floating, floating. At the same time, strange to say, I had the feeling that I was not moving at all! Though I smoked a good deal of cannabis that summer, I was in no danger of getting hooked, and when Carter returned to his native California I gave up the habit for good and have not been tempted since.

Years later, when even Louie was no longer in touch with me, I took to burning frankincense and myrrh, as well as *kifr* allegedly made in accordance with a recipe that had been found in an ancient Egyptian papyrus. I obtained them by post from an agency which catered for the ritual needs of witches and warlocks, together with a supply of the thick charcoal discs on which they could be safely burned. The odours of the frankincense and the myrrh, though not the *kifr*, were much stronger and more distinctive than those of the different incenses that had been burned at my incense-burning parties. Each odour communicated something. It had a *meaning*. That is to say there is an olfactory language of smells and scents, just as there is a visual language of form and colour and an aural language of sound. Dogs, for example, understand this olfactory language, at least on their own level of intelligence, while human beings are acquainted with it only to a very limited extent. We can distinguish between different perfumes, we can recognize the food in front of us by its smell, and we can tell whether another person is sick or well, and what kind of emotional state they are in, by their body odour; but that is about all. Evidently we have a lot to learn in this area. In any case, even if we succeed in developing a sense of smell as keen as that of a dog, that is still a long way from our being able to understand the meaning of scents, as distinct from understanding the associations to which they give rise. The *Vimalakirti-nirdesa*, an important Mahayana scripture, appears to envisage the possibility of human beings being able to do this. It speaks of a world in which everything is made of fragrances and in which Fragrance-Accumulated, the Buddha of that land, communicates the Dharma by means of fragrance. As a bodhisattva from that land tells Vimalakirti, the eponymous hero of the scripture, 'The Thus Come One in our land does not employ words in his exposition. He just uses various fragrances to induce heavenly and human beings to undertake the observance of the precepts.'[11] Another important work, *The Awakening of Faith in the*

*Mahayana*, uses the image of perfume and what it terms 'perfuming' to elucidate a serious problem. This problem arises out of the fact that the leading of the spiritual life involves, by its very nature, the positing of a dichotomy between samsara and Nirvana, the conditioned and the Unconditioned. How, then, shall a mortal attain the Immortal State, or a conditioned being achieve the Unconditioned? That is the question. According to *The Awakening of Faith in the Mahayana*, just as our worldly clothes have no scent of their own but can acquire one, so our worldly, samsaric mind is perfumed by Suchness (a Mahayana term for the Unconditioned), and it is because they are perfumed by Suchness that sentient beings, though defiled by greed, hatred, and delusion, are able to aspire to the attainment of Enlightenment. In other words, the dichotomy is not absolute, but can be transcended.

**Notes**

1. Marcel Proust (1871–1922), the great French novelist, composed *Remembrance of Things Past* (*À la recherche du temps perdu*, more recently translated as *In Search of Lost Time*) – a novel in seven parts – from 1909 until his death. A theme of the novel is an exploration of what Proust called voluntary and involuntary memory, the first being partial, the second bringing one much closer to the 'essence' of the past. An example of the latter occurs in a scene in which the narrator tastes a madeleine (a kind of small cake) and immediately a complete experience from childhood fills his mind – a memory of eating a piece of madeleine given to him by an aunt. In fact in the novel it is the taste rather than the smell of the delicious cake that evokes the memory; but the meaning of Sangharakshita's train of thought is clear.

2. Sangharakshita and Buddharakshita (see note 17, p. 55) received their samanera or 'lower' ordination together at Kusinara on 12 May 1949 (see *A History of my Going for Refuge*, Windhorse Publications 1988, pp. 30–33). Soon afterwards their paths diverged: Sangharakshita went to Benares to stay with Bhikshu Jagdish Kashyap while Buddharakshita left for Ceylon (*RR*, pp. 429–30). From March 1950 Sangharakshita was based in Kalimpong and that autumn he travelled to Sarnath where on 24 November 1950 he received the bhikshu or 'higher' ordination (*A History of My Going for Refuge*, op.cit., pp. 33–6).

3. In 1952 Sangharakshita spent several weeks in Calcutta, staying at the Maha Bodhi Society headquarters while writing his biographical sketch of Anagarika Dharmapala (*FMK*, ch. 18). In 1954 he became editor of the *Maha Bodhi* journal and in this capacity regularly spent time in 'the city of dreadful noise' checking proofs and engaging in other work for the monthly publication – as well as giving lectures. (See for instance his chapter 'Proof-reading at 110°F' in *ISGW*, p. 113 and the introduction to *Beating the Drum*, Ibis Publications 2012).

4. As told in *ISGW*, ch. 1., 'The Scent of Gardenias'.

5. As recounted in *MAS*.

6. Samuel Taylor Coleridge (1772–1834), the great English poet, literary critic, and philosopher, lived from 1816 with the physician James Gillman and his wife in Highgate where, despite the struggle with opium addiction, he managed to complete his *Biographia Literaria* and produce some other work. Sangharakshita has regarded Coleridge as second only to Shakespeare among the greats of English literary history. See also 'My Five Literary Heroes' in this volume.

7. As related in *RR*, p. 35.

8. The art students called themselves the English Mystical School, or New English Mystical School. It was with them (and others) that Sangharakshita visited Glastonbury Tor in 1969. The experiences they had are recounted in his poem, 'On Glastonbury Tor' (*Collected Poems*, pp. 439–45).

9. See *1970: A Retrospect*, at www.sangharakshita.org/a-retrospect.html#toc-19.

10. Parliament Hill Fields (from which one could at one time see the Houses of Parliament) are at the south-east corner of Hampstead Heath, that great green and open space that runs from Hampstead to Highgate in North London. Kenwood House, a former stately home, now restored and open to the public, is at the northern edge of the Heath.

11. *The Vimalakirti Sutra*, trans. Burton Watson, Columbia University Press 1997, ch. 10: 'Fragrance Accumulated', p. 117.

# And on his Dulcimer he Played

I have sometimes been asked if I had any regrets as I looked back over my life. To this I usually replied that I wished I had learned to play a musical instrument, either the harpsichord or the organ, or perhaps the sitar. Reflecting on this recently I realized that my usual reply to the question of whether I had any regrets was misleading, implying as it did that I had never learned to play as much as a tin whistle. The fact is that I *did* once play an instrument. When I was eight or nine, and confined to bed with alleged heart disease, I was given a shiny black dulcimer, with a hole in the middle and wires that could be tightened by turning a screw, and on this dulcimer, like the Abyssinian maid in *Kubla Khan*, I played, picking out tunes – or at least sequences of notes – with a little hammer. This could not have been my first experience of music. I have vague recollections of sitting on the floor near my mother as she played the piano. All her brothers and sisters played the piano and they may well have learned to play on this very instrument, for it was the old family piano which on the death of her father had passed to Auntie Kate,[1] my mother's eldest sister, and from her to my mother. She did not have it for long. When I was four or five it disappeared, most likely passing into the keeping of Uncle Jack, my mother's youngest brother but one, who lived not far from us.

Looking back at what I have just written, it occurs to me that the dulcimer was not the only musical instrument on which I learned to play. There was, in fact, another instrument, on which I learned to play very early in life, on which I have played regularly ever since, and which only recently has begun to show signs of wear and tear. This instrument is my own voice. I do not remember my mother ever singing to me, or teaching me any songs; but what I did not learn at home I certainly learned at what was then called Infant School, which I started attending (at first very unwillingly) when I was four. There, together with the other children of my own age, I learned to sing a number of songs, of varying quality as to both words and music. These included 'Sweet and Low', which was a setting of a poem by Tennyson,[2] the rather mawkish 'Away in a Manger', which was really a hymn,[3] and a song from which we learned how the violet acquired its name and which involves angels. It consisted of only four lines, and ran:

> She came one day from a sky of blue,
> And angels found her beneath the dew.
> They said, 'Little one, your eyes are wet,'
> And so they called her Violet.

I could not understand why the angels had called her Violet because her eyes were wet rather than because she came from a sky of blue. However, as a child I was a quite fond of this song, and used to give solo performances of it, until my voice broke, at family gatherings. When I came to the word 'Violet', it was my custom to end the word on as high a note as I could manage, which usually earned me a round of indulgent applause. It was also at Infant School, I think, that I first sang 'O God, our help in ages past'. I certainly have vivid memories of my singing it at Junior School, which I started attending after the conclusion of my long period of confinement to bed and wheelchair. The famous old hymn was usually sung at morning assembly, as well as on special occasions such as Empire Day, and the sound of 300 or more youthful voices raised in the mournful, dirge-like tune that, for me, is inseparable from the words, rings still in my ears. Not that I ever forgot the words of the hymn, especially the solemn ones that remind us of the fleeting, dreamlike nature of human life.

> Time, like an ever rolling stream,
> Bears all its sons away;
> They fly, forgotten, as a dream
> Dies at the opening day.[4]

Far from my forgetting them, the words remained deeply imprinted on my consciousness, there to blend, years later, with the *Diamond Sutra*'s teaching of the transitoriness of all conditioned things. I was still in Junior School when it put on a performance of *The Pirates of Penzance*[5] all the parts being taken by the children themselves. I was cast as a pirate and with my fellow pirates sang 'Let's vary piracy-ee with a little burglary' to a catchy tune that was to remain with me for the rest of my life. All the tunes were catchy, and none more so than 'Poor Wandering One', the lovely aria sung at one of the high points of the action by Mabel, the opera's noble heroine. In Senior School, to which I was promoted when I was twelve or thirteen, we had a proper music teacher. He should rightly have been called our *singing* teacher, for there was no question of any of us being taught to play a musical instrument. Not that he did not give us the beginning of a musical education. Tall and portly, Mr Scheu had a pale face and black hair parted down the middle. He was German, a convinced Nazi, and an excellent teacher, who threw himself into his work with an energy and enthusiasm that succeeded in arousing the interest of even the dullest and most backward members of the class. Besides greatly improving our singing, he taught us a wide variety of songs, from traditional English ballads and rounds to Handel arias. He also prepared us for our first orchestral concert, which took place at the Methodist Central Hall, Tooting Broadway, in front of an audience of children drawn from all the schools in the district. The principal item on the programme was Mendelssohn's overture *The Hebrides,*[6] and in the course of the weeks preceding the concert Mr Scheu took us through the piece almost bar by bar, playing as much of it as he could on the piano, and telling us what to look out for on the day. Although this was my first *live* orchestral concert, I had certainly heard orchestral music before. My father possessed a small collection of gramophone records, prominent among which was Gershwin's *Rhapsody in Blue.*[7] I was very fond of this work, which I had nicknamed 'The aeroplane', from the way in which the solo clarinet soared up into the sky, as it were.

By the time the Central Hall concert took place there had been a major change in the external circumstances of my life. The family had moved from the upstairs flat where I had been obliged to spend so much time in bed to the semi-detached council house on the other side of Tooting. We now had a very much bigger garden, an indoor toilet, a proper bath, and constant hot water. The change meant that I had a longer walk to school, which I did not mind. It also meant that I could join the local unit of the Boys' Brigade, which for the next four years was to play an important part in my life.[8] On Sunday mornings we gathered for an hour of prayer, hymn-singing, and exhortation by the unit's 'captain'. Our favourite hymn was a suitably martial one.

*Onward Christian soldiers*
*Marching as to war,*
*With the cross of Jesus*
*Going on before....*
*Hell's foundations tremble*
*At the shout of praise.*
*Brothers, lift your voices,*
*Loud your anthems raise!*

We indeed lifted our voices with a will, which it was all the more easy for us to do inasmuch as the tune to which these rousing words were sung was a march, with a steady beat, like that of a victorious army.[9] But there was one change that affected me even more deeply, and for much longer, than my joining the Boys' Brigade. This was the fact that the family now had a wireless set. Before long I was spending as many evenings as I could on my own in the sitting-room, listening to the wireless. Though I enjoyed the popular songs of the day (or at least some of them), I 'listened in' only to classical music, which meant that I was a devotee of the Third Programme, as I think it was called. For me at that time Classical music meant orchestral music, and orchestral music meant either overtures (Beethoven, Mozart, Weber) or symphonies (Beethoven, Mozart, Haydn). My favourite composer was Beethoven. I was passionately fond of *all* his symphonies (except the Ninth, which I do not remember hearing at that time), as well as of the *Egmont* and *Coriolanus* overtures and *Leonora* no. 3. They thrilled and excited me, rousing my emotions to fever pitch, and carrying me out of myself on a wave of ecstasy that seemed to touch the heavens. Mozart was hardly less of a favourite than Beethoven, though he affected me differently. Of his symphonies, it was the last three, especially no. 39 in E-flat, that gave me the most intense pleasure, a pleasure that was so intense as to be almost painful. Haydn's works were played less frequently than those of Beethoven or Mozart, I think, but I always enjoyed them, and came to love the 'Hen' and the 'Clock' symphonies. In the course of my months and years of 'listening in' I noticed that as well as the staple symphonies and overtures there were certain works that were played again and again. They included Bach's *Brandenburg Concerto* no. 3 (it was always no. 3), Debussy's *Prélude à l'après-midi d'un faune*, Delius's *On Hearing the First Cuckoo in Spring* (it was played all the year round), and Sinding's *Rustle of Spring*, which I must have heard a dozen times then, but have not heard since.[10]

In the middle of 1940 I was evacuated to Devonshire, World War II having started the previous year with Hitler's invasion of Poland. This naturally brought my musical evenings to an abrupt end. On my return to London the following year, however, I at once restarted them and they continued to be an important part of my life for the next two years and more. But although I was as passionately fond of music as ever, music now had serious rivals for my time, my energy, and my emotional investment. The most dangerous of these rivals, at least until I discovered Buddhism and realized I was a Buddhist, was poetry, of which I was hardly less fond than I was of music, and which I had been writing for a number of years. Sometimes the two passions clashed, sometimes they co-operated, as when I put into the mouth of Beethoven a blank verse monologue in which he expostulated with Goethe for what he considered his servility to princes,[11] and also when I wrote a series of stanzas modelled on Baudelaire's *Les Phares*.[12] Whereas Baudelaire had written about the great painters, I wrote about the great composers. The poem has not survived, but fragments of it still linger in my memory. The stanza on Beethoven began, perhaps predictably, 'Beethoven, blast of hurricane and storm', and I assume I must have gone on to mention his more tender side. 'Bach, endless time where echoes cease to be' and 'Lost in the gulf of that immensity/ Wherein he adumbrates the source of things' are all I can remember of the stanza devoted to Bach. The grandiloquent nature of the language suggests that when I wrote it I had in mind the *Toccata and Fugue in D minor*, my first encounter with which was probably the greatest single musical experience of my life.[13] The stanza devoted to Mozart, unlike the stanzas on any of the other great composers, has survived in my memory complete. It ran:

*Mozart, an elegant despairing mien,*
*Poised like a skater in the evening shade*
*That trembling falls on some rococo queen*
*Sighing in palaces of purest jade.*

Strictly speaking, this is nonsense. At the same time, it does give an idea of the kind of impression Mozart's music made on me at that time. It was *elegant*, and it was *poised*, in that it had perfect balance and control. It was also *rococo*, by which I meant that it was light and airy, without the least trace of dullness or heaviness. *Queen* and *palaces* suggested refinement and aristocracy, as did *jade*, though it was an aristocracy not of birth but of the mind. As for *despairing, evening shade*, and *sighing*, they reflected my feeling that running through much of Mozart's music there was a vein of melancholy. My characterization of Mozart in this stanza, written when I was sixteen or seventeen, is probably rather one-sided, but it shows how carefully I listened to him and the other great composers. In 1943, when I was eighteen, I was conscripted, and once again my musical evenings came to an abrupt end, as did many other things that were important to me. Only twice in the course of the next four years did I have an opportunity of imbibing a few drops of what Byron once called 'the brandy of the damned'.[14] The first time this happened I was in India, to which the Signals unit to which I belonged had been sent a year after my conscription. Having spent the evening in Delhi, I was walking the last few hundred yards back to camp through the darkness, the stars brilliant overhead, when there came to me from somewhere in the distance, through the stillness and silence of the night, the familiar sound of the slow movement from Mozart's *Eine Kleine Nachtmusik*. It was a magical moment. The second time it happened I was in Singapore, to which my unit had been posted shortly after VJ Day[15] and it happened when I saw Walt Disney's

*Fantasia*. Once again I heard old favourites like Bach's *Toccata and Fugue in D Minor*, Beethoven's *Pastoral Symphony*, and Schubert's *Ave Maria*, only this time I heard them as orchestrated by Leopold Stokowski and as illustrated, in the case of the three compositions I have mentioned, by Disney's undulating railway track, dancing centaurettes, and upward-soaring Gothic arches.[16]

Early in 1947 I left Singapore for India, where for the next seventeen years I was occupied with the study, practice, and realization of the Dharma, at first as a freelance wandering ascetic, then as an ordained Buddhist monk.[17] In 1964 I returned to England and took up residence at the Hampstead Buddhist Vihara, where I lived for the next two years. I held meditation classes at the Vihara, and gave lectures there and at other venues. One of these lectures was on 'Buddhism and the Problem of Death', and at the end of it I was approached by a tall, well-dressed young man who said he wanted to tell me something. Thereafter he came regularly to my lectures, visited me at the Vihara, and started giving me lifts to my engagements in and around London in his VW. The young man's name was Terry Delamare, and it was in this way that there developed between us what was to be one of the most important friendships of my life. Terry had a flat near the Vihara, and soon I was spending time with him there. Besides talking (we had a lot to say to each other), we listened to records on Terry's record player. We had much the same musical tastes, our favourite records being those of the Mozart and Haydn symphonies and of Elgar's *Enigma Variations*, all of which we played over and over again. Unfortunately, Terry had long been the victim of chronic depression, and although he accompanied me on my 1966–7 'farewell' visit to India the change of scene gave him no relief from his suffering, as we had hoped it would. He killed himself on 14 April 1969, four years after our first meeting, as I have related in *Moving Against the Stream*. Shortly before Terry's death I had started a new Buddhist movement in London, so that for the next few decades I had little time for the enjoyment of music. Not that music was entirely banished from my life, or that I had lost the capacity to enjoy it. Indeed, as our new Buddhist movement spread I was often away on tour, which meant that I was sometimes able to attend operas and concerts in cities other than my native London. Thus over the years I saw an *avant garde* production of Handel's *Giulio Cesare* in Düsseldorf,[18] heard a brilliant performance of Vivaldi's *The Four Seasons* in Prague[19] and heard a suitably solid performance of Brahms' *German Requiem* in Berlin[20] In more recent years, when I have done little or no travelling, CDs and Radio 3 have made it possible for me to explore the whole heritage of Western music, from Thomas Tallis and Palestrina to Prokoviev and Philip Glass. This exploration has enabled me to deepen my appreciation of old favourites like Bach, Beethoven and Mozart, as well as to discover new favourites, like Sibelius and Richard Strauss. One of Strauss's shorter works has in fact come to have a special significance for me. This work is his *Four Last Songs*, especially the fourth song, 'Sunset'.[21] I am now at the sunset of my life, and friends have asked me what kind of funeral I would like to have. Though I have no strong preference in this connection, I would like music to have a part in my obsequies. I would like Jeremiah Clarke's *Trumpet Voluntary* (version with kettle-drum)[22] to be played at my cremation or burial and Strauss's 'Sunset', preferably as sung in German by Elisabeth Schwarzkopf, to be played at whatever memorial service is held afterwards. If my consciousness is hovering round, I shall certainly listen.

### Notes

1. Sangharakshita writes of Aunt Kate and other aunts to whom "only the creator of the Aunts in *Mill on the Floss*" could do justice in *RR*, pp. 9–10.

2. From the second canto of Tennyson's poem 'The Princess', published in 1847.

3. Sung widely since Victorian times as a Christmas carol and still popular today.

4. By hymn writer Isaac Watts (1674–1748) based on Psalm 90. It is often sung to the tune 'St Anne' by William Croft (1678–1727) who composed it whilst organist at St Anne's Church, Soho.

5. *The Pirates of Penzance; or, the Slave of Duty* is a comic opera by librettist W.S. Gilbert (1836–1911) and composer Arthur Sullivan (1842–1900). It was first performed in 1879.

6. Felix Mendelssohn Bartholdy (1809–1847) composed the overture (also known as *Fingal's Cave*) in 1830 after visiting the cave on the Hebridean island of Staffa. Sangharakshita writes about the concert in *RR*, p. 28.

7. George Gershwin (1898–1937), the American composer and pianist, wrote *Rhapsody in Blue* for solo piano and jazz band in 1924.

8. See *RR*, ch.4, 'Here Comes the Boys' Brigade'.

9. This hymn by Sabine Baring-Gould (1834–1924), an Anglican priest and scholar, was written in 1865 originally as a processional hymn for children. The tune, 'St Gertrude', through which it became famous, was composed by Arthur Sullivan in 1871.

10. Perhaps only the last of these well known composers and their works requires a note. Christian Sinding (1856–1941) was a Norwegian composer who wrote for the piano, both solo and in combination with other instruments. His 'Rustle of Spring' for solo piano, was written in 1896 and became a huge success beyond his own country.

11. Sangharakshita's poem was based on a story told by Goethe's friend, Bettina von Arnim (its veracity has been questioned) about the meeting of the two German geniuses in Teplitz (then part of the Austro-Hungarian empire) in 1812. As the two men strolled along together they were met by the empress Maria Ludovica of Austria and her entourage. Whilst Goethe politely bowed and stepped aside, Beethoven strode straight through their midst, afterwards berating his companion for his servile behaviour. 'There are countless nobles,' he remonstrated, 'but only two of us!'

12. Charles Baudelaire (1821–1867), the French poet, essayist and art critic. *Les Phares* or 'The Beacons' is a poem of eleven verses, the first eight of which celebrate one of the great European artists. It was included in his collection *Les Fleurs du Mal* (*The Flowers of Evil* or *The Flowers of Suffering*) first published in 1857.

13. Johann Sebastian Bach (1685–1750) composed the *Toccata and Fugue in D Minor* (BMV 565) for organ. No autograph manuscript survives to give the date of composition. (It was published only in 1833, owing to the efforts of Felix Mendelssohn).

Sangharakshita recalls first hearing the piece when he was fifteen or sixteen. 'Stunned, overwhelmed, annihilated by those majestic chords, I went about for several days in a kind of waking trance' (*RR*, p. 67).

14. It seems it was, in fact, George Bernard Shaw (1856–1950), the Irish playwright, essayist and writer, in his play *Man and Superman*, 1903, Act III.

15. Victory over Japan Day. This was 15 August 1945 when the Allies announced that Japan had surrendered, signalling the end of the Second World War. On 2 September a treaty was signed. Conscript Dennis Lingwood (later Sangharakshita), who was at that time stationed in Calcutta for a few weeks, was sent to Singapore to await demobilization (*RR*, pp. 131–3).

16. *Fantasia* is an animated film released by Walt Disney in 1940. Its eight sections feature the music of classical composers from Bach to Stravinsky played by the Philadelphia Orchestra. Leopold Stokowski (1882–1977) was the orchestra's musical director from 1912 to 1940.

17. As told in his memoirs: *RR, FMK*, and *ISGW*.

18. During a trip to visit the Essen Buddhist Centre and Order members and mitras in the area in autumn 1989 (*TBE*, p. 144). The performance was given by the Deutsche Oper am Rhein with a female singer taking the lead role.

19. Sangharakshita was accompanied on his visit to Prague by Anomarati, then chairman of the Buddhistsiches Tor (FWBO Buddhist Centre in Berlin).

20. Sangharakshita made a number of visits to Berlin, notably in 1998 to open the Buddhistsiches Tor (Buddhist Centre) in Hessische Strasse, not far from the Reichstag. In 2012 the Centre moved to larger premises in the suburb of Kreuzberg where it attracts many people to classes and events held there.

21. Richard Strauss (1864–1949), the German Romantic composer especially of operas and Lieder. His *Four Last Songs* (*Vier Letzte Lieder*) for soprano and orchestra were written in 1948, the year before he died. The fourth is 'Im Abendrot' or 'Sunset'.

22. Jeremiah Clarke (c.1674–1707) was organist at the Chapel Royal. He composed *The Prince of Denmark's March* around 1700. The piece came to be associated with Henry Purcell and known as the *Trumpet Voluntary* (so called because, though played on the

organ, it makes use of the organ's trumpet stop). More recently an orchestral arrangement including trumpet, organ and kettledrums was devised by conductor Sir Henry Wood (1869–1944).

# IV

# Dancing Round the Maypole

'Dance, children, dance,
Dance round the Maypole,
Lifting your feet
In time with the music!'

Thus spoke the teacher
In my happy schooldays,
Spoke in the playground
On May Day morning.

From the top of the Maypole
Hung marvellous streamers
Of many different colours,
All bright in the sunshine.

Each child seized the end
Of a streamer, and with it
Danced round the Maypole
In time with the music.

Fifteen or twenty
Happy London children
Dancing round the Maypole
On May Day morning!

Clockwise and anti-
Clockwise we danced
In our asphalted playground,
Backwards and forwards,

Weaving and un-
Weaving round the Maypole
Wonderful patterns
With our bright-coloured streamers.

And the tall old Maypole
Looked down benignly
On the dancing children,
Looked down and blessed us.

Fifty years later
No tall old Maypole,
No children dancing
On May Day morning.

No bright-coloured streamers,
No wonderful patterns.
In the empty playground
Only the asphalt.

## The Warning Voice

'Don't touch the red-hot pokers,'
Our kindly teacher said.
'They're sure to burn your fingers,
And you'll wish that you were dead.'

We stood and gazed upon them,
Inquisitive and scared,
For red and sulphur-yellow
Those red-hot pokers flared.

Beyond the purple pansies
And marigolds aglow,
Untouchable for ever
They stood in fiery row.

It was in the playground-garden;
We were very, very young,
And every word was gospel
That fell from teacher's tongue.

We are older now, and wiser;
The warning voice is spurned.
Life's reddest red-hot pokers
We touch – and are not burned.

## Then and Now

We waved our little Union Jacks,
And stood and sang God Save the King.
Now 'Empire' is a dirty word,
And loyalty a shameful thing.

Nelson and Drake are villains now,
We wish that they had never been,
Give the thumbs down to our history
And never sing God Save the Queen.

## Queens Past and Present

Elizabeth Tudor
Was frequently ruder
Than queens are today.
She boxed courtiers' ears,
Swore roundly at peers
And had plenty to say
For herself in English, French, Latin, Greek, Spanish, and Italian.
She could ride a stallion
As well as a man,
*And* flutter a jewelled fan
With the best of the saucy, aristocratic girls
Who arranged her red curls...
What a pity
That in London's city
Our Sovereign Lady today
Should be so polite, well mannered, and grey!

# The Economic Argument
*The People of Denmark Reject the Euro 28 September 2000*

'The economic argument
Is sure to win the day'
Said businessman to banker,
And who more wise than they?

Oh could they not remember
What long ago was said
By him they call their master:
'Man lives not just by bread'?

The bread may be well buttered
On both sides, but even so
In tones of proud defiance
The Viking breed shouts 'No!'

Oh may that shout be echoed
From Albion's doubtful shore,
And the businessmen and bankers
Rule over us no more!

## The Double Root

Poetry has a double root
In nursery rhyme and prophecy;
Mother Goose and Apollo
Are its twin progenitors.
But mother doesn't croon nursery rhymes any more,
And the poets are all in hiding.
English poetry's on its last legs,
Lost between pop lyric and Laura Riding.

## Poet and Muse

*After looking into a biography of Robert Graves*

The poet has his Muse, the terrible White
Goddess who is the sole object
Of his adoration, and to whom
His whole life is consecrate. But naturally
The Muse has her attendants, her personal
Assistants, and there may even be
A Deputy Muse or two to whom,
When not in the mood, she from time to time
Delegates a portion of her authority, and all these
Divine and semi-divine ladies
Collaborate happily
(Or not so happily, as the case may be)
In the production
Of the poet's *oeuvre*, and in the completion
Of a learned treatise
In which he gives a comprehensive account
Of the religious-cum-anthropological-
Cum-sociological-cum-linguistic
Theory behind
His poetic practice.

## The Listener

The poet listens for the inevitable word,
The word which from eternity has waited
To reveal itself to him.

Having heard it, he takes a diamond pen
And with tears of gratitude inscribes it
On a jade tablet upheld by angels.

# Three Arthurian Poems

I

## The White Hawthorn
*A Recollection of Burne-Jones' 'The Beguiling of Merlin'*

If it could speak, the white hawthorn,
What would it say?
*Merlin and wily Vivien*
*Wandered this way.*

If it could speak, the white hawthorn,
What could it tell?
*Vivien wrested from Merlin*
*A mighty spell.*

If it could speak, the white hawthorn,
What then the sound?
*With the spell Vivien pent Merlin*
*Far under ground.*

If it could speak, the white hawthorn,
What were the sighs?
*Female beauty can overbear*
*Even the wise.*

II
## Love and Duty

Guinevere loved the King
Much less than she esteemed,
And so of gallant Lancelot
She dreamed and dreamed and dreamed.

One day the dream became so deep
That it was dream no more,
And she and gallant Lancelot
Stood on a lonely shore,

And standing on that lonely shore
They heard a dreadful sound,
A sound as of the Crack of Doom,
As split the Table Round;

And thus the lawless passion
Of Arthur's guilty queen
Broke up the goodliest fellowship
That e'er on earth was seen.

Let love and duty coincide,
Lest both of them be hurled
To ruin, and the Crack of Doom
Be heard around the world.

III
## The Cell of Glass

Merlin, in his cell of glass
Imprisoned, sees the centuries pass;
Sees the nations come and go
Like clouds in Autumn, fast or slow;
Sees cities rise and cities fall
Like flowers in Springtime, one and all.
Grieved or rejoicing, inly wracked,
He sees, and sees – but cannot act.

# In Krakow

## In the Great Square

Love is of so delicate a nature, I said,
Quoting the old Indian poet,
That it cannot bear the burden of wisdom;
But you seemed not to understand.
Perhaps, in your case, love can bear the burden of wisdom.
We were sitting in the great square of Krakow,
Drinking tea, surrounded by our friends,
And listening to the gypsy musicians.
The musicians could understand
That love cannot bear the burden of wisdom.
Did not their ancestors come from India, long ago?


II

## To Michal, my Interpreter

In your apt mouth
My silver words are transmuted into gold;
In your young life
My frozen sap puts forth leaves and flowers.

III
## On the Balcony

Breakfast was on the balcony. The sparrows were there too,
Chirruping loudly, and flying in and out of the eaves.
Below, men were working in the fields. A cock crew.
'It's too early', someone said, 'for the storks.'

# Guhyaloka, September 1999

Drenched in silence, drenched in sunlight,
I survey the valley round,
Where the pines stand green and upright
And the grey dwarf oaks abound.
Between sheer cliffs of limestone
I muse the livelong day,
Wrapped in silence, wrapped in sunlight.
The world is far away.

Drenched in silence, drenched in moonlight,
I listen to the sound
Of the darkling owl's tu-whooing,
Hear the bat's wings hovering round.
With scent of pine for incense
I meditate and pray
Wrapped in silence, wrapped in moonlight.
The world is far away.

Drenched in silence, drenched in starlight,
With peace my thoughts are crowned
And I sense within this 'being'
A 'not-being' more profound.
No one – nothing – for companion
I sit till break of day
Wrapped in silence, wrapped in starlight.
The world is far away.

**East is East**

East is East and West is West
And ever the twain shall meet.
Opposites belong to each other,
Like sour and sweet.

East is East and West is West
Each for himself discovers.
Love and hate are near akin,
Fratricidal, yet brothers.

## To My Teacher, Chetrul Sangye Dorje

You revealed to me the face of the Green Goddess
And spoke of the scholars of old.
I could only guess your meaning.

You showed me a handful of seed pearls
Taken from the ruins of a stupa.
I could only guess your meaning.

You sent me a ceremonial scarf,
White as the snows of Kanchenjunga.
I could only guess your meaning.

You sent me two packets of medicine,
Compounded from rare Himalayan herbs –
Medicine over which you had repeated thousands of mantras.
I could only guess your meaning.

Now you send me a thangka depicting
A white, naked dakini.
She is smiling, and holds
A chopping-knife and skull-cup filled with golden nectar.
Once again, O inscrutable guru, I can only guess your meaning.

## The Six Elements Speak

I am Earth.
I am rock, metal, and soil.
I am that which exists in you
As bone, muscle, and flesh,
But now I must go,
Leaving you light.
Now we must part.
Goodbye.

I am Water.
I am ocean, lake, rivers and streams,
The rain that falls from clouds
And the dew on the petals of flowers.
I am that which exists in you
As blood, urine, sweat, saliva and tears,
But now I must go,
Leaving you dry.
Now we must part.
Goodbye.

I am Fire.
I come from the Sun, travelling through space
To sleep in wood, flint, and steel.
I am that which exists in you
As bodily heat, the warmth of an embrace,
But now I must go,
Leaving you cold.
Now we must part.
Goodbye.

I am Air.
I am wind, breeze, and hurricane.
I am that which exists in you
As the breath in your nostrils, in your lungs,
The breath that gently comes, that gently goes,
But now I must go,
For the last time,
Leaving you empty.
Now we must part.
Goodbye.

I am Space.
I contain all,
From a grain of dust to a galaxy.
I am that which exists in you
As the space limited by the earth, water, fire, and air
That make up your physical being,
But now they have all gone
And I must go too,
Leaving you unlimited.
Now we must part.
Goodbye.

I am Consciousness.
Indefinable and indescribable.
I am that which exists in you
As sight, hearing, smell, taste, touch and thought,
But now I must go
From the space no longer limited by your physical being
Leaving nothing of 'you'.
There is no one from whom to part,
So no goodbye.

Earth dissolves into Water,
Water dissolves into Fire,
Fire dissolves into Air,
Air dissolves into Space,
Space dissolves into Consciousness,
Consciousness dissolves into – ?
HUM

## The Great Burning

The year will soon be at an end
And it is time to start sweeping up the fallen leaves,
Yellow, brown, and red leaves
From oak, beech, birch, and elm,
Time to start gathering them up into baskets
In readiness for the great burning.
Only the leaves of the holly are green
And have not fallen,
Glossy-green with – brilliant amidst them – red berries.

## Remembering Arthadarshin

The wooden hut stands empty amid the pine trees;
No one climbs up the slope to water my garden.
Owls hoot all night, but in the cold dawn
The sound of a voice chanting the Refuges is heard no more.

## The Silver Spoon

On my birthday
You gave me a silver spoon with a bear handle.
'In Tibetan Buddhism', I said,
'Silver is one of the three pure metals,
The others being copper and gold.'
Now, I use your spoon every day,
Stirring my tea with it,
Eating kiwi fruit with it,
Gripping the handle tightly
Because I cannot feel the touch of your hand.

## To Michal, with a Photograph

'Have it taken together with birch trees,' you said, referring
To the 'official' photograph that was to be sent to our friends
    in the Ukraine.
Like the Russians, the Ukranians love the birch tree,
So here am I, leaning against the black and silver trunk
Of the old birch tree on which I looked out from my study win-
dow each morning, all those years ago.

I hope the Poles, too, love the birch tree
And that you will like this photo of your white-haired old friend.

## I am Sitting in the Late Afternoon Sunshine ...

I am sitting in the late afternoon sunshine,
An old man with tired bones and a heart empty of desires.
Nearby, a bird is singing in the trees,
And a puff of wind is soft against my cheek.
Soon the sun will be setting, and I wonder
If tonight I shall see the stars.

# Epigrams

Crows, in their collective spite,
Will peck to death a crow that's white.
We humans show as little sense
When forced to deal with *difference*.

The world continues on its crazy course;
Where love is needed, they resort to force.

We realize that war has snags
When men come home in body bags.

A cobra in a basket
Remains a cobra still,
Don't just suppress the kleshas;
With the sword of Wisdom, kill.

*The Lure of Domesticity*
Another youthful hero bites the dust,
By dreams deluded, and consumed with lust.

In vain we flee before the King of Death;
We feel upon our necks his icy breath.

## Justice and Pity

I saw a woman, beautiful but blind,
Lying upon the ground in pools of blood
And asked her name. My name, she said, is Justice.
And who has given you these cruel wounds,
That thus your very lifeblood drains away?
Her name is Pity, Justice said, and died.

## Haikus

The grey clouds are my friends.
They visit me every evening
With messages from the West.

What is the wine you bring me, Cupbearer?
Ah, it is the bitter wine of separation.
But at the bottom of the cup
There is the taste of union.

Beauty such as yours
Is for seeing, not touching.
Perhaps not even for seeing
Except with closed eyes.

The ship sails on its way
Leaving behind a brilliant wake
On which the moon shines
Dazzlingly.

Looking Back

V

# The Search

One bright, sunny morning in the middle of June 2010, Paramartha and I left Madhyamaloka for Ipswich, with Paramartha at the wheel. Our journey had a double objective. We were to visit the Ipswich Buddhist Centre,[1] where I was to give a talk, as well as meet members of the local sangha, and we were to search for traces of my Lingwood ancestors, who we knew came from that part of Suffolk. On the way we visited Bury St Edmunds, a place I had not seen before, where we spent a couple of hours looking round the cathedral, and where we had lunch in the cathedral refectory. From Bury we drove straight to Ipswich, and soon we were being warmly greeted by Swadipa[2] and Carol,[3] with whom we were to stay. In the evening, after I had rested, Harshaprabha,[4] an old friend of ours, took us out to a quiet Italian restaurant for dinner. After the meal he drove us round the town, of which we had not seen much during our visit the previous year. We saw the marina, where I was astonished by the enormous number of dinghies and other boats, the docks, and an early Norman Foster building[5] – a controversial one, according to Harshaprabha. We also saw, on a house in the old part of the town, a plaque that informed us that the house opposite was the birthplace of the great Cardinal Wolsey, Ipswich's most famous son.[6]

After breakfast the following day Paramartha and I set out for Felixstowe, which before the war was a popular holiday resort. The reason for our going there was that I very much wanted to see the sea, a pleasure I had not had for some time. As the product of an island race I was very conscious of the sea, and as all my ancestors on the spear side were from Suffolk I was particularly conscious of the North Sea. Indeed, since I first encountered it in my teens in Kate Freiligrath Kroeker's translation, Heine's cycle 'The North Sea' has been one of my favourite longer poems.[7] Be that as it may, there we were on the deserted beach that morning, Paramartha and I. Except for the wind, it was a perfect June day. The sun was bright, the sky without a cloud. I walked down the sand to within a few feet of the white surf, and stood there looking out over the rollers to the distant horizon, where the Prussian blue of the sea met the eggshell blue of the sky.

From Felixstowe we drove to Battisford. Thanks to the internet, Paramartha had discovered that my great-grandfather Edward Lingwood was born in Battisford in 1828, and in the absence of other clues we had decided that it was in Battisford that we would begin our search for traces of my Lingwood ancestors. The village was rather scattered, and we had to drive round for a while before finding the lane that led to the parish church. It was built of cobbles, like so many Suffolk churches, had a quaint belfry like structure at one end instead of the more usual round tower, and was dedicated to St Mary. Finding the door unlocked, we entered and spent the next fifteen or twenty minutes looking round the church's well lit interior. There was a memorial tablet on one of the walls, and there were red heraldic shields in two of the windows, but these did not relate to any member of the Lingwood family, though it was more than likely that my great-grandfather was baptized in the ancient stone font. We therefore continued our search in the graveyard. It was overgrown with grass and weeds, and the graves were not in neat rows, as in a modern municipal cemetery, but scattered, as if whenever a new grave was needed the sexton simply dug it wherever there was an unoccupied space. Moreover, the ground was very uneven, so that I had to tread carefully. This meant that soon Paramartha was not only ahead of me but out of sight round the other side of the building. I paused, and stood in the hot sun surveying the scene. Before long Paramartha was back. He had found something, he said quietly with a broad smile. I followed him as quickly as I could to the back of the church. Close to the wall there was a grave with a small double headstone. The inscriptions on all the other headstones we had seen were illegible, as the soft sandstone had weathered over the years, but the inscription on the double headstone could be read quite easily, probably because the grave was protected by the wall. Two children were buried there. One was Arthur, who was born in 1841 and died the same year, aged only a few months; the other was Elizabeth, who was born in 1840 and died in 1849. They were the children of Edward and Sarah Lingwood, the headstone said, which meant that they were my great-grandfather's brother and sister.

We left Battisford well pleased with the start we had made. It was more than we had dared hope for from the first day of our search. We had not driven for more than half a mile along the road out of the village, a road bordered on both sides by trees in the full glory of their summer leafage, when Paramartha suddenly slowed down, then stopped. He had seen on the other side of the road, at the entrance to a driveway, a sign that said 'St John's' and the name had jogged his memory. He had come across it while researching my ancestry on the internet! We therefore parked just inside the driveway, and Paramartha strode up to the house to make enquiries. Minutes later he was talking to whoever it was had come to the door in response to his knock. As he afterwards told me, he had apologized to the lady for disturbing her but explained that he had with him an old gentleman whose family may have had a connection with the house. Naturally she wanted to know the family's name. When he said it was Lingwood she told him that the family had indeed once occupied the house and that she had a box of papers relating to its history. Paramartha hurried back to me with the news, whereupon I walked with him up the driveway and introduced myself to the lady to whom he had spoken, who by this time had emerged from the house. Soon the three of us were seated on chairs under the trees. Her name was Pat Knoch, the woman told us. She was eighty, had lived at the house for some years and it was called St John's because the Knights of St John had occupied the site until the time of the Dissolution of the Monasteries under Henry VIII.[8] The Knights had planted the holm oak under which I was sitting. Having given us this information and more besides, she went back into the house to fetch what she called her Lingwood box. Paramartha and I "looked at each other in a wild surmise".[9] Was providence, or our good karma, about to vouchsafe us the miracle of a breakthrough in our search for traces of my ancestors? When at last the box came we were not disappointed. A cursory inspection showed that it contained wills, personal letters, photographs, obituaries and other items of interest. A treasure had fallen into our hands. It had fallen into them by accident, or rather by virtue of a whole series of accidents. Had we not been driving along that particular road that morning Paramartha would not have spotted the sign that said 'St John's'. Had his memory not been jogged by the sign we would not have stopped, and he would not have gone up to the house to make enquiries. Had Pat Knoch not been at home at the time, we would not have known of the existence of the Lingwood box. Finally, had Pat Knoch not been of a generous, trusting disposition she would not have allowed us to take away the precious box and photocopy its contents. Indeed, it was clear that she shared in our joy, and was glad to have been of assistance to us in our search.

Paramartha and I had been so absorbed in our fresh discovery that we had forgotten about lunch, and it was only when we were on the road again that we realized we had not yet eaten. Swadipa had recommended the Red Lion, this being the only vegetarian pub in Suffolk, perhaps in all England. As it was situated a little off the beaten track we experienced some difficulty finding it, and eventually we had to pull into the side of the road and phone Swadipa for directions. Though it was mid-week we found the place full, which suggested that vegetarianism had made some headway in Suffolk. We secured a table in a quiet corner, some distance from the bar, and while waiting for our meal dipped into the Lingwood box, which we of course had not left in the car. After the meal, which was a reasonably good one, we drove straight back to Ipswich. I went to my room and rested, as in the evening I would be giving a talk at the Ipswich Buddhist Centre. Paramartha went and had the entire contents of the Lingwood box photocopied. The result was 200 pages of material.

I had opened the new Ipswich Buddhist Centre the previous year, and this time I had been asked to bless the centre's newly completed chapter room.[10] This I did by chanting a few Pali verses, after which I shared with my closely packed auditors some of my recent reflections.[11] First, though, I spoke of Paramartha's and my search for traces of my Lingwood ancestors and of the remarkable discovery we had made that very day. That search would probably bring us back to Ipswich again, and thus my ties with the local sangha would be further strengthened. I then adverted to the events of the past year, and in particular to the change from 'Western' to 'Triratna' in the nomenclature of our Order.[12] This enabled me to speak on the subject of the Three Jewels, i.e. on the Buddha or Perfectly Enlightened One, the Dharma or body of truths taught by the Buddha, and the Sangha or spiritual community of those practising the Dharma. Usually, I said, the three were enumerated in this order, which was the chronological one, as it were, the Dharma having originated from the Buddha, and the Sangha from the Dharma. But the order could be reversed. There was no Sangha without the Dharma, and no Dharma without the Buddha. It was the Dharma that made the Sangha. Without the united practice of the Dharma by its members the Sangha was no more than an ecclesiastical institution or a social club. I then spoke about the Buddha. It was important that we knew about the life of Shakyamuni, the historical Buddha, for it was ultimately on him that we depended for what knowledge of the Dharma we possessed. The most reliable source of information about that life was the Pali scriptures. Besides providing us with the earliest account of his teaching, those scriptures tell us a good deal about his personal appearance, his way of life, his manner of teaching, his relations with his disciples, and with a wide variety of other people, from princes to peasants, and from ascetics to well-to-do farmers. We can also get a sense of the Buddha's living presence by going on pilgrimage to the places where he was born, where he gained perfect Enlightenment, where he gave his first teaching, and where he passed into Parinirvana. This, or something like it, was what I said that evening, though at somewhat greater length. I also answered a few questions.

On our second and last whole day in Suffolk it was dull and overcast. But Paramartha and I did not allow our spirits to be dampened, and after breakfast we left for the village of Barking where my great-great-great-grandfather Edward Lingwood of Eye was buried. He was buried in the parish church of St Mary. His grave was an altar grave, that is to say it was situated immediately in front of the altar. I sat in the car, and Paramartha went to investigate. On his return he reported that the area in front of the altar was carpeted and he had been unable to see whether or not there was a grave underneath. We therefore drove to Battisford, where Paramartha gave back the Lingwood box to Pat Knoch and thanked her for allowing us to photocopy the contents.

Before he left she insisted on his taking photographs of the Victorian flush toilet and of the Maltese cross above the door, the well known badge of the Knights of St John. The Lingwood box having been returned to its owner as promised, Paramartha and I were soon on our way to Eye, some thirty miles to the north. When we were a few miles from our destination we happened to see a cemetery by the roadside, and as the gates stood wide open we drove in. Just inside the entrance, on the right, there was a small chapel, and beyond it several acres of old graves. While Paramartha went in search of inscriptions I stayed near the car and studied a row of new graves on the left of the path, some of them with bunches of fresh flowers on them. They were all close together, and had small white headstones of what may have been marble. Some graves, I noticed, were very small, so that I wondered if they might hold not a dead body but only a handful of ashes. Paramartha returned from his search to say that he had not found anything of interest. Here, as elsewhere, the headstones were of sandstone, which meant that any inscriptions on them soon became illegible. We therefore resumed our journey north.

Eye was not a village but a town. It dated back to the end of the eleventh century, when William the Conqueror granted the lordship of Eye to William Malet, who built a castle and established a market. Before long there was a flourishing town on the spot. Towards the end of the fourteenth century the church of St Peter and St Paul was built, and it was enlarged a hundred years later, when the hundred-and-one foot tower was added. Both church and tower were built of knapped flints which, glittering in the dull morning light, contrasted well with the dressed stone that had also been used. The building was, in fact, a fine specimen of East Anglian medieval architecture, and testified to the wealth of the town in the middle ages. The interior was no less impressive than the exterior. It had a nave with two side aisles, a high, arched wooden roof, and a wooden rood screen that connected the end pair of pillars. Paramartha and I were not the only visitors and we wandered round looking at the memorials to departed worthies, at the carved woodwork, at the richly coloured and gilded panels depicting various kings and saints, including (as I later discovered) the martyred King Edmund and St Edward the Confessor, and at the very gothic cover of the stone font. There was no sign of the Lingwood name anywhere, and soon we were out of the town and on our way to Brome.

The door of the parish church of St Mary, Brome, was open, but as the sky was still overcast it was dark inside. Paramartha groped his way round the nave to a light switch but the single electric bulb gave only a feeble light and I could see very little. Nonetheless, I managed to make my way to the Cornwallis family tombs, on the other side of which Paramartha was moving about. There must have been four or five tombs all crowded together to the left of the altar. In the gloom it was difficult for me to make out their shadowy forms but I passed my hand over the bare head of the recumbent figure on the tomb nearest, then over the 'gable peak' headdress of the recumbent figure by his side, a headdress that told me that the couple had lived in the early Tudor period. The stone was cold to the touch. I thought of a passage in 'The Eve of St Agnes', in which Keats describes the ancient beadsman and the castle chapel:

> The sculptur'd dead, on each side, seem to freeze,
> Emprison'd in black, purgatorial rails:
> Knights, ladies, praying in dumb orat'ries,
> He passeth by; and his weak spirit fails
> To think how they may ache in icy hoods and mails. [13]

The sky had now cleared, and after the darkness and cold of the church it was pleasant to wander among the crumbling headstones in the warm sunshine, looking for inscriptions that were legible. As usual, Paramartha took the lead in the search, forging ahead, and moving rapidly from one headstone to another. After fifteen or twenty minutes he motioned me to follow him to the back of the church. Side by side, their headstones against the cobbled back wall of the church there were five coffin-shaped tomb graves. The inscriptions were all quite legible, the graves were those of my great-great-great-great-grandfather Thomas Lingwood of Brome, his wife, and three of their sons. It was very quiet there behind the church. I stood regarding the five graves for a few minutes, then turned away and slowly walked back to the car with Paramartha. The day's search had ended in an important discovery, and it was time for us to leave Brome for Ipswich, the dead for the living, and the past for the world of the twenty-first century.

We were in a mood of quiet satisfaction as we drove back to Ipswich, eating the sandwiches Carol had made for us on the way, and not talking very much. On reaching the town we did not drive straight to Swadipa's and Carol's hospitable home. Instead, we drove through Gainsborough Road, for it was in a house in this road that my great-grandfather Edward Lingwood of Battisford had spent the last years of his life and we wanted to see what it looked like. As far as we could judge, the houses were all late Victorian, but not having an address we could not tell in which of the houses, if in any, my great-grandfather had lived. In the afternoon, after resting for a couple of hours, I had tea with Srivandana at her flat. Our last evening in Ipswich passed quietly. After dinner with Swadipa and Carol, I spent the rest of the evening in my room, reflecting, while Paramartha had a long talk with Swadipa downstairs.

The following morning was a morning of farewells. Paramartha and I thanked Swadipa and Carol warmly for their hospitality. They assured us that we were welcome to come and stay with them next year and continue our search, which was by no means finished. Torrential rain lashed us on the way back to Birmingham, and we arrived at Madhyamaloka in time for lunch. For me, at least, our three days in Suffolk had been a holiday. I greatly enjoyed driving through the beautiful Suffolk countryside, spending more time in the open air than usual, exploring the old parish churches and viewing the long unvisited North Sea. I was also glad to have had a little more contact with the Ipswich sangha. Perhaps Paramartha and I would return next year, and continue our search for traces of my Lingwood ancestors.

# The Ancestors

It was the year 1528. King Henry VIII had been on the throne for nineteen years, the great Cardinal Wolsey was still Lord Chancellor of England, and in Rushmere St Michael in the county of Suffolk, on the 2nd of August in that year, Robert Lynghoode was making his will. Very likely he was dying, perhaps of the plague, for it is clear from the terms of the will that his six children are all under age, besides which his wife Joan is pregnant with a seventh child, and that he is concerned for their future welfare. After declaring that he is 'in good mind and whole remembrance' he leaves his soul to God Almighty and Our Lady and all the holy company in heaven (for England is still Catholic) and his body to be buried in the church of Saint Michael of Rushmere. Perhaps his conscience was troubling him, for his first bequest is to the high altar of Rushmere church 'for my tithes forgotten'. There are also bequests to the high altars of three other churches in the locality and a bequest to Rushmere church for repairs. His principal bequests are to his children Nicholas, Elizabeth, Margery, Laurence, Thomas, Robert, together with the unborn child, to each of whom he leaves five marks sterling, a cow, and a quantity of barley. Should one of his children die before reaching the age of twenty, the five marks is to go to an honest priest to say mass for the testator and his friends in Rushmere church. Should two of them die, an honest secular priest is to have ten marks to say mass for a whole year. Should more than two children die before reaching the age of twenty the money is to go to their mother. Relatives and friends are not forgotten. To his brother Steven Lynghoode he bequeaths one of his black cattle at Waldsdyke, and to Ellen Gyldorne, who may be a servant, a measure of barley. Finally, Robert Lynghoode of Rushmere leaves all his remaining goods to his wife Joan, whom he makes his executrix. He directs her to deliver all his children's money to Sr Thomas Bedingfeld and Sr Laurence Mayewe for them to hold for the benefit of the children until such time as they should require it.

The will is witnessed by Sr Thomas Bedingfeld, Sr Robert Clarke, and John Leslyn.

Sir Thomas Bedingfeld of Oxburgh belonged to an East Anglian family well known to historians of the Tudor period. He was High Sheriff of Norfolk and Suffolk in 1522 and died in 1538 after making a nuncupative will in which he left everything to his wife Alice, daughter of William London, Mayor of Norwich. His brother Sir Edmund Bedingfeld (1479/80–1553) was knighted in 1523 for demonstrating bravery in the French wars and eventually inherited from his brother Robert Bedingfeld the great estate of Oxburgh Hall, Kings Lynn, Norfolk. Following Henry VIII's divorce he was entrusted with the care of Katherine of Aragon at Kimbolton Castle. It was the father of the brothers, Sir Edmund Bedingfeld (1443–1496) who built Oxburgh Hall where Henry VII and his queen once stayed. Oxburgh Hall is now a National Trust property. Sir Henry Bedingfeld (1509–1583) of Oxburgh, the son of Thomas Bedingfeld and nephew of the younger Sir Edmund Bedingfeld, had the care of the Princess Elizabeth (the future queen Elizabeth I) when on the orders of Queen Mary she was transferred from the Tower of London to Woodstock in Oxfordshire.

It should be noted that Sir Thomas Bedingfeld is both entrusted with the children's money until they are of age *and* is a witness to Robert Lynghoode's will, whereas Sir Laurence Mayewe is only entrusted with the children's money and Sir Robert Clarke and John Leslyn are only witnesses to the will. This suggests that Robert Lynghoode had a closer connection with Sir Thomas Bedingfeld than with the three other men, which indeed is not unlikely. Sir Thomas's father originally came from Bedingfeld, which is situated in the same part of Suffolk that my Lingwood ancestors came from, so the two families may well have known each other for several generations.

Robert Lynghoode's will was of great interest to me. It told me quite a lot about my ancestor. He was married to a woman named Joan, had at least six children, and died at a comparatively early age. He was quite well-to-do, being in a position to leave money, a cow, and a quantity of barley to each of his children, as if to set them up in life as soon as they became of age. His wife was left the residue of his estate, which no doubt meant a house and land and the means of providing for herself and the children until they grew up and could fend for themselves. The bequest to his brother suggests that he had land in Waldsdyke as well as in Rushmere. That he makes bequests to so many churches does not necessarily mean that Robert Lynghoode was especially pious. Probably it was no more than what a person of good standing in the community was expected to do in those days. More significant is the fact that he expresses a wish to be buried in Rushmere church, i.e. not in the graveyard like ordinary folk, and apparently takes it for granted that his wish will be respected.

Besides his will, there were two other sources of information about Robert Lynghoode of Rushmere. One is a genealogy included in the Lingwood family papers (LFP); the other, the Suffolk Subsidy Returns for 1524. In the genealogy Robert Lynghoode is styled constable, a term that in this connection means an officer who, under a High Sheriff, is responsible for the maintenance of law and order, probably within a certain area. It is not clear whether Robert Lynghoode served under Sir Thomas Bedingfeld or under some other occupant or occupants of the post of High Sheriff of Norfolk and Suffolk. The subsidy of 1524 was granted by parliament to Henry VIII to finance the war in France. It was a graduated tax, spread over four years. In the first two years land and houses paid one shilling for each pound of their yearly value. Those who had moveable goods valued at £20 and upwards paid one shilling for each pound. According to the Suffolk Subsidy Returns of 1524 Robert Lynghoode paid, or was assessed at, the sum of £16.8s.0d – it is not clear which it was. In either case he must have been quite well to do, as indeed is evident from the terms of his will.

Robert Lynghoode of Rushmere thus emerges from the early Tudor records as a substantial Suffolk yeoman, a man of some position in his community, a responsible father and husband, a good Catholic, and with contacts – even friends – among the gentry of East Anglia. On the whole it is a not unattractive picture.

Nicholas Lingwood of Badingham, yeoman, Robert Lynghoode's eldest son, farmed at Badingham, had four sons and three daughters by his wife Margery, and according to the Suffolk Subsidy Returns of 1568 he paid, or was assessed at, the sum of £10. He died in 1591, his wife in 1563.

Next in line is John Lingwood of Dennington, yeoman, Nicholas Lingwood's eldest son, who was born in 1548 and died in 1597. He married (1) Margaret Connold of Laxfield and (2) Mary. He had five sons and a daughter. One of the sons bore the unusual name of Wulfran.

John Lingwood of Swaffing, yeoman, John Lingwood's eldest son, was born in 1575, married Mary, and by her had three sons and three daughters, plus an unnamed child.

The record for Thomas Lingwood of Hynten St Blythburg, yeoman, who was born in 1600, is sparse. All that is known of him is that, unusually for the philoprogenitive Lingwoods, he had only one child, a son.

This son, Thomas Lingwood of Badingham I, yeoman, did a little better than his father in the generative department. He had two sons, and died in 1683.

Thomas Lingwood of Badingham II, yeoman, the elder of Thomas Lingwood I's two sons, married Annis Aldous, and died in 1698, leaving two sons and four daughters.

Thomas Lingwood of Brome I, gentleman, the elder of Thomas Lingwood of Badingham II's two sons, was born in 1688, died in 1748, and was buried in the graveyard of Brome parish church. His wife was Mary Peake of Wickenham Skeith, who was born in 1695 and died in 1763. They had one son, though the records may be incorrect and there may have been other children. Thomas Lingwood of Brome was the first of my Lingwood ancestors to be styled gentleman. All his ascendents, from his father to Thomas Lingwood of Badingham up to and including Robert Lynghoode of Rushmere, are styled yeoman. It is an interesting example of upward social mobility.

Thomas Lingwood of Brome II, gentleman, was born in 1736 and died in 1815, leaving a will. Like his father, he was buried in the graveyard of Brome parish church. He married Mary Lathbury, who was born in 1735 and died in 1802. They had twelve sons and three daughters.

It was the coffin shaped tomb graves of Thomas and Mary Lingwood and three of their children that Paramartha and I found behind the back wall of the parish church of St Mary, Brome, when we visited Suffolk in June 2010.

The last will and testament of Thomas Lingwood of Brome II is dated 1809, which means that he made it seven years before his death, the witnesses being Mary Kelly, Richard Kelly, and J. Bellman. The will is prolix, repetitive, and entirely devoid of punctuation, and must have been drawn up by a lawyer. After a simple invocation of the Deity (for England has long been Protestant), the testator appoints three of his sons as his executors. They are Thomas Lathbury Lingwood, Peter Lathbury Lingwood, and Decimus Lathbury Lingwood, and the three names occur again and again throughout the will like a kind of refrain. He gives them 'all and every my messuages, farms, lands, tenements and hereditaments and all other my real estate whatsoever situate, lying, and being in, Brome, aforesaid, and Thrandeston in the said County, or in any other Town, Parish, or place near or adjoining thereto as are freehold or charter hold...(punctuation added).' He then proceeds to make sundry bequests, the gist of which is as follows:

1. The interest from a sum of £1,500 in consolidated bank annuities is to continue to be paid annually to Robert Page and Mary Page (Thomas's daughter) and is to be paid for the rest of their natural lives.

2. He bequeathes to his granddaughter Mary Page (daughter of the above) the sum of £100, to be paid on her attaining her 21st birthday.

3. He also asks his executors to set up from the moneys from his estate a fund to pay annuity of £10 to Mr Thomas Bond, yeoman, of Starson, in the county of Norfolk.

4. A similar fund to be set up to pay annuity of £10 to Ann Pretty (who lives with him).

5. Lastly, he directs that the residue of the monies from the sale of his real and personal estates be divided and shared alike amongst his children, namely, Thomas Lathbury Lingwood, Peter Lathbury Lingwood, Joseph Lathbury Lingwood, Charlotte Edmonds (his daughter), Edward Lingwood, Decimus Lingwood, and Benjamin Lingwood.

In 1811 Thomas Lingwood of Brome added a codicil to his will in his own hand. The codicil was witnessed by Ann Pretty. In it he bequeaths £500 each to his granddaughters Mary and Charlotte Page, the amounts to be paid to them within six months of their attaining the age of twenty one. The genuineness of the codicil may have been questioned, for in 1815 Edward Lingwood of Eye, Thomas's eldest son, confirmed that the codicil was indeed in his father's handwriting.

The will and its codicil do not really tell us much about Thomas Lingwood of Brome. They tell us what he owned, which evidently was quite a lot, but they tell us nothing about the man himself. He may have left generous bequests to his two granddaughters because he was particularly fond of them, but on the other hand he may have done so just because that was what was expected of a wealthy grandfather. Our only other source of information about him comes from an item in the *Norfolk Chronicle* of 22 June 1782, which reports on the General Meeting of the 'Diss Association for apprehending and prosecuting Horse-Stealers'. At this meeting 'the Gentlemen residing in or near the said Hundred, associated for prosecuting Horse-Stealers, held the fifth Day of this Instant June in the King's Head at Diss, the Treasurer's Accounts for the last Year were settled, and it was agreed that Mr Benjamin Fincham of Diss, aforesaid, should be continued Treasurer for the Year ensuing, and that the Articles of this Association should remain in full Force, and that the Reward of Ten Guineas, together with all reasonable Charges, be continued to be paid by the Treasurer to any Person or Persons who shall apprehend, and prosecute to Conviction, the Stealers of any Horse, Mare, or Gelding, from any of the undermentioned Subscribers.' Among the undermentioned subscribers is Thomas Lingwood of Brome, which suggests that he would have shared, to an extent at least, the interests and opinions of the other landowners and gentlemen farmers of East Anglia.

Thomas's sons must have been no less prosperous than he was. One of them, Thomas Lathbury Lingwood, could afford to give his only son a university education. This son was Robert Maulkin Lingwood, born in 1813. A Cambridge graduate (B.A. 1836, M.A. 1840), he was a botanist and entomologist, was in the Channel Islands and in Ireland with the distinguished C.C. Babington (a correspondent of Charles Darwin), discovered and named various plants, and was a member of a number of scientific bodies. He was High Sheriff of Herefordshire in 1848, and in 1860 he became Deputy Lord Lieutenant of the County. Robert Maulkin Lingwood married his first cousin Elizabeth Lingwood, daughter of Benjamin Lingwood, but they had no issue. He died in 1887, at Lystone House, Llanwarne.

While he was at Cambridge Robert Maulkin Lingwood applied to the College of Arms for a grant of arms. In 1835, since he was able to 'prove his pedigree' to their satisfaction, the application was accepted. The grant was made not to Robert Maulkin himself, but to his grandfather Thomas Lingwood of Brome, and to all the latter's male descendants. Among the LFP there is a sketch of the armorial bearings of the family, together with the motto CREDE DEO. In traditional heraldic terms the Arms are: Azure a saltire, engrailed, erminoise, between fleur de lis, or Crest: A Talbot's Head, erminoised erased, and ear sable with mural crown gules.

Edward Lingwood of Eye and Needham Market, the eldest son of Thomas Lingwood of Brome II, was born in 1770 and died in 1849, and was buried in front of the altar of Barking parish church. He married Hannah Ward, who was born in 1766 and died in 1798, at the age of 32. They had two children, Edward and Hannah. It was his altar grave that Paramartha was unable to see as the area in front of the altar was covered by a carpet.

Edward Lingwood of Battisford, the only son of Edward Lingwood of Eye and Needham Market, was born circa 1797 and baptized 12 June 1797 at Eye. In 1827 he married Sarah Haywood, and they had eleven sons and three daughters. He died in 1864, after living in retirement at

The Elms, Stowmarket, and was buried in the graveyard of Battisford parish church, of which he had been 'Perpetual Churchwarden'. According to the Census of 1851, Edward Lingwood of Battisford, then aged 53, lived at St John's, farmed 400 acres, and employed sixteen men and eight boys. There lived at home with him seven children, including Edward, his eldest son, as well as two male and two female lodgers.

St John's – or The Manor House, as it was also known – was the large, tree-surrounded house Paramartha and I had come across on the first day of our search for traces of my Lingwood ancestors. It was where we met Pat Knoch, its present occupier and owner or custodian of the Lingwood box, from whom we learned that the property had once been occupied by members of the Lingwood family. Though we could see that the house was old, despite its relatively modern frontage, at the time we had no idea how old it really was or how long and varied was its history. That history began with the mention of Battisford Manor in the Domesday Book where it is described as a farm. According to a note in the LFP, 'a priory was founded on the spot in the time of Herbert Losinga, bishop of Norwich, by Radulfus Fitzbrian and Emma, his wife. It was dedicated to St Leonard and endowed by them with lands and tithes'. More information is to be found in the National Trust Listing Text (grade II). After describing St John's as it exists today, in great detail, it goes on to say: 'The house is built upon the moated site of the Preceptory of the Knights Hospitallers founded here in circa 1154 and dissolved in 1540'. In the reign of Elizabeth I the property was owned by Sir Thomas Gresham, Lord of the Battisford and St John's Manors, and the founder of the Royal Exchange. Dame Anne, Sir Thomas's wife, rebuilt the house in 1570, and in the course of the rebuilding 'many rafters were reused from a large open hall of late C13 or early C14'.

Sarah Lingwood was born in 1803 and died in 1879. She appears to have been an educated, intelligent, and pious woman, and came from a prosperous and well-connected family. Her brother Edward Haywood was Bar-at-law of the Inner Temple. He married Christine Annette Campbell of Brighton, daughter of the late Daniel Campbell, cousin to the Duke of Northumberland and to Lord Carbery. In the LFP there are typewritten copies of two letters from Sarah to her and Edward's third son, Henry Lingwood, then seventeen and living first at Wickham Market, Suffolk, and afterwards at Crabtree, near Plymouth, Devonshire.

The first letter is headed Battisford and dated 19 September 1848. Sarah was writing because his brothers were all fully employed. His father was busy carting barley, which suggests that the harvest was well under way. There followed news of various members of the family. Tom had that day gone to Woolpit bullock fair instead of his father, who did not like to leave home. They had been surprised to see Horace, who came with a friend to see the balloon at Stowe, probably one of the hot-air balloons popular at the time. They had heard of a situation for James at Yarmouth, but his father had not yet decided. Mr Page had taken great pains to make enquiries. Sarah probably had an ear for music, for she commented that Mr Cooper, who married Henry's sister Sarah, played the flute beautifully. His sister had come with him, and Sarah had found her a most pleasing amiable person and quite liked her. She and Sarah junior had gone for a ride to Brice and would spend the next day with Sarah senior's mother. Other news was that Mr Moores and Mr Wood had been at St John's shooting, which probably means shooting pheasants; that her brother and his wife had been at Bosmere, but had not come to St John's; that Mr Edmonds had left ten shillings for him, which he was not to spend on 'those hateful things', cigars. He had not given so much to his sister Sarah, who was a 'most extraordinary woman for her age'. What made her daughter so extraordinary Sarah did not say. Finally, she had admonished him, her dear boy, to walk in the strait path, for 'he that walketh uprightly walketh safely'.[14] That God might abundantly bless him in this life and save him for ever was, she assured him, the very frequent prayer of his mother.

Sarah Lingwood's second letter to her son Henry, now eighteen and working in a Mill in or near Plymouth, bears no date but is marked 'To be posted Battisford, Saturday evening.' The envelope is stamped 'Ipswich 1 July 1849' and 'Plymouth 3 July 1849.' She writes:

My dear Henry,

I was truly glad to receive your interesting letter for which I was looking most anxiously – fearing perhaps mine had not reached you – I wish my dear boy you had not so many hours to work without rest, and rejoice at your determination to do your best and when we are in the path of duty, we may hope and expect God's blessing on our honest endeavours – nevertheless nothing would give us more pleasure than to find you were promoted to some place in the Mill, where you had less to do. I am thankful you do not omit to go to church – I am glad you like Plympton church, because I conclude you can go there in all weathers, and it is not good to roam from church to church, if we know where to go to hear God's word rightly preached.

I should like much to see the glorious view of the ocean at Plymouth and am thankful that every opportunity you have of taking a walk, that you can command such lovely views.

I was very pleased with the green plant, I think I have found it out – it is so fleshy, that probably it will not dry well, but Sarah will be glad to have whole specimens of what you find, but a blossom pleases me much. Sarah went to Burstal on Wednesday and is to return to-night. James is gone to the train to meet her. James came home last Monday – he is rather taller but not stouter I think; he is full of spirits – he seems to like his occupation much and is improved in manner. He received your letter and will answer it he says when he goes home, which he is to do next Thursday – he has his meals alone at the back of the shop, to be in waiting when called.

Sarah half expects Mr. C.C. next week to go with her to the Flower Show at Ipswich; the children being all at home I should prefer his visit another time. My Brother & his wife are still in Dublin staying with Mrs. Putland – Mrs. H. is of "immense consequence" so my Brother says. I should like to see the Slate quarry – is not Plymouth Dock cut out of slate? When the flints are ground what coloured earthenware is it used for? White?

I think I heard from Horace just after I wrote to you; he seems very comfortable and contented and I hope will continue so – he wrote quite a long letter. – I was afraid he would miss the gun.

We have two large hay and stover stacks got up very well –

Mr. & Mrs. R. Lingwood have been on a trip to the Lakes.

Your father has given up all thoughts of hiring Roydon Hall which I am glad of – Edward and Thos. are very anxious to go to the Norwich Show. Thos. has been ailing and taking medicine every day since you left – I hope however this illness has been for his good in some respects and I have no longer any cause for uneasiness: you understand this.

There are 4 young peafowls, they are very pretty, and are kept in the partridge coop by the walnut tree. The peahen hatched 5 chickens but soon walked them to death. Sarah has 12 Ducks hatched.

I have had a very bad face-ache all the week, but it is much better. Do you get any Beer, as I read whiskey cider is the usual drink? I am sure you will smile at my odd mixture of subjects – (you write where instead of were very often in your letters).

Sarah is just returned and left all friends well at Burstal. She went to the Ipswich Museum and to some gardens at Bramford. She had a long ride on "Jack" she is very much obliged for the plant – I must bid you good night with my kind love and best wishes –

Your most affectionate

Mother

A mixture of topics indeed! Henry may well have smiled reading his mother's letter. As she does in the first letter, Sarah shows herself to be solicitous for both the material and spiritual welfare of her son, and perhaps even more for the latter than the former. Though thankful that he still goes to church, she appears not to be concerned what kind of church he attends, whether Anglican or Nonconformist. Her principal concern is that he should be able to hear God's word rightly preached. In this she is firmly Protestant, even Evangelical. Yet though she is pious, Sarah is not parochial. She has a strong desire to see the ocean, which she has either not seen or saw a long time ago, and she wonders if Plymouth Dock was not cut out of slate, and would like to know of what colour was the earthenware made from ground flints. Horizons were expanding in remote, rural, Suffolk. People went on trips to the Lake District, Ipswich had its own museum, and the fact that someone had gone to meet a train could be mentioned without comment.

The walnut tree mentioned by Sarah in her letter, beside which was the partridge coop where she kept her peafowl chicks, was no longer to be seen at St John's. It had been blown down in a storm during her time at the house, Pat Knoch told Paramartha and me. Neither were there any peacocks there, as there may have been when Sarah lived in the old house. I had no difficulty imagining them strutting haughtily about the place, displaying their magnificent plumage and bringing a touch of oriental splendour to the sober English countryside.

Thomas Lingwood, the second son of Edward and Sarah Lingwood, was born in Battisford in 1832, but spent the greater part of his life at Shrub House, Brockford. He evidently inherited the strong religious feelings of his mother. According to an obituary in the LFP, he was for much of his life devoted to mission work, holding Sunday services in the old oak beamed house at Brockford, fitting up the barn as a mission hall when numbers increased, and erecting a gospel hall on his land at Brockford six years before his death. We have no clue as to the precise nature of his religious views. Probably he was an evangelically-inclined protestant and, like his mother, believed that thirteen people should be able to "hear the word of God rightly preached". He may also have been dissatisfied with the lukewarm ministrations of the local Anglican clergy.

But Thomas Lingwood's interests were not exclusively religious. He was a lover and breeder of horses, a subject on which his advice was frequently sought, and for sixty years he never failed to appear at the Woodbridge Horse Fair. He was an active member of several local charities, and a keen horticulturist whose garden was greatly admired for its wealth of old fashioned flowers, including a fine display of roses. He died in 1915, at the age of 83. A large number of people attended his funeral, which was held in the Gospel Hall, from which his oak coffin was taken to Wetheringsett Cemetery on the shoulders of tenants from his estate. He never married. In his will he provided for the upkeep of the Gospel Hall, and for the disposal of his books on religion. He also left generous legacies to his numerous nephews and nieces, as well as to his housekeeper and various friends.

In the LFP there is a photograph of Thomas Lingwood, and beside it a photograph of his twin sister Sarah Lingwood Cooper. He has a broad forehead, deep set eyes, and full lips similar to those of my father. His expression is one of strength and kindness, and he wears a kind of bow-tie. Sarah is seated, and reads a newspaper. Behind her is a fireplace and a clock the hands of which point to 1.55. Her face is thin, her nose aquiline, and she wears on her head a small cap. Both brother and sister are in their fifties, even their sixties.

James Grace Lingwood, the fourth son of Edward and Sarah Lingwood, was born in 1832. His second name was that of one of his three godparents, a Mr Grace. A note to a genealogical tree in the LFP describes him as an artist, but we do not know if he ever went to art school or practised as an artist professionally. From Sarah's letters to his brother Henry we know that as a young man he worked in a shop in Yarmouth and seemed happy there. He never married, and died in 1863, aged 30. Behind the bare facts there may well be a story of blasted hopes and unfulfilled aspirations.

Two of Edward's and Sarah's sons emigrated to Canada. They were Septimus Robert (known as Robert), their seventh son, born in 1835, and William Herbert, their eleventh son, born in 1845. Robert went first, when he was in his early twenties, and William followed later. Both brothers married in Canada, and founded, in Robert's case at least, a branch of the Lingwood family in that country. Initially, Robert leased a farm in Nichol township, but the venture was not a success. He then became a director of a company drilling for oil, and with his brother William went into the brewing and canning business.

One of the most interesting aspects of the lives of the two brothers in Canada is their membership of the Fergus Company, a militia organized for defence against the Fenian Raids of 1865–66.[15] Once the Fergus Company was ordered to go to Sarnia.[16] They went by wagon to Guelph, where they were joined by the Elora Company and took the train to Sarnia. There was no confrontation with the Fenians. On another occasion the Fergus Company went to Niagara, where they were in a skirmish with the Fenians under General O'Neill.[17] The Fenians were repulsed. According to family tradition, Robert was wounded in the hand during the fighting, the wound festered, and it had to be amputated. Later he moved from Fergus to Guelph, where he died of TB in 1875, leaving four sons, four daughters, and a handwritten will.[18] Edith Wilson, who put together the Lingwood box, was his granddaughter. In the LFP there is a photograph of Captain Robert Lingwood in his militia uniform. William Herbert Lingwood returned to England in about 1900, and after enduring much hardship eventually settled in Stowmarket, where he died, blind, in 1924, leaving one child, a daughter, then living in the United States.

Edward Lingwood of Ashfield, the eldest son of Edward Lingwood of Battisford and his wife Sarah, stayed at home and made his contribution to the history of the Lingwood family, including the line that ends with the present writer. He was born in 1828, and educated at Eye Grammar School. In his late twenties he married Catherine Sophia Sheldrake (known as Kate), the daughter of Edward Sheldrake of Ixworth Priory. They had fourteen children, at least four of whom died in infancy. The census of 1861 records Edward Lingwood as farming 232 acres in Ashfield, Suffolk, and employing thirteen men and five boys. He was then 32. Subsequent censuses show him as living, successively, in Wetheringsett-cum-Brockford, Thwaite, Bramford, and in St Margaret (Ipswich), all in Suffolk. An obituary in the LFP gives a summary of his career: "He started farming at the age of 20, at Ashfield; and in later years he acted as agent for Lord Thurlow. For some time he was a well-known follower of the Essex and Suffolk Foxhounds, his favourite meet being at Hintlesham Park gates. About fifty years ago he was a member of the Needham Market Bowling Club, and he would ride a dozen miles in order to participate in his favourite game. He was for a long period a member of the Stowmarket Farmers' Club, and was one who read papers in various districts on sheep breeding. The noted flock of the later Mr. Henry Lingwood was developed from sheep drawn from the deceased gentleman's flock when he relinquished farming 25 years ago.

During his long period of activity Mr. Lingwood represented parishes in which he resided on the Stowmarket or Hartismere Boards of Guardians; in politics he was a staunch Conservative, for considerable periods he held the position of churchwarden or overseer. He was an ardent collector of birds' eggs, and had a wonderful knowledge of bird-life in general, travelling long distances to hear and see rare specimens. Up to the date of his death he could quote the Latin name for almost any English bird." Edward Lingwood spent the last years of his life in retirement at his residence in Gainsborough Road, Ipswich, where he died in 1909, his wife Kate having died earlier that year. They were survived by six sons and two daughters.

In the LFP there are two three-quarter-length photographs of Edward Lingwood of Ashfield and his wife Kate. Both are seated beside a table. He looks to his left, she to her right. Edward has the same broad forehead and deep set eyes as his brother Thomas, as well as the same full lips, but he is bearded and his expression is sad, even tragic. Between his hands he holds an open book or magazine. Kate has a thin, pale face, and about her lips there is a hint of a smile. Her smooth dark hair is parted in the middle and surmounted by a small cap. She has a full skirt and full sleeves, and appears to be reading. On the table at her elbow there is a row of books.

One of those books could have been *Prayer and Praise at Eventide*, a copy of which, inscribed to him in her own hand, Kate gave to her son Philip Francis Lingwood, my grandfather. I found this book at the bottom of a cupboard when I was a child and read the inscription. In the house at that time there were only two other articles that had belonged to my grandfather, a silver-mounted amber cane and a wooden dispatch case, and all that I really knew about him was that he had died young. Even now I know very little more than that. There are two reasons for this. The first is that the Lingwood box contained no information about him, the compiler being more concerned with the fortunes of the descendants of Septimus Robert Lingwood in Canada. The second is that he died when my father was three years old, so that the latter had no personal recollections of him to pass on to me.

Philip Francis Lingwood, the seventh son of Edward Lingwood of Ashfield and his wife Kate, was born in 1873 at Occold, Suffolk. At some point he came to London, where in 1896 he married Anna Ellen Butters, born 1872, the daughter of Walter Butters, a farm labourer, of Besthorpe, Norfolk, and his wife Caroline.[19] They had two children, Philip Edward Lingwood, born at Woolwich, Kent (now part of Greater London) in 1899, and Helen Frances Lingwood, born in 1902. He died in 1902, at Charlton, London. Anna Ellen lived until 1952, having remarried after the death of Philip Francis, and had two more children.

As a child I knew that my grandfather had died young, but I also knew, from what I heard – or overheard – from my elders, that there was a mystery about his death, or at least something unexplained. One version was that he had caught a chill after going for a swim and had died of pneumonia. Another version of the story was that he had picked up a deadly infection from certain diplomatic papers that had arrived from the Far East, papers he had handled in the course of his duties at the War Office. If there was any truth in this account, the papers may well have been kept for a while in the wooden dispatch case, which had soon passed into my possession, along with the silver-mounted amber cane. The case was lined with green beige and it could be locked. On its polished back a crest was picked out in gold. The crest was in the form of a shield, on the shield there was a horizontal bar, on the bar a row of three balls. I do not know if the crest was my grandfather's, or that of a previous owner of the case. It also seems that my grandfather had a fine copperplate handwriting, on account of which he was given the task of making out the commissions that went to the queen for signature. However, hearsay is not evidence, as a libel lawyer once reminded me, and I cannot vouch for the truth of all the things I heard – or overheard – as a child.

Though she had a framed photograph of my grandfather hanging in her kitchen, not far from a similar one of her deceased second husband, I can remember my grandmother speaking of him only once. This was when I was fourteen or fifteen. My mother and I were alone with her one day, and my mother, who was like a daughter to her, happened to remark that over the years her memories of her first husband must have gradually faded. "Oh no!" my grandmother at once exclaimed, a joyous expression lighting up her face. "It's all as fresh as if it were yesterday!"

Philip Edward Lingwood, who was born in 1899 and was the only son of Philip Francis Lingwood and his wife Anna, married in 1920 Catherine Florence Margaret Ketskemety (known as Florrie to her brothers and sisters and Kit to her husband and his relations). They had two children, Dennis Philip Edward, who was born in 1925, and Joan Doreen, who was born in 1926 and died in 2001, leaving a husband Edward Turner (known as Eddie), and four children, John, Maria, David, and Kamala (known as Kay). Philip and Florrie/Kit were divorced in 1946 and both remarried, the former once, the latter twice. Philip Edward died in 1971, and Florrie/Kit in 1990, after being twice widowed.

Philip Edward, my father, grew up in Besthorpe, Norfolk, and in Tooting, South London. After leaving school he worked for, or was apprenticed to, a jeweller, along with several other boys. The boys all 'lived in', and my father more than once told me, when I was a child, how he and the other boys used to play tricks on the jeweller's elderly housekeeper. When World War I began he was fifteen, and it was not long before he enlisted, giving a false age. He served in the trenches, was badly wounded, was invalided back to England, and while recovering in St Benedict's Hospital, Tooting, met my mother, who was working there as a VAD.[20] Later he trained as a French Polisher at the Lord Roberts Workshops.[21]

Had Philip Francis Lingwood, his father, not died young, my father probably would have had a very different life. He certainly would not have grown up in Tooting, and though he may have enlisted he almost certainly would not have met my mother, so that, had I been born at all, I would have been born to a different mother and with a different genetic inheritance. In a word, I would not have been quite me, and would have had a different kind of life.

But speculation is a waste of time. I have had the life I have had, and it has been a life very different from that of any of my Lingwood biological ancestors or, for that matter, from the life of any of my Ketskemety ancestors. I have never married, and at 85 I am unlikely to do so, and I therefore will have no biological descendants. I will, I trust, have many spiritual descendants, in the form of the members of the Triratna Buddhist Order. In other words, my spiritual descendants will be all those who, whether in Suffolk, in England, or in any other part of the world, Go For Refuge to the Three Jewels, and who study, practise, and communicate the Buddhadhamma as taught by me in the course of sixty and more years.

# Reflections

The discovery of the Lingwood box was important for me. Before it, I had known of my paternal Lingwood ancestry only that my grandfather was from a good Suffolk family and had died young. Now I knew a good deal more than that. Thanks to the contents of that box, I was suddenly swept back over four centuries of English history, over a dozen generations of Lingwoods, to the reign of Henry VIII and to Robert Lynghoode of Rushmere, the first of my known Lingwood ancestors. I was in a position similar to that of one who, having been adopted at an early age and brought up by adoptive parents, one day discovers that he has real parents and is a member of a real, biological family. The difference between us was that his discovery related to the present, whereas mine related to the past.

To discover one's true parents is to learn something about oneself, and to discover a whole series of previously unknown ancestors is to learn even more, and to learn it with greater certainty. The basic fact about my Lingwood ancestors was that they were farmers. Generation after generation they had ploughed, sowed, harvested, and gathered into barns. Farming was therefore in my blood, along with other ingredients, and it was natural that when, in a foreign country, I acquired a stone cottage and four acres of hillside land, I should have cultivated those four acres as a matter of course. During the seven years that I lived at the cottage I grew maize and buckwheat, cared for my hundred orange trees, and saw to it that there were vegetables for the table and flowers for the shrine.[22] There were good practical reasons for my doing this, but I did not do it only for these reasons. I also did it because engaging with the soil gave me a deep inner satisfaction. It was the kind of satisfaction that Edward Lingwood of Battisford must have experienced when carting barley a hundred years earlier.

Ancestry is far from being merely biological. It is also cultural and religious, and the different ancestries can overlap, the biological with the cultural, the cultural with the religious. Probably the most important part of our cultural heritage is language, through which so much of our knowledge and experience is mediated. In my own case, I inherited from my Lingwood ancestors not only some of my genes but the language in which I think, speak, and write. From my Ketskemety ancestry I inherited it only to a limited extent, for until two generations ago that side of my family spoke not English but Hungarian, of which I know hardly a word. Not that this really mattered. I grew up speaking, as my native tongue, one of the world's great languages, through which I had immediate access to one of the world's great literatures. I have always been thankful that I spoke the language that Shakespeare and Milton spoke and have been able to enjoy their works in the original, as well as the works of so many other poets, dramatists, novelists, historians, philosophers, and essayists who have contributed to the creation of the glory that is English literature. Nor is that all. Much has been translated into English from other languages, both ancient and modern, eastern and western, to the cultural enrichment of the English-speaking world. Among the works translated have been the Buddhist scriptures. Had none of them been translated it would not have been possible for me, as a boy of sixteen or seventeen, to discover the Dharma.

Proper names are an integral part of any language. As I look back over the line of my paternal ancestors I see four Thomas Lingwoods, three Edwards, two Johns, two Philips, one Robert, and one Nicholas – but no Dennis. There was no Dennis until 1925 when I was born and baptized Dennis Philip Edward at the parish church of St Nicholas, Tooting. The person responsible for this innovation in the matter of names was my aunt Helen, my father's sister, who was also my godmother. 'Dennis' must have been a name she particularly liked; but I have never liked it, and would much rather have been called Edward, or even Philip. I was not the only one who disliked the first of my baptismal names, my dislike being shared by at least one other person. This was old, red-faced Thomas Whitehead (known to the family as Uncle Tom), my bluff, hearty godfather.[23] As a small child I often heard him declare, as I sat perched on his knee, 'He's not Dennis. He's little Phil.' Whether my two godparents had argued the point over the baptismal font at my Christening I never knew. Years later I was to undergo more than one change of name. From Dennis I became first Dharmapriya, then (for a few hours) Dharmarakshita, after that Sangharakshita, and finally Urgyen Sangharakshita.[24]

The change from Dennis to Dharmapriya and its successors was much more than a simple change of name. It marked a change of religion on my part. Dennis and the two other names I was given at the font were my baptismal names. They bore witness to the fact that I had undergone the rite of admission into the Christian church. The change from Dennis to Dharmapriya was therefore an event of singular moment. It was a change from being a member of the Christian church to being a member of the Buddhist sangha, from being a Christian, albeit a very nominal one, to being a believing and practising Buddhist. At the same time, this did not mean that I ceased to appreciate and enjoy Christian art, though I appreciated it aesthetically, without giving intellectual assent to its doctrinal content. Even when I was a small boy, and had as yet no definite religious ideas, whether Christian or non-Christian, I was unaccountably drawn to old churches. Visiting them, and photographing them with my box camera, was one of the highlights of my summer holidays at Shoreham-by-Sea with my parents and my sister.[25] It was therefore only natural that I should have felt at home in the parish churches of Suffolk, where so many of my Lingwood ancestors were baptized, were married, where they sang hymns and heard sermons, and where, finally, they were buried.

There followed from this, inevitably, the thought of impermanence and death as the fundamental reality of the human condition. I cannot claim, however, that my search for traces of my Lingwood ancestors, or the discoveries I made about them, gave me any fresh or original insights into that reality, though they reinforced, and underlined, the insights I already had. My discoveries did, however, give me a more vivid sense of how one generation succeeds another, and of how important it is that within the span of human life allotted to us we take full advantage of our spiritual opportunities, especially if we are so fortunate as to be able to study and practise the Dharma.

Though I have biological ancestors I certainly will not leave behind me any biological descendants; but perhaps, in years to come, there will be spiritual descendants of mine who will, one day, search for traces of me in Tooting and Kalimpong, Hampstead and Moseley, and elsewhere. I wonder what they will discover.


**Notes**

1. FWBO activities in Ipswich began in 1986 with meditation classes run by Rex Smart (Saddharaja). From these small beginnings a thriving FWBO (from 2010 Triratna) community has grown that over the years has seen the establishment of chapters of Order members, residential communities, a Right Livelihood business, and, in January 2009, the purchase of premises at 4 Friars Bridge Road to permanently house the Buddhist Centre. Sangharakshita officially opened the new Centre in July that year.

2. Swadipa (b. 1947) was working as Consultant Obstetrician and Gynaecologist at Ipswich Hospital when he attended a talk at Ipswich Public Library. The talk was on Dr Ambedkar; the speaker was Order member Sumana. In 2008 he himself was ordained. Since retiring he has been fully engaged in the life and work of the Ipswich Buddhist Centre where he is currently Mitra Convenor for men. He and Carol were delighted to offer accommodation to Sangharakshita both on the visit referred to here and the previous year when Sangharakshita opened the Ipswich Buddhist Centre.

3. Carol (b. 1947 in Ipswich) was ordained as Charumani in 2014. She was a reception class teacher in an independent girls school in Ipswich when, in 1999, she went along to the Ipswich Buddhist Centre to learn to meditate. She retired in 2007 and asked for ordination the same year. She, too, is involved in many of the Ipswich Centre's activities.

4. Harshaprabha (b. 1953) went along to an FWBO class in 1974, and the following year attended a lecture given by Sangharakshita, 'Enlightenment as Experience and Non-Experience'. They met not long afterwards when Sangharakshita visited the men's community where Harshaprabha was living. With mutual visits, letters and cards, a friendship sprang up between them that has continued to this day. In 1981 Harshaprabha, a trained architect, founded Octagon Architects and Designers, a

Buddhist Right Livelihood business that continued until 2002. In 1991 he started up FWBO (Triratna) activities in Colchester. In 2004 he spent a year in Guelph, Ontario, sowing the first Triratna seeds in Eastern Canada. That it was Guelph and no other Canadian town is rather striking for Guelph is the place to which some of Sangharakshita's forebears had emigrated (see pp. 199–200 and note 18 below). Furthermore, when the great Buddhist missionary Anagarika Dharmapala visited North America for the second time in 1896, he made a visit to just one Canadian town. That town was – Guelph! (*Anagarika Dharmapala: A Biographical Sketch*, Sangharakshita, Ibis Publications 2013, p. 51). Harshaprabha now lives in Ipswich where he works part-time for the local borough council and is involved with the Ipswich Buddhist Centre. He also continues to support Triratna activities in Eastern Canada.

5. Norman Foster (b.1935), the English architect, designed the Willis building soon after founding the now famous Foster Associates in 1967. The Willis building was constructed between 1970 and 1975, one of Britain's first hi-tech developments. Notable for its lack of right-angles, it is coated in smoky glass and topped by a roof garden.

6. See note 12, p. 120.

7. Heinrich Heine (1797–1856), the German poet and writer, made several visits to the East Frisian island of Nordeney where he wrote many of the verses included in his cycle, *The North Sea* (*Die Nordsee*) written 1825–6. Kate Freiligrath Kroeker's *Poems Selected from Heinrich Heine* was first published in London in 1887.

8. The Knights of St John, also known as the Hospitallers, originated in the eleventh century in a Jerusalem hospital dedicated to St John the Baptist for the tending of sick and weary pilgrims. At the time of the First Crusade (1096–1099) they ceased humanitarian work to become a military order with a papal charter for the defence of the Holy Land. When the Holy Land came under Islamic rule, the Knights' headquarters were removed first to Cyprus, then Rhodes, and then to Malta – their emblem is the Maltese Cross. The first record of the Order's activities in Battisford is under King Henry II (1133–1189) and refers to a preceptory or hospital of the Knights. Under Henry VIII the property was confiscated and given in 1544 to one Sir Richard Gresham.

9. From John Keats' (1785–1821) sonnet 'On First Looking into Chapman's Homer' (1816).
> *Or like stout Cortez, when with eagle eyes*
> *He stared at the Pacific – and all his men*
> *Look'd at each other with a wild surmise...*

10. The name of the room was intended to echo the chapter rooms in cathedrals and was to be used for study and discussion, especially by members of the Order.

11. Selected highlights can be viewed at www.youtube.com/watch?v=9nLAdJo1VeY

12. In January 2010 the Friends of the Western Buddhist Order and its Indian counterpart, Trailokya Bauddha Mahasangha Sahayaka Gana, were renamed the Triratna Buddhist Community.

13. From John Keats' *The Eve of St Agnes* (1819), second stanza.

14. *The Bible*, Proverbs 10.9.

15. The Fenian Brotherhood (named after a legendary band of Irish warriors) were Irish Republicans based in the United States who carried out raids on British army forts and customs posts in Canada in a bid to bring pressure on Britain to withdraw from Ireland.

16. A town on Lake Huron in south-western Ontario.

17. General John O'Neill (1834–1878), a member of the Fenian Brotherhood, led a number of the Fenian raids.

18. During his year living in Guelph, Harshaprabha (see note 4 above) visited nearby Fergus and looking round the graveyard there discovered the gravestone of Robert Lingwood. Next to Robert Lingwood's grave was the grave of his daughter Jessie (1865–1866) and son Henry (1867–1880). Nearby was the grave of Florence Evelyn Lingwood, fourth daughter of John Campbell Ross (died 21 November 1924).

19. Anna Butters of Besthorpe is the 'Nana' of whom Sangharakshita writes in *A Mosaic of Memories* (see this volume pp. 34–7).

20. The Voluntary Aid Detachment was founded in 1909. During the First World War tens of thousands of volunteers – two-thirds women and girls – provided field nursing services at home in Britain and abroad. Vera Brittain's *Testament of Youth* (1933) recounts her experiences as a VAD nurse in World War One.

21. Named after Field Marshal Earl Roberts (1832–1914) the workshops were for the retraining of wounded ex-servicemen.

22. This stone cottage was the Triyana Vardhana Vihara in Kalimpong (the name was given by Sangharakshita's teacher, Chetrul Sangye Dorje). It came with four acres of terraced hillside which Sangharakshita cultivated as described here (see also *PT*, p. 40). The Vihara was his base from 1957 until he left India for England in 1964.

23. Uncle Tom also appears in *My First Eight Years*, see Neighbours and Early Friends, pp. 20–1.

24. Dennis Lingwood left the army demobilization camp where he had been stationed in Singapore early in 1947 and, in search of a context to lead a spiritual life, returned to India, where he had first landed in 1944. From the spring of that year (1947) he adopted the name 'Dharmapriya' (he who loves the Dharma – see *RR*, p. 202). It is with this name that he 'went forth' and with this name he spent his two year wandering period. On 12 May 1949 at Kusinara he received the sramanera monastic ordination from U Chandramani who gave him the name 'Dharmarakshita' ('he who is protected by the Dharma'). However, another disciple of U Chandramani who had been given the same name protested until the elderly preceptor decided the newly ordained sramanera should be Sangharakshita (*RR*, pp. 400–1). 'Urgyen' is a variant of 'Uddiyana' the place where Padmasambhava was born. (He is sometimes known as Urgyen Padmasambhava.) This name was given to Sangharakshita by his Tibetan teacher Kachu Rimpoche on 21 October 1962 in the context of a Padmasambhava abhishekha or initiation held at the Triyana Vardhana Vihara (*PT*, pp. 83–4).

25. See *RR*, p. 29.

Book Reviews

VI

# Buddhism Without Beliefs?

Stephen Batchelor
*Buddhism Without Beliefs: A Contemporary Guide to Awakening*
Riverhead Books, New York 1997, pp. 127.

Why does one write book reviews? This was the question that occurred to me recently, when I resumed writing them after an interval of several years.

On reflection I concluded that one engaged in this minor form of literary activity principally for four reasons. In the first place, through a review one can draw attention to a book that might otherwise be undeservedly neglected. Then one can point out particular beauties in a work, especially if it is a work of imagination, in this way not only delighting in those beauties oneself but perhaps being the cause of others delighting in them too. Again, reviewing a book enables one to correct factual inaccuracies, expose muddled thinking, and challenge one-sided views. Finally, by obliging one to engage closely with the product of another mind, writing a review helps one to clarify and refine, even to modify, one's own ideas.

Most of these reasons entered into my decision to review *Buddhism Without Beliefs*, of whose appearance on the scene I was made aware through excerpts published in the Spring 1997 issue of *Tricycle*, the American Buddhist review. As I later discovered, these excerpts were taken from three sections of the book, sections headed, respectively, Agnosticism, Imagination, and Culture, the lengthiest being taken from the first section. With certain elements in Batchelor's thinking I found myself very much in agreement, for instance his insistence on the importance of the agnostic imperative in Buddhism and his contention that dharma[1] practice was more akin to artistic creation than technical problem-solving. I therefore procured a copy of the book from which the *Tricycle* excerpts had been taken. Unfortunately, *Buddhism Without Beliefs* proved to be something of a disappointment. To begin with, it was a slim volume of 127 pages including ten pages of Sources and Notes, whereas I had expected a more substantial work. That it was only a slim volume was no accident, as I afterwards realized. Moreover, the author.... But to give reasons for my disappointment is in effect to start reviewing the book, and since it is best to proceed systematically, I shall look at (1) those points in it that are acceptable and (2) those that are unacceptable, (3) examine Batchelor's idea of a belief-free, agnostic Buddhism in detail, (4) offer a few general observations, and (5) ask myself what I have learned from the exercise.

The work consists of fifteen short essays divided into three groups. The first group, collectively entitled Ground, contains essays on, respectively, Awakening, Agnosticism, Anguish, Death, Rebirth, Resolve, Integrity, and Friendship; in the second, entitled Path, essays on Awareness, Becoming, Emptiness, and Compassion, while the third, entitled Fruition, contains essays on Freedom, Imagination, and Culture. In looking both at the points that can be accepted and those that are unacceptable, rejoicing in the former and deploring the latter, I shall deal with them in the order in which they occur in the book. Obviously I shall not be able to deal with all such points, or even to deal with each essay individually. I shall try, however, to cover all the points that to me seem important.

(1) Batchelor begins at the beginning, going back to Siddhartha Gautama's awakening (as he calls it, instead of the more usual Enlightenment) and to his giving, as the Buddha, his first discourse, delivered to his five former ascetic companions in the Deer Park at Sarnath, near Benares. This is where many expositions of Buddhism begin; but Batchelor, in addition to summarizing the discourse, draws attention to the fact that each of the four ennobling truths (as he calls them) of Anguish, its origins, its cessation, and the path leading to its cessation, which together form the core of the discourse, requires being acted upon in its own particular way. Anguish has to be *understood*, its origins have to be *let go of*, its

cessation has to be *realized*, and the path leading to its cessation has to be *cultivated*. Thus 'Buddhism' (the inverted commas being Batchelor's) suggests a course of action; the four truths are challenges to act. Though more Buddhists may be aware of the distinction between the first discourse's four ways of action than our author thinks, his emphasis on the importance of action certainly deserves to be taken seriously by all Buddhists. As Professor Richard F. Gombrich has recently pointed out, albeit from within a different perspective, karma or 'Action', in the word's primary sense of morally relevant action, lies at the heart of the Buddha's world view;[2] such action being, as he goes on to point out, not only physical and vocal but also mental. Though Batchelor nowhere mentions Going for Refuge, Going for Refuge to the Buddha, the Dharma, and the Sangha is likewise an action – the central, definitive act of the Buddhist life, by virtue of which one is a follower of the Buddha. It is in fact as a direct consequence of our Going for Refuge, after 'hearing' the Buddha-word, that we seek to understand, to let go of, to realize, and to cultivate. Thus karma in the sense of morally relevant action, and the act of Going for Refuge, can in truth no more be separated from the first discourse's four actions than these can be separated from one another. Together they form 'an interwoven complex of truths' (p.4) even richer than the one envisaged by Batchelor.

As I have noted, Batchelor speaks of the four *ennobling* truths rather than of the four *noble* truths (the usual translation of *arya-satya*.) This enables him to speak of the Buddha's experience of these truths as ennobling, so that awakening granted to his life a natural dignity, integrity, and authority, and this in its turn enables him to distinguish between authority which is natural and non-coercive and that which consists in imposing our will on others 'either through manipulation and intimidation or by appealing to the opinions of those more powerful than ourselves' (p.6). The distinction is an important one, and in view of the widespread modern habit of lumping true authority together with false and rejecting both he could well have said more about it. Though unfortunately he does not do this, at least he recognizes that there are degrees of awakening, thereby implicitly also recognizing that there are degrees of ennoblement and, therefore, degrees of true authority. In other words, there is a spiritual *hierarchy* – a hierarchy of degrees of awakening or ennoblement or true authority – and this hierarchy is a true hierarchy, as opposed to the false or at least conventional hierarchy based on earthly power and worldly position. Batchelor appears not to see this, though it follows from the distinction he himself draws between the two kinds of authority, for on the page immediately preceding the one where he speaks of degrees of awakening he uses the word hierarchy in a pejorative sense that suggests he lumps true hierarchy together with false hierarchy in the same simplistic manner that people lump together true and false authority (pp. 11 and 12).

Awakening is an individual matter, and Buddhism declined as fewer and fewer Buddhists succeeded in achieving this state. Batchelor in effect attributes the decline to increased monasticization and he may well be right, at least to an extent. He is certainly right when he points out that the traditional explanation for the decay of the religion relies on the Indian idea of the 'degeneration of time', as he calls it, a notion that regards the course of history as a process of inexorable decline. 'According to this notion, those who lived at the time of the Buddha were simply less degenerate, more "spiritual", than the corrupted mass of humanity today' (p. 12). Batchelor does not enlarge on the topic, but in its Buddhistic form as the doctrine of the three periods of the Dharma – the period of the True Dharma, the period of the Image (or Counterfeit) Dharma, and the period of the Destruction of the Dharma, in which we are now living – the idea of the 'degeneration of time' influenced the course of the Far Eastern Buddhism profoundly. Yet though the consciousness of living in the Dark Age of Buddhism precipitated doctrinal and spiritual developments of enormous importance, in my view there can be little doubt that the notion of an *inevitable* decline of Buddhism is inconsistent with both the spirit and the letter of the Buddha's teaching. Social and political conditions admittedly may be less (or more) supportive of the practice of the Dharma at one period, or in one place, than another, but *intrinsically* it is no more difficult to practise it now than it was in the past. The idea of the 'degeneration of time', and therewith the doctrine of the three periods of the Dharma, is one that can have no place in Western Buddhism. Likewise there can be no place in Western Buddhism for the inverted form of the idea, according to one popular version of which, humanity having entered the Age of Aquarius, spiritual progress will henceforth be collective and automatic.

Since Batchelor's idea of a belief-free, agnostic Buddhism will be examined later, I shall not look now at those points in his essay on Agnosticism that I find acceptable. The next two essays, on Anguish (the term Batchelor uses when referring to *dukkha* as personal experience of the kind of suffering caused by self-centred craving) and on Death, do not require much in the way of comment. Both strike a meditative note. In the first he takes the reader through a simple exercise in respiration-mindfulness and in the second through a meditation on death. The guidance he offers here is obviously based on personal experience and moreover is framed, in both cases, by heartfelt reflections that from time to time crystallize into aphorisms that are themselves appropriate subjects for reflective meditation. Not only do we try to forget the idea that the only certainty in life is that it will end, but 'Everyone collaborates in everyone else's forgetting' (p. 22). Similarly, 'Evasion of the unadorned immediacy of life is as deep-seated as it is relentless', so that 'Even with the ardent desire to be aware and alert in the present moment, the mind flings us into tawdry and tiresome elaborations of past and future' (p. 25). Batchelor also reminds us, in connection with Siddhartha's encounter with the four sights, that when the questioner realizes that he himself is the question, such a question is a mystery, not a problem, and that 'It cannot be "solved" by meditation techniques, through the authority of a text, upon submission to the will of a guru' (pp. 26–7). Other aphorisms are 'Reflective meditation is a way of translating thoughts into the language of feeling' and 'How extraordinary it is to be here at all' (p. 32), the second of which put me in mind of Spinoza's wonderment at the fact that there should be anything rather than nothing. Less aphoristic, but equally true and no less worthy of reflective meditation, is a sentence that comes towards the end of the essay on death: 'To meditate on the certainty of death and the uncertainty of its time helps transform the experience of another's death from an awkward discomfiture into an awesome and tragic conclusion to the transience that lies at the heart of all life' (p.33).

The essay on Rebirth opens with the declaration 'Religions are united not by belief in God but by belief in life after death' (p.34). Buddhism, of course, teaches rebirth, and Batchelor recognizes that the Buddha himself accepted the idea and found this 'prevailing Indian view' (p.35) sufficient as a basis for his ethical and liberating teaching. Although he taught dharma practice to be meaningful whether or not we believe in rebirth (a quotation to this effect from the Pali canon prefaces the essay), the evidence does not suggest that he held an agnostic view on the matter. Is it then true that, as often claimed, you cannot be a Buddhist if you do not accept the doctrine of rebirth? Batchelor is aware that, from a traditional point of view, it is indeed problematic to suspend belief in the idea of rebirth, since many basic notions then have to be rethought, 'But if we follow the Buddha's injunction not to accept things blindly, then orthodoxy should not stand in the way of forming our own understanding' (p.36). Orthodoxy and blind belief, it would seem, are synonymous! Not that the idea of rebirth presents no difficulties. Unfortunately Batchelor drags across the trail the old red herring of the alleged incompatibility of the idea of rebirth and the central Buddhist idea that there is no eternal self. However, he is right when he points out that the mere fact of rebirth does not entail any ethical linkage between one existence and the next. He is also right in pointing out that 'While the Buddha accepted the idea of karma as he accepted that of rebirth, when questioned on the issue he tended to emphasize its psychological rather than its cosmological implications. "Karma", he often said, "is intention": i.e., a movement of the mind that occurs each time we think, speak, or act' (p.37). Though Batchelor does not actually tell us this, the fact that karma is *cetana* implies that skilful actions are to be performed not so much because they will result in a good rebirth (the cosmological reason) as because they will help us understand, let go of, realize, and cultivate (the psychological reason). What he does however tell us, and very rightly, is that the Buddha 'denied that karma alone was sufficient to explain the origin of individual experience' (p.37).

The point is an extremely important one; so important I wish Batchelor had enlarged upon it, the more especially as he makes it clear that the Buddha's denial that karma alone suffices to explain the origin of individual experience is in contrast to 'the view often taught by religious Buddhists' (p.37). Who these religious Buddhists are he does not say (in his vocabulary 'religious Buddhists' means, apparently, those Buddhists who are not agnostic Buddhists), but they certainly include those Tibetan lamas and their disciples who, as I know from personal experience, not only teach but strongly, even vehemently, insist that karma alone is sufficient to explain the origin of individual experience. In the words of an eminent Gelugpa lama, '*All* happiness and suffering is the *exclusive* result of our *individual* karmic deeds created through *past* lives' (my italics).[3] He could hardly have expressed himself more clearly. The Buddha was no less clear. There are at least three passages in the Sutta Pitaka of the Pali canon in which he speaks of the various *non*-karmic factors in human experience, and in one of these, addressing the Wanderer Sivaka of the Top-Knot, he explicitly rejects the view of those recluses and brahmins who, like the Tibetan lamas and their disciples, hold that 'whatsoever pleasure or pain or mental state a human being experiences, all that is due to a previous act.' Holding such a view, he declares, 'they go beyond personal experience and what is generally acknowledged by the world. Wherefore do I declare those recluses and brahmins to be in the wrong.'[4]

Though it might seem that there are only two options, either to believe in rebirth or not, Batchelor is convinced there is a third: to acknowledge, in all honesty, *I do not know*. If it is a question of either knowing or not knowing *in the absolute sense* then, clearly, we do not know and should admit it. Such acknowledgement is not incompatible with a *provisional* belief in rebirth as the more reasonable of the two options (or of the three, if we include the Christian and Muslim option of post-mortem but not pre-natal existence). Nonetheless Batchelor's emphasis on the desirability of agnosticism in connection with the question of rebirth is a welcome one; especially when one considers the kind of fantasies in which some religious Buddhists, as he calls them, have indulged in this regard.

Also welcome is his emphasis, in the essays on Resolve and Integrity, on the fact that dharma practice can embrace a range of purposes (all subordinate to the supreme purpose, awakening) and on the fact that ethical integrity is rooted in empathy. Thus at times we may concentrate on 'creating a livelihood that is in accord with our deepest values and aspirations. At times we may retreat: disentangling ourselves from social and psychological pressures in order to reconsider our life in a quiet and supportive setting. At times we may engage with the world: responding empathetically and creatively to the anguish of others' (p.42). Though Batchelor himself does not draw the conclusion, such a position tends to undermine the monk–layman dichotomy: at one time in our Buddhist life we may be living more as a monk, at another more as a layman. More specifically, at different times, and for longer or shorter periods, we may be working in a team-based right livelihood business, enjoying a solitary retreat, raising funds for a third-world social project, teaching meditation, or writing a book on the Dharma. As for his emphasis on the fact that integrity is rooted in empathy, Batchelor reminds us that it requires courage and intelligence as well, because every significant ethical choice entails risk, since we cannot know in advance the consequences of the choices we make and have to learn from concrete mistakes. He also reminds us that ethical enquiry is not the same thing as moral certainty and that 'While moral conditioning may be necessary for social stability, it is inadequate as a paradigm for integrity' (p.48).

But welcome as his emphases on resolve and integrity are, still more welcome is Batchelor's assertion that dharma practice is embodied in friendship, and that 'Our practice is nourished, sustained, and challenged through ongoing contact with friends and mentors who seek to realize the dharma in their own lives' (p.49). Despite the fact that the Buddha stressed the importance of spiritual friendship (*kalyana-mitrata*), even declaring it to be the whole of the holy life (*brahmacharya*)[5], books on Buddhism rarely mention the subject, and it is therefore all the more heartening to find Batchelor devoting an entire essay to it. Besides singing the praises of friendship, and emphasizing its significance and value, he points out that the forms of Buddhist friendship have changed over history and that today a new model may be needed. He is very much alive to the fact that true friendship can be compromised by issues of power, and warns, 'We should be wary of being seduced by charismatic purveyors of Enlightenment.' Our true friends 'seek not to coerce us, even gently and reasonably, into believing what we are unsure of. These friends are like midwives, who draw forth what is waiting to be born' (pp. 50–1).

Like the essays on Anguish and Death, those on Awareness, Becoming, and Emptiness strike a meditative note, as Batchelor leads us through an exercise in the expansion of awareness, a reflection on the five primary factors of mental life, and a contemplation of the fact that things are devoid of intrinsic, separate being. In the course of so doing he reminds us that 'To meditate is not to empty the mind and gape at things in a trance-like stupor' (apparently a point that still needs to be made) and that 'emptiness', which he admits is a confusing term, although used as an abstract noun 'does not in any way denote an abstract thing or state' (pp. 64–5 and 81). The essay on Compassion introduces us to a variant of the *metta bhavana* or 'development of (universal) loving kindness' practice which Batchelor rightly sees not just as a separate exercise but also as a means to developing mindfulness and loosening the grip of self-centredness. 'Insight into emptiness and compassion for the world', he reminds us, 'are two sides of the same coin' (p.88). But there are dangers. The exaggeratedly altruistic person may come to think of himself as the saviour of others, thus risking messianic and narcissistic inflation.

Freedom – spiritual freedom, the freedom of awareness – is of the essence of Buddhism, and it is not surprising that Batchelor should devote space to the subject. His essay on Freedom is not so much an essay on it as a paean to it, and we are left with a sense of exhilaration at the prospect of our being free *from* confusion and craving, free to realize our creative potential, and free to be *for* others. What perhaps *is* surprising is that the last two essays in *Buddhism Without Beliefs* should be devoted to Imagination and Culture. Studies of the Buddhist, or at least the Buddhistic, culture of this or that 'Buddhist' country are not unknown, but to devote an entire section of a book on Buddhism to the subject of imagination is to my knowledge unprecedented – and very welcome. Batchelor sees imagination as the faculty through which authentic vision finds expression in concrete and vivid forms. For him, therefore, 'dharma practice is more akin to artistic creation than technical problem solving' (p.103), as I noted at the beginning. 'The technical dimension of dharma practice (such as training to be more mindful and focused) is comparable to the technical skills a potter must learn in order to become proficient in his craft. Both may require many years of discipline and hard work' (p.103). The potter's raw material is clay. Similarly, 'The raw material of dharma practice is ourself and our world, which are to be understood and transformed according to the vision and values of the dharma itself' (p.103). Moreover as soon as imagination is activated in the process of awakening, the natural beauty of the world is vividly enhanced and our appreciation of the arts enriched. Great works of art in fact succeed in capturing both the pathos of anguish and a vision of its resolution, while the Buddha's four ennobling truths themselves provide us with 'not only a paradigm of cognitive and affective freedom but a template for aesthetic vision' (pp.105–6). Batchelor does not go so far as to describe the Buddha himself as an artist (though he might well have done), but he does say of him that his genius lay in his imagination. 'He succeeded in translating his vision not only into the language of his time but into terms sufficiently universal to inspire future generations in India and beyond. His ideas have survived in much the same way as great works of art. While we may find certain stylistic elements of his teaching alien, his central ideas speak to us in a way that goes beyond their reference to a particular time or place. But unlike ancient statues from Egypt or Gandhara, the wheel of dharma set in motion by the Buddha continued to turn after his death, generating ever new and startling cultures of awakening' (p.107).

Such a culture of awakening is forged, according to Batchelor, from the tension between an indebtedness to the past and a responsibility to the future. We have to distinguish between what is central in the Buddhist tradition and what peripheral, between elements vital for the survival of dharma practice and alien artefacts that might obstruct that survival. Nor can a culture of awakening exist independently of the specific social, religious, artistic, and ethnic cultures in which it is embedded. Resisting creative interaction with those cultures, dharma practice today could end up as a marginalized subculture, a beautifully preserved relic. On the other hand, through losing its inner integrity and critical edge it could end being swallowed up by something else, such as psychotherapy or contemplative Christianity. In any case, a culture of awakening – a culture in which the Buddha's eightfold path is cultivated – is always an expression of a community. 'Community is the living link between individuation and social engagement. A culture of awakening simply cannot occur without being rooted in a coherent and vital sense of community, for a matrix of friendships is the very soil in which dharma practice is cultivated' (p. 114). At this point I started wondering where I had heard it all before, and just where I had seen the idea of a culture of awakening being translated into action. But that is another story. Like the essays on Agnosticism, Friendship, and Imagination, that on Culture is something of a departure and therefore deserves, like them, to be given serious consideration by Western Buddhists.

(2) Being able to agree with a respected fellow Buddhist is pleasant, having to disagree with him is painful. When one has looked at those points in *Buddhism Without Beliefs* that are acceptable, and rejoiced in them, it is with reluctance that one turns to those points that are unacceptable and that have, therefore, to be deplored and rejected. For this reason I shall touch on only some of the more significant of these latter points which, fortunately, are few in number. In any case, my principal disagreement with Batchelor is in connection with his advocacy of a belief-free, agnostic Buddhism, and with this I shall deal separately later.

If it is true that 'Religions are united not by belief in God but by belief in life after death' (p. 34), then it follows that they are united by the belief that consciousness – for want of a better term – is separate from the physical body and can exist independently of it. Similarly, if consciousness exists independently of the body, it follows that it cannot be explained in terms of brain function. To believe that it can be so explained is materialism, just as to believe the contrary is idealism or at least immaterialism. Batchelor appears to believe that consciousness *can* be explained in terms of brain function. At least he dismisses the notion that consciousness cannot be explained in terms of brain function as an 'article of faith' adopted on account of 'ancient Indian metaphysical theories' (p.37). It is odd, he thinks, that a practice concerned with anguish and the ending of anguish should be obliged to accept these ancient theories and, along with them, the article of faith in question. But if the belief that consciousness cannot be explained in terms of brain function is an article of faith, the belief that it *can* be so explained is no less so, inasmuch as the brain of which consciousness is supposedly an epiphenomenon is 'material' and belief in the existence of 'matter' is as much an article of faith as belief in the existence of 'spirit'. Since Batchelor dismisses the notion that consciousness cannot be explained in terms of brain function, it is not surprising to find him rejecting 'a transcendent absolute in which ultimate meaning is secured' and insisting 'Dharma practice starts not with a belief in a transcendent reality but through embracing the anguish experienced in an uncertain world' (p.40). Dharma practice may indeed begin in this way (though how one 'embraces' anguish is not clear), but this does not mean that it cannot begin in any other way. *Logically* speaking it begins with the 'existence' of what may be described as a transcendent Absolute, for as the Buddha declares in the *Udana* 'There is, monks, an unborn, unbecome, unmade, uncompounded; if there were not, there would be known no escape here from the born, become, made, compounded' (i.e. there would be no ending of anguish)[6]. Batchelor also insists 'Dharma practice can never be in contradiction with science', since the former's concern 'lies entirely with the nature of existential experience' (p.37). But if consciousness can be explained in terms of brain function, and if the physical organism is indeed 'capable of consciousness' when in the course of evolution it reaches a certain degree of complexity (p.29), then it would seem that inasmuch as existential experience is unthinkable apart from consciousness such experience is, like consciousness itself, the concern of science rather than religion, so that there is nothing left for dharma practice to concern itself with. Here Buddhism is subsumed under science, and 'dharma practice' becomes no more than an applied science. Probably Batchelor would not agree that such was the case, but none the less it is what appears to follow from certain of his assumptions. Moreover, he is convinced that 'One of the great realizations of the [eighteenth century] Enlightenment was that an atheist materialist could be just as moral a person as a believer – even more so' (p. 35). But if an atheistic materialist can be moral, then on the basis of his reasoning it should be possible for a materialist scientist – one who by definition shares Batchelor's rejection of a transcendent Absolute – not only to practise what in effect is the Dharma but to practise it without ceasing to be a materialist.

When discussing friendship Batchelor rightly points out that our true friends do not seek to coerce us, and that it is possible for friendship to be compromised by issues of power (pp. 50–1, 53). In other words true friends do not seek to exercise power over us, and perhaps do not even consider themselves as being morally possessed of such power. Here power is equated with coercion or the exercise of force or authority without regard to the wishes or desires of the person or persons who are its object. This is the sense in which I use the term when I speak of the power mode as contrasted with the love mode, as I call them, and maintain that power has no place within the sangha or spiritual community and that members of the sangha or spiritual community relate to one another solely in accordance with the love mode. So far all is clear and there would seem to be no disagreement between Batchelor and me. However, towards the end of the essay on Friendship he speaks of the possibility of imagining a community of friendships in which diversity is celebrated rather than censured, smallness of scale regarded as success rather than failure, and in which 'power is shared by all rather than invested in a minority of experts' (p. 54). Here power is clearly power in the sense of coercion. That this is the case is indicated by the fact that only a few lines back he says 'true friendship has tended to be compromised by issues of power' and before that 'true friends seek not to coerce us' – thus equating power and coercion. In speaking of the possibility of a community of friendships in which 'power is shared by all rather than invested in a minority of experts' he is therefore speaking of the possibility of one in which force or authority is exercised not by a few over the rest but by everybody over everybody, which is absurd, unless it is to be exercised not internally but externally, i.e. over a person or persons not belonging to the community. Batchelor has in fact imposed on his community of friendships a 'democratic' constitution, complete with equal rights for all, without considering whether this form of constitution is the appropriate one for a spiritual community. He has also failed to see that the idea of power being shared by all is inconsistent with his earlier recognition that there are degrees of awakening and ennoblement, and therefore of authority, for if there are degrees of authority (whether coercive or non-coercive) there are, correspondingly also degrees of power, and if some have more power than others then power cannot be said to be shared, i.e. equally shared, by all. The difficulty is partly due to the fact that Batchelor nowhere defines power, or tells us in what sense (or senses) he uses the term, thus ignoring a contemporary philosopher's warning that 'it is disastrous to talk of power without first engaging in an analytical exercise of some complexity'.[7]

Two of the points on which I disagree with Batchelor relate to the Path, disagreements regarding which are a serious matter, pertaining as they do to the very means by which Enlightenment or Nirvana is to be achieved. Both these points arise in connection with the cultivation of awareness. Having spoken of awareness, in the sense of stopping and paying attention to what is happening in the moment, as 'a reasonable definition of meditation', Batchelor goes on to describe it as 'a process of deepening self-acceptance' (p. 59). The first point is by far the more unacceptable of the two and hence the more decisively to be rejected, ignoring as it does all higher spiritual experience. Stopping and paying attention to what is happening in the moment may be a reasonable definition of mindfulness or awareness (*sati*), which is indeed an important practice, but is totally inadequate as a definition of meditation (*samadhi*), which besides mindfulness or awareness includes the eight *vimokshas* or 'emancipations' and the nine *samapattis* or 'attainments'. Without a full experience of these higher states awakening is incomplete, though of course there can be degrees of meditative experience even as there can be degrees of awakening. That such is the case is clear from what the

Buddha, speaking to Ananda, says of his own attainment of Enlightenment:

> And so long, Ananda, as I attained not to, emerged not from these nine attainments of gradual abidings, both forwards and backwards, I realized not completely, as one wholly awakened, the full perfect awakening, unsurpassed in the world with its gods, Maras and Brahmas, on earth with its recluses, godly men, devas and men; but when I attained to and emerged from these abidings suchwise, then, wholly awakened, I realized completely the full perfect awakening unsurpassed ...[8]

In reducing meditation to stopping and paying attention to what is happening in the moment Batchelor is in effect precluding the possibility of Enlightenment. Such reductionism is not uncommon in Buddhist circles today and was not unknown in the past. As Professor Richard F. Gombrich has recently shown in *How Buddhism Began*, in a fascinating chapter entitled 'Retracing an Ancient Debate: How Insight Worsted Concentration in the Pali Canon', the ambiguity of the term *prajna* or insight led to a differentiation between release by both insight *and* meditation (the kind of release exemplified and taught by the Buddha) and release by insight alone. This led to the development of the idea that Enlightenment could be attained without meditation (i.e. without any experience of the *samapattis*), simply by means of *prajna* in the sense of a process of intellectual analysis.[9] Batchelor's affinities would seem to lie with the modern representatives of this kind of development. Just as they emphasize *vipassana* or insight in the intellectual sense at the expense of *samatha* or calm, similarly he reduces meditation to stopping and paying attention to what is happening in the moment. The result in both cases is the elimination of meditation in the normative Buddhist sense.

'Self-acceptance' is one of the catchphrases of Californian psychobabble, and it is a pity to see a respected Buddhist like Batchelor falling victim to this usage and to its underlying ideology. Not only is awareness 'a process of deepening self-acceptance' (p.59) but 'There is nothing unworthy of acceptance' (p.59). Indeed, awareness 'embraces' whatever it observes, though Batchelor at least warns us, rather confusingly, that to embrace a mental state like hatred does not mean to indulge it but to accept it for what it is (p.60). The root of the confusion, and thus of the wrong view and wrong practice which that confusion entails, is a misuse of the word 'accept', which means: 'To take with pleasure; to receive kindly; to admit with approbation' (*Johnson*); 'To receive with favour; to approve' (*Webster*); 'To tolerate or accommodate oneself to ... to receive with approval' (*Collins*); 'regard with favour' (*Concise Oxford*). Johnson in fact, after giving his definition of 'accept', makes the precise meaning of the word perfectly clear by adding, with his usual perspicacity, 'It is distinguished from *receive*, as *specific* from *general*; noting a particular manner of receiving.' Thus it is obvious that there can be no question of a Buddhist, least of all a Buddhist meditator, ever regarding the unskilful mental state of hatred (to take Batchelor's example) with pleasure, or approval, or toleration, or favour. For Buddhism it is axiomatic that hatred, like all other unskilful mental states, is to be rejected, even though in most cases the rejection will admittedly be a gradual process rather than instantaneous. So axiomatic is it that actual quotations from the scriptures are hardly needed, and it is perhaps sufficient simply to refer to the *Dhammapada*'s 'Kodhavagga' or Chapter on Anger and to the references and citations in the Pali Text's Society's *Pali-English Dictionary* under '*kodha*'. The proper attitude to unskilful mental states, as well as to unskilful speech and unskilful bodily action, is not acceptance but awareness in the sense of recognition (i.e. recognition of the fact of their unskilfulness), followed by the taking of measures to rid oneself of those states. In the case of skilful mental states, speech, and bodily action, awareness will be followed by measures to cultivate and develop them. All this is clear from the Buddha's teaching of Right Effort (*samyak- vyayama*), the sixth factor of the Eightfold Path, which is fourfold, consisting in the effort to prevent the arising of unarisen unskilful qualities, to suppress arisen unskilful qualities, to develop unarisen skilful qualities, and to maintain arisen skilful qualities. Here there is no talk of the unskilful being 'accepted' or 'embraced'. Dharma practice involves not a weak, and probably indulgent, 'self-acceptance', but an unflinching self- knowledge that recognizes both one's strengths and one's weaknesses and which, while accepting and encouraging the former, no more hesitates to reject the latter than a man who, in the traditional comparison, finding a dead snake round his neck hesitates to fling it off.

My remaining points of disagreement with Batchelor, apart from those connected with his advocacy of a belief-free agnostic Buddhism, are two in number, and since they relate to topics on which he touches only lightly I shall deal with them briefly, even though each of them represents the tip of an ideological iceberg of enormous dimensions. Concluding his essay on Compassion, which he rightly describes as the heart and soul of awakening, Batchelor says: 'It becomes abundantly clear that we cannot attain awakening for ourselves: we can only participate in the awakening of life' (p.90). With the first half of the sentence I have no quarrel, but what is this *awakening of life*? The phrase suggest a *collective* attainment of Enlightenment, in which the individual participates by virtue of the fact that 'life', as represented by humanity as a whole, has reached a higher stage of evolution. Here Batchelor appears to have fallen victim, at least momentarily, to that particular strain of New Age thinking according to which the Age of Aquarius is upon us and we shall all ride to Enlighten-ment on the crest of an evolutionary wave. Such thinking is inconsistent with his own rejection, in the essay on Awakening, of the Indian idea of the 'degeneration of time', an idea of which the New Age notion of auto-matic spiritual progress for everyone is the 'positive' counterpart. The second of these two remaining points of disagreement is not dissimilar to the first. In the essay on Freedom Batchelor speaks of awakening as 'that awesome freedom into which we were born but for which we have sub-stituted the pseudo-independence of a separate self' (p.99). Into which *we were born*? The phrase suggests either that freedom is our *destiny* (cf. 'the man born to be King'), in which case it is redolent of New Age ideology, or that we as infants are born free and awake and only later, when we have learned to speak and say 'I', develop a separate self, in which case the phrase is suggestive of a Rousseauistic, or a Wordsworthian, idealization of infancy as a state of innocence and purity and the child as not only 'best Philosopher' but 'best Buddhist'.

(3) Eastern Buddhists, and Western Buddhists to the extent that they are followers of this or that form of Eastern Buddhism, often give their assent to propositions for which there is no proof. They assent to such propositions either because they are to be found in the scriptures or because they encounter them in the teachings of their own lama or guru. Some are of a 'scientific' nature, relating as they do to such areas of modern knowledge as history, geography, and astronomy, and of these propositions some, again, have not only not been proved true but have been shown to be demonstrably false. We now know that the Buddha was not born in 1030 BCE, that the earth is not flat, and that the sun and moon do not revolve round Mount Meru. Batchelor's 'agnostic Buddhist' is therefore perfectly right in not regarding the Dharma as a source of 'answers' to what are really scientific questions and right in seeking such knowledge 'in the appropriate domains' (p.18). This is no more than what all Buddhists should do. At the same time, we must be careful just where we draw the line between the respective spheres of Buddhism, correctly understood, and the different sciences. Batchelor says of the agnostic Buddhist that he is not a 'believer' with claims to 'revealed information about supernatural or paranormal phenomena' (p.18). This is rather too sweeping, for we must be open to the possibility of there being phenomena which are inexplicable in scientific terms, though some scientists may, of course, *believe* that science will be in a position to explain them one day.

Batchelor's agnostic Buddhist is also perfectly right in founding his agnostic stance on 'a passionate recognition that *I do not know*' (p.19). This is a recognition that is badly needed in many parts of the Buddhist world, where only too often 'infallible' lamas and 'omniscient' gurus think they know when in fact they merely believe, and therefore I hope that agnosticism *in this healthy sense* will blow like a refreshing breeze through gompas, viharas, zendos, meditation centres, and international Buddhist conference halls everywhere, scattering to the four winds of heaven whatever pseudo-answers, dogmatic assertions, and exaggerated claims prevail in those places. There is much that we do not know, whether regarding the world, regarding Buddhism, or regarding ourselves. In every field of knowledge, what we know is infinitesimal compared with what we do not know. Nowhere is this more true than in the case of Buddhism. In speaking about the Dharma we ought, therefore, always to distinguish between what we know from direct personal experience (e.g. that respiration-mindfulness can lead to the attainment of the dhyanas), what seems reasonable to us according to the evidence at our disposal, (e.g. that people are reborn after death), and what we accept on the testimony of the scriptures (e.g. that the Buddha was Enlightened). These categories are illustrative rather than definitive, and we must in any case always bear in mind that with regard to the second and third of them, at least, considerations of a more general philosophical nature cannot be excluded.

The breeze of a healthy agnosticism has of course blown, from time to time, through the corridors of Western thought. According to Batchelor, the methodological principle that T.H. Huxley expressed positively as 'Follow your reason as far as it will take you' and negatively as 'Do not pretend that conclusions are certain which are not demonstrated or demonstrable' runs through the Western tradition, from Socrates, via the Reformation and the (eighteenth century) Enlightenment, to the axioms of modern science. This is what Huxley, who coined the term 'agnosticism' in 1869, called the 'agnostic faith', and Batchelor believes that the Buddha shared this faith, for he, too, followed his reason as far as it would take him and did not pretend that any conclusion was certain unless it was demonstrable (p.17). There are several points to be made here. In view of the fact that for a thousand years the Western tradition was a Christian tradition one cannot really say of Huxley's agnostic principle that it 'runs through' that tradition. It is also doubtful if Socrates was an agnostic, for while he regularly exposed the pretensions of those who, though they claimed to know, in fact merely believed, he also asserted the immortality of the soul, accepted the pronouncement of the Delphic oracle regarding himself, and maintained that there was a daimon who at times directed him to refrain from a certain course of action. It is even more doubtful to what extent the agnostic principle runs through the Protestant Reformation, for did not Martin Luther, its great inaugurator, not only preach salvation by faith rather than works but go so far as to call reason a whore? There is no doubt that the principle runs through the (eighteenth century) Enlightenment. At the time of the French Revolution the breeze in fact became a hurricane that blew down, at least for the time being, all manner of ancient idols. Unfortunately it also set up an idol of its own in their place, an idol called Reason, which in the form of a young woman from the Opera was taken in procession to the cathedral of Notre Dame, set on the high altar, and worshipped with the singing of hymns.[10] Batchelor does not set up any idols, not even an idol called Agnosticism, but he certainly believes that 'Buddhists' (to borrow his own inverted commas) do something very much like this in relation to Buddhism, and to this aspect of his thinking I must now turn. But first there is a final point to be made in connection with his claims on behalf of Huxley's 'agnostic faith'. The Buddha definitely believed that you should 'follow your reason as far as it will take you', but this does not mean that there is not in man a higher faculty capable of taking him beyond reason. The Dharma is explicitly stated to be *atakkavacara*, 'beyond reason' or 'inaccessible to logic'.[11] This was why the Buddha initially hesitated to communicate his discovery of it to the world.[12]

According to Batchelor, Buddhists make the mistake of turning 'four ennobling truths to be acted upon' into 'four propositions of fact to be believed' (p.5). They do this because 'the crucial distinction that *each truth requires being acted upon in its own particular way* (*understanding* anguish, *letting go of* its origins, *realizing* its cessation, and *cultivating* the path) has been relegated to the margins of specialist doctrinal knowledge' (p.4). I have already questioned Batchelor's assertion that 'Few Buddhists today are probably even aware of the distinction' between these four kinds of action (p.4), and it is still more questionable whether the four truths were, in fact, turned into four propositions on account of a failure to make this admittedly important distinction. Batchelor does not tell us exactly when the 'mistake' was originally committed, or just who committed it, but he appears to believe that it was committed shortly after the Buddha's death, perhaps even before it, and that it was subsequently committed by all Buddhists except for a handful of iconoclastic Indian tantric sages and others who were, presumably, the forerunners of his belief-free, agnostic Buddhism. He does, however, tell us into just what propositions the truths were – and are – turned. 'The first truth becomes: "Life Is Suffering"; the second: "The Cause of Suffering Is Craving"' – and so on. (p.5). But if we turn to the *locus classicus* of the Buddha's teaching of the four truths, the *Dhammacakkapavattana Sutta* or Discourse setting in motion the Wheel of the Doctrine, what do we find? We find the Buddha telling the five ascetics:

> 'Now this, monks, is the noble truth of pain [or suffering, *dukkha*]: birth is painful, old age is painful, sickness is painful, death is painful, sorrow, lamentation, dejection, and despair are painful. Contact with unpleasant things is painful, not getting what one wishes is painful. In short the five groups of grasping are painful.
>
> 'Now this, monks, is the noble truth of the cause of pain: the craving, which tends to rebirth, combined with pleasure and lust, finding pleasure here and there, namely the craving for passion, the craving for existence, the craving for non-existence'....

And so on[13]. Here we obviously have a number of *propositions*. In particular we have the proposition 'The five groups of grasping (*pancupadana-kkhandha*) are suffering' and the proposition 'The cause of pain is craving'. Having affirmed these and the other two propositions (i.e. those relating to the cessation of suffering and the way thereto), the Buddha goes on to declare that he has, respectively, understood, let go of, cultivated, and realized them. Here there is no question of four ennobling truths to be acted upon being 'neatly turned', in Batchelor's phrase (p.5), into four truths to be believed (or if there is, it is the Buddha himself who is responsible for the transformation), much less still is there any question of the turning being due to a failure to make the crucial distinction that '*each truth requires being acted upon in its own particular way*' (p.4). Believing in a proposition of fact is *not* incompatible with acting upon it. Indeed, action presupposes belief, whether explicit or implicit. It was only because the five ascetics had come to *believe* that their erstwhile companion had in fact attained Enlightenment (they did not *know* this) that they were able to *believe* the four noble truths and act upon them. This is not to say that belief may not sometimes be blind; Batchelor equips with initial capital letters the words making up the propositions into which, he alleges, the first two truths were 'turned'. This would appear to signal his conviction – I had almost said his belief – that belief is blind almost by definition. For him therefore, action, i.e. acting upon the four truths, and belief, i.e. believing in the four truths as propositions of fact, are not only distinct but separate, not only separate but mutually exclusive. Nor is this all. Action and belief being mutually exclusive, for Batchelor it follows that dharma practice consists in acting upon the four truths to the exclusion of all beliefs, and although he *might* argue that he believed in the four truths, but not as propositions, the fact of the matter is that a belief is necessarily expressed in propositional form. It is his advocacy of this belief-free dharma practice that characterizes the agnostic Buddhist and distinguishes him from those Buddhists who, by turning the four truths into propositions to be believed and thus the Buddha's teaching into a 'religion' (for Batchelor a pejorative term), make it possible for 'Buddhist [to be] distinguished from Christians, Muslims, and Hindus, who believe different sets of propositions' and for 'The four ennobling truths [to] become principal dogmas of the belief system known as "Buddhism"' (p.5).

We have seen that for the Buddha, in the *Dhammacakkapavattana Sutta* (and elsewhere), belief in a proposition of fact is not incompatible with acting upon such a proposition. It remains for us to see what consequences flow from this position, as well as what consequences flow from the contrary position adopted by Batchelor, namely, that in the case of the four truths, at least, action and belief are incompatible, even mutually exclusive.

Belief in the four truths as propositions of fact is not incompatible with action upon them because neither the belief nor the acting is ever absolute. There are *degrees* of such belief and *degrees* of such acting, the latter being usually commensurate with the former. We have no hesitation in setting out on a journey to Rome, for example, because we really do believe that such a place exists and that if we take the right road we will sooner or later arrive there. On the other hand, there are occasions when we are not sure – perhaps cannot be sure – either that the goal on which we have set our heart exists or that, assuming it really does exist, that we have adopted the right means for its achievement. Nonetheless, believing that it exists and that the means we have adopted are the right ones, we go on employing those means until such time as experience confirms both our belief in the existence of the one and our belief in the rightness of the other – or does *not* confirm them. Belief of this kind is relative, not absolute; qualified, not unqualified; provisional, not final; and tentative, not certain. It is on account of this *provisional* belief – as for the sake of convenience it may be termed – that we accept the four truths as propositions of fact and act upon them in the particular way each requires and according to the degree of our belief. Actual *knowledge* of the four truths comes only with the attainment of the Transcendental Path. Not that provisional belief is ever mere belief. It is belief that enjoys the support of evidence and arguments which, though they may not be conclusive, are yet sufficiently strong for us to be willing to take the risk of acting upon the belief. Provisional belief is therefore also rational belief. In the case of the five ascetics, they were initially unimpressed by the Buddha's claim to be Enlightened and refused to listen to his teaching. Only when he had convinced them with an argument ('Have you ever known me to speak like this before?'[14]) did his declaration ('The Tathagata is an Accomplished One, a Fully Enlightened One').[15] become for them a proposition of fact to be (provisionally) believed. Similarly, it was only on account of their provisional, rational belief in the four truths he subsequently taught them that they were able to act upon those truths and, by so doing, come to know them for themselves and attain Nirvana.[16] Here there is a progression from ignorance and scepticism to actual knowledge (or transcendental knowledge, as *pace* Batchelor I prefer to call it), via the successive stages of a provisional belief which, as it is confirmed by experience, becomes less and less provisional and provides an increasingly firm basis for further action. The path is thus a graduated path in which, as the Buddha said when comparing the Dharma and Vinaya to the Great Ocean, 'there are progressive trainings, progressive obligations, progressive practices, there being no sudden penetrations of supreme Knowledge.'[17]

Since the path is a graduated path instruction must be methodical, beginning at the beginning, and not introducing more advanced teachings until the disciple has mastered the more elementary ones. We find the Buddha adopting this approach on a number of occasions. He adopted it with Anathapindika, the wealthy merchant who was to be one of his principal supporters:

> Then did the Exalted One discourse unto Anathapindika, the housefather, with talk that led gradually on, thus: of charity and righteousness and the heaven-world; of the danger, uselessness, and defilement of the passions, and of the profit of giving up the world. And when the Exalted One saw that the heart of Anathapindika, the housefather, was made pliable and soft without obstruction, uplifted and calmed, then did he set forth the Dharma teaching of the Buddhas, proclaimed the most excellent, that is, suffering, the arising of suffering, the ceasing of suffering, and the way leading to the cessation of suffering.[18]

A discourse of this kind is known (in Pali) as an *anupubbikatha* or 'graduated discourse', dealing as it does with the ever higher values of charity (*dana*), righteousness (*sila*), the heaven-world (*sagga*), and the path (*magga*). It was to provide, in the centuries that followed, the pattern for discourses and systematic expositions of the Dharma throughout the Buddhist world, in the case of the Mahayana being associated with the concept of *upaya kausalya* or 'skilful means'. In twelfth century Tibet, for example, we find 'Teacher' Drom, Atisha's chief disciple, leading a pious, but perhaps simple-minded, layman to a deeper understanding of the meaning of dharma practice in the following manner:

> One day an old gentleman was circumambulating the Ra-dreng monastery. Geshe Drom said to him, 'Sir, I am happy to see you circumambulating, but wouldn't you rather be practising the dharma?'
> Thinking this over, the old gentleman felt it might be better to read Mahayana sutras. While he was reading in the temple courtyard, Geshe

Drom said, 'I am happy to see you reciting sutras, but wouldn't you rather be practising Dharma?'

At this, the old gentleman thought that perhaps he should meditate. He sat cross-legged on a cushion, with his eyes half-closed. The teacher Drom said again, 'I am so happy to see you meditating, but wouldn't it be better to practise the Dharma?'

Now totally confused, the old gentleman asked, 'Geshe-la, please tell me what I should do to practise the Dharma?'

The teacher Drom replied, 'Renounce attraction to this life. Renounce it now. For if you do not renounce attraction to this life, whatever you do will not be the practice of Dharma, as you have not passed beyond the eight worldly concerns. Once you have renounced this life's habitual thoughts and are no longer distracted by the eight worldly concerns, whatever you do will advance you on the path of liberation.'[19]

Strange to say, this anecdote from the *Kadamthorbu* or 'Precepts Collected from Here and There' features as the epigraph to the second part of *Buddhism Without Beliefs*, on the Path, though Batchelor appears to have mistaken its meaning. He appears to believe that practices such as circumambulating monasteries, reading Sutras, and even meditation as practised by the old gentleman, are a complete waste of time. They are a waste of time because they form part of *religion*, along with exotic names, robes, and insignia of office. Buddhism became a 'religion' when the four ennobling truths to be acted upon were turned into four propositions of fact to be *believed*. Authentic dharma practice therefore has nothing to do with practices and observances of a 'religious' nature. For Batchelor, as we have already seen, acting upon the four truths and believing them as propositions of fact are incompatible, even mutually exclusive. Curiously enough, in his 'reworking' of Geshe Wangyal's translation of the anecdote from the *Kadamthorbu* he substitutes for Drom's final reply, which is sufficiently plain, straightforward, and practical, a version 'heard from Tibetan lamas' (p. 122). 'When you practise', Drom is made to say, 'there is no distinction between the Dharma and your own mind' (p. 55)

– a gnomic utterance that could well have left the old gentleman feeling more confused than ever.

Batchelor illustrates his thesis that the four truths are simply injunctions to act, and have nothing to do with belief or with religious practices and observances, by referring to a passage in *Alice's Adventures in Wonderland*. In this passage Alice enters a room to find a bottle marked with the label 'Drink Me'. As Batchelor points out, the label does not tell Alice what is inside the bottle but tells her what to do with it. Similarly, 'When the Buddha presented his four truths, he first described what each referred to, then enjoined his listeners to act upon them' (p.7). For reasons I have never quite understood, Lewis Carroll's classic children's story has always been popular with a certain type of British Buddhist (the late Christmas Humphreys was fond of describing the work as 'pure Zen'), and it is interesting to find Batchelor citing it in this connection. Apparently all we have to do is act upon the four truths without asking any questions, just as Alice drank the contents of the little bottle simply because the label told her to do so. Not that the 'wise little Alice' of the story was going to do such a thing in a hurry. Though Batchelor does not mention the fact, she decides to look first and see whether the bottle is marked 'poison' or not, 'for she had read several nice little histories about children who had got burnt, and eaten up by wild beasts, and many other unpleasant things, all because they *would* not remember the simple rules their friends had taught them such as, that a red-hot poker will burn you if you hold it too long; and that, if you cut your finger *very* deeply with a knife, it usually bleeds; and she had never forgotten that, if you drink much from a bottle marked "poison", it is almost certain to disagree with you sooner or later.'[20]

Apparently Batchelor has not read any such nice little histories, for he evidently thinks we should be less wise than Alice and drink the contents of the bottle without first seeing whether they will disagree with us or not. In Alice's case there was only one bottle, it was not marked 'poison', and drinking its contents only made her grow smaller. Today anyone who follows the White Rabbit down the rabbit-hole into the Wonderland of the spiritual supermarket will find themselves confronted not by one bottle but hundreds, of all shapes, sizes, and colours, and all marked 'Drink Me' – some of them in very large letters indeed. Among the bottles there is one, usually also marked 'Buddhism', that contains the four truths. Why should we drink the contents of this bottle rather than the contents of one – or more – of the various other bottles? All bear the same injunction: 'Drink Me'. Admittedly, the label on the yellow 'Buddhist' bottle tells us what ingredients its particular contents contain. As Batchelor says, when the Buddha presented his four truths, he first described what each referred to. But the labels on all the other bottles also describe what their respective bottles contain, some of them at great length and in very forcible terms. Some, indeed, describe not only the advantages to be gained from drinking the contents of their particular bottle but the terrible things that will happen to one if one does *not* drink them. One might argue (if argument was permitted) that the contents of the Buddhist bottle are described by the Buddha; it is the Buddha who enjoins us to act upon the four truths, and since he is the Buddha, having himself understood anguish, let go of its origins, realized its cessation, and cultivated the path, we have no alternative but to comply. But how do we know that the Buddha is what he is said to be, i.e. Enlightened? Like the five ascetics, we need to be convinced of the fact, and it is only evidence and argument that will convince us. Once convinced, we are in a position to develop the degree of rational faith sufficient to enable us to start acting as he enjoins. We may also need to be convinced that 'anguish' is, in fact, caused by craving, that craving really can be made to cease, and that there is a path leading to its cessation. There are people who doubt all these things, and who are no more prepared to comply with an injunction to act upon the four truths than they are prepared to observe the Ten Commandments. Batchelor's assertion that action and belief are incompatible not only rules out 'the dogmas of the belief system known as "Buddhism"' (p.5) but precludes both the possibility of developing a rational belief and the following of a graduated path. Authentic Buddhist practice consists in acting upon the four truths, to the total exclusion of practices and observances of a religious nature ('religion' is equivalent to belief), and we act upon them simply because we are so enjoined. Strictly speaking, indeed, there is no question of any 'because'. We are told to act upon them, and we act, just as Alice was told 'Drink Me' and she drank – except that in our case we are not, it seems, allowed to harbour any doubts. Buddhist agnosticism thus turns out to be a form of authoritarianism. The Buddha speaks – or Batchelor speaks in his name – and we have no option but to obey.

(4) That 'le style est l'homme même' and that 'the medium is the message' may well be clichés, but there is still a good deal of truth in them. An author's choice of words, as well as the way in which he actually uses those words, can often reveal something of his conscious and unconscious intentions. In the preface to *Buddhism Without Beliefs* Batchelor tells us that he has tried to write a book on Buddhism in ordinary English that avoids the use of foreign words, technical terms, lists, and jargon. This is obviously a laudable aim. But he also tells us, 'The one exception is the word "dharma", for which I can find no English equivalent' (p.xi), which is really rather ingenuous, suggesting as it does that he has found English equivalents for all the other Buddhist terms. The reader is thus lulled into a false sense of security and into an uncritical acceptance, therefore, of words such as awakening, freedom, awareness, and meditation as being the actual equivalents of traditional Buddhist terms and as providing us with a vocabulary adequate to the discussion of important aspects of the Dharma. It is also noteworthy that although he professes to write in ordinary English there is a whole class of words that Batchelor repeatedly employs not in accordance with standard usage but only pejoratively. Such are the words religion, belief, spiritual, mystical, transcendental, holiness, hierarchy, ritual, and institution. Even 'Buddhism', within inverted commas, is employed in this way. All these words, in their pejorative sense, Batchelor associates with what he terms 'religious Buddhism' (also pejorative). Words such as freedom, democratic, secular, and pluralist, together with the fashionable 'vulnerability' and 'empowerment', he on the contrary associates with belief-free, agnostic Buddhism. Moreover, Batchelor is not above occasionally playing to the populist gallery, as when, speaking of the challenging of certain views, he declares, in ringing tones as it were, 'The doors of awakening were thrown open to those

barred from it by the strictures and dogmas of a privileged élite. Laity, women, the uneducated – the disempowered – were invited to taste the freedom of the dharma for themselves' (p. 13).

Batchelor indeed is stronger in rhetoric than in argument, in assertion than in demonstration. There is in fact very little in the way of actual argument in his book, which is probably why it is such a slender production. Reading it, I was reminded of the occasion when, nearly thirty years ago, I heard a solemn-voiced Norman O. Brown slowly and deliberately reading extracts from his forthcoming book *Love's Body* to an audience of some three hundred American undergraduates. The reading was received in complete silence. There were no questions afterwards. No questions were expected. The oracle had spoken. *Buddhism Without Beliefs* will certainly not be received in silence. Questions will certainly be asked (they are being asked already), despite the fact that much of the book is written in an oracular, categorical style that gives one the impression that Batchelor is speaking *ex cathedra*. This impression is heightened by his noticeable fondness for the imperative mood, sentences in which mood are scattered throughout the book. None of this is surprising. Reliance on rhetoric rather than argument, an oracular, categorical style, an *ex cathedra* delivery, and a fondness for the imperative, are all characteristics of the language of authoritarianism.

This is not to say that Batchelor himself necessarily has an authoritarian personality. The authoritarianism is inherent in his intellectual position, according to which acting upon the four truths and belief in them are incompatible, so that authentic dharma practice consists in our acting upon those truths simply because we have been enjoined to do so, anything of the nature of ('religious') belief, even rational belief, being entirely excluded. Nor is it to say that Batchelor's reliance on rhetoric is a matter of personal choice. This too is inherent in his intellectual position, for if one is convinced that dharmic practice consists simply in compliance with, or obedience to, an injunction, not much room will be left for argument. Batchelor is in fact not unaware of the danger of 'falling prey to the bewitchment of language' (p.40), and if he does fall prey to that bewitchment himself to an extent, it is due as much to the logic of his position as to inadvertence. Similarly, if there is a trace of messianism in his attitude, this is not because he is unaware of 'the danger of messianic and narcissistic inflation' (p.90), much less still because he has any messianic pretensions, but rather because he is genuinely convinced that he, perhaps alone in his generation, has discovered what the Buddha *really* taught and how it can be made relevant to Western culture.

Disagreement with a respected fellow Buddhist is painful, as I observed earlier, even as agreement is pleasant. Though there is much in Batchelor's book that I find unacceptable and which I deplore, fortunately there is also much that is acceptable to me and in which I can rejoice. Similarly, though I am obliged to reject his basic thesis as illogical and as a serious misrepresentation of the Dharma I can, at the same time, not only appreciate his sincerity of purpose but sympathize with his position. It is not easy to be a Western Buddhist. Inheritors as we are of an enormously rich and complex spiritual tradition that does not always speak with a single voice and comes to us embedded in a variety of colourful alien cultures, it is not easy for us to separate the essential from the non-essential, to decide what is relevant to our spiritual needs and what is not, or to determine the exact nature of the relationship between Buddhism on the one hand and Western culture on the other. If some of us, in our struggle to make sense of Buddhism for ourselves and others, should happen to overestimate the importance of this or that aspect of the Dharma, or allow ourselves to be carried to extremes of affirmation and denial, as Batchelor does with his advocacy of a belief-free, agnostic Buddhism, this is understandable and forgivable. Extremism will always find a following, and *Buddhism Without Beliefs* will no doubt find many appreciative readers. This need not dismay us. People come into contact with the Dharma in a variety of ways. Many, I know, have come in contact with it through reading Lobsang Rampa's *The Third Eye* or Christmas Humphreys' *Buddhism*, or as a result of seeing a Bruce Lee film, and I am confident that at least some of those in whom an interest in Buddhism is awakened by *Buddhism Without Beliefs* will sooner or later find their way to more adequate sources of information. The end of the golden string now being in their hand, they have only to wind it into a ball.

(5) What, then, have I learned from writing this review? I must confess I have not learned anything I did not know before, though the exercise has certainly helped clarify some of my perceptions and this is always useful. It is clearer to me than ever that the Dharma is an ocean, and that its depths are not to be plumbed by reason alone, that the human mind is capable of mingling truth and falsehood to such an extent that in some cases 'A Hair perhaps divides the False and True' and it is difficult to separate them, that ideologically speaking Buddhism's near enemies can be more dangerous than its distant ones, that language must be looked at no less clearly than its content, and that for one seeking to understand and explain the Dharma sincerity is not enough. Finally, it is clearer to me that while the writing of reviews may be a minor form of literary activity, so long as new books on Buddhism continue to be published it is possible for it to perform a useful, even a necessary, function.

*This review was first published in the Western Buddhist Review, vol. 2, August 1997.*

### Notes

1. Quotations from Batchelor's book, and references (without quotation marks) to specific points he makes, adhere to Batchelor's own typographical conventions.

2. Richard F. Gombrich, *How Buddhism Began*. Athlone Press 1996. pp. 48–9.

3. Thrangu Rinpoche, *King of Samadhi*. Rangjun Yeshe Publications 1994, p. 89. According to the same author, ibid., p. 47, children die of starvation in Africa due to their lack of merit.

4. *Samyutta Nikaya* 36 (S.ii.3.21). See *The Book of Kindred Sayings*, part IV, trans. F.L. Woodward. Luzac 1956, p. 155.

5. *Samyutta Nikaya* 45 (S.v.1.2). See *The Book of Kindred Sayings*, trans. F.L. Woodward, Luzac 1930, p. 2. Woodward translates *kalyana mitrata* as 'friendship with what is lovely.'

6. *Udana* viii, 3, trans. Gombrich, op. cit., p. 42.

7. Peter Morris, *Power: a Philosophical Analysis*. Manchester University Press 1987, p. 4.

8. *Anguttara Nikaya* 9.iv.41. See *The Book of the Gradual Sayings*, trans. E.M. Hare. Pali Text Society 1978, p. 295.

9. Gombrich, op. cit. pp. 96 et seq.

10. For a colourful description of the ceremony see Thomas Carlyle, *The French Revolution*, Chapman and Hall 1871, vol. iii, pp. 193–4.

11. *Majjhima Nikaya* 72. See *The Middle Length Discourses of the Buddha*, trans. Bhikkhu Nanamoli and Bhikkhu Bodhi. Wisdom Publications, 1995, p. 593.

12. Bhikkhu Nanamoli, *The Life of the Buddha*, Buddhist Publication Society 1978, p. 37.

13. *Samyutta Nikaya* 56 (S.xii.2.1). See Edward J. Thomas (trans.), *Early Buddhist Scriptures*, Kegan Paul, Trench, and Trubner 1935, p. 30.

14. Nanamoli and Bodhi (trans.), *Majjhima Nikaya* 26, op. cit., p. 265.

15. ibid., p. 264.

16. The *Ariyapariyesana Sutta* (*Majjhima Nikaya* 26) does not actually mention the Four Truths. The *Dhammachakkapavattana Sutta* (*Samyutta Nikaya* 56 (S.xii.2.1)) speaks of them as having been taught to the five ascetics.

17. *Udana* 5.5 in Peter Masefield (trans.), *The Udana*, Pali Text Society, 1994, p. 97.

18. *Vinaya Pitaka* ii, 6, 4. See F.L. Woodward (trans.), *Some Sayings of the Buddha*, Buddhist Society 1973, p. 96 (changing Woodward's 'Norm' to 'Dharma').

19. Geshe Wangyal, *The Door of Liberation*, Maurice Girodias 1973, pp. 141–2.

20. Lewis Carroll, *Alice's Adventures in Wonderland*, (1865), ch.1, 'Down the Rabbit Hole'.

# Asian Commitment

David Snellgrove
*Asian Commitment: Travels and Studies in the Indian Sub-Continent and South-East Asia*
Orchid Press, Bangkok 2000, pp. 635.

David Snellgrove's first exposure to Asia took place during the war, and after demobilization he had looked forward to a career in the ICS, a career in which a life of practical good works in the Indian subcontinent would be combined with local scholarly researches. The achievement of political independence by India and Pakistan put paid to that youthful dream, and Snellgrove, who had already developed 'a consuming interest' in Tibetan Buddhism, was faced by the prospect of a life of scholarly research for its own sake. Scholarship, however, proved to be only tolerable when combined with new ventures in foreign lands, and *Asian Commitment* is the very readable – and lavishly illustrated – record of how, over a period of more than fifty years, the author sought to live simultaneously in the two worlds, the world of scholarship and the world of travel. Not that any of his experiences during the war years was wasted. During that period, he tells us, he learned resourcefulness in travel of all kinds and in dealing with superior authorities and difficult bureaucracies. He met for the first time men and women of very different cultural and religious backgrounds, and learned later, when he lived as one of them, to accept their ways almost as though they had become his own.

*Asian Commitment* is divided into two parts. Part I covers the period 1943 to 1982, in the course of which the author made ten journeys to India and the surrounding region, including Nepal, Sikkim, Bhutan, and Ceylon (he refuses to call it Sri Lanka), besides making a number of journeys to places of Buddhist interest within India itself. The stories of these travels are told, to a great extent, through the medium of letters, often very lengthy, which Snellgrove wrote at the time to his parents, his sister, and various academic colleagues. This introduces a directly personal element into a narrative that might otherwise have been a dry account of distances traversed, places visited, and ancient manuscripts and paintings discovered. Thus we learn about his dealings with the School of Oriental and African Studies, about his being snowed up in a 14-foot-square room in Dolpo, a remote frontier region of Nepal, with the local Lama and six other persons, and about his grief when a favourite horse has to be put down. We also learn about the various companions of his travels, especially Pasang, the young Sherpa who became a lifelong friend and who ended his days as a producer of peach brandy in his native Nepal, and in memory of whom *Asian Commitment* has been written. Snellgrove evidently is a man with a gift for friendship, so much so that his book, like his life, might be described as being dedicated not only to scholarship and travel but also to friendship.

In 1967, during his seventh visit to India, Snellgrove started to feel a sense of disillusion with India and Nepal, a sense that was later to take possession of him. 'For me everything changes here for the worse,' he writes from the Nepal Valley to a friend. 'Temples and stupas are in ever greater decay. Even the great Bodnath stupa is filthy and covered with green mould. There are more and more foreigners, and Tibetan books, paintings and *objets d'art* command such fantastic prices that I am out of the market.' Eleven years later, writing from the same place, he complains that the valley had been rendered even more hideous by 'development projects' and even more filthy due to the increasing population and the absence of sanitation. Nor were these the only changes for the worse. The ending of all cultural relations with Tibet, combined with the pressure of 'Nepal-style' education was gradually undermining what remained of Tibetan civilization and culture in the northern frontier areas. It seemed that there would be even fewer Tibetan-speaking areas in Nepal where scholars like him could study Tibetan Buddhism, and in 1979–80 and 1982 he made his last two journeys to the subcontinent.

The next five years were spent working on *Indo-Tibetan Buddhism*, probably his most important book, and it was not until 1987 that he was able to resume his Asian travels. This time they were in South-East Asia, where between 1987 and 1999 he made fifteen journeys. These journeys are chronicled in Part II of *Asian Commitment*, and they took him to the Malay archipelago and Funan, to the Hindu-Buddhist states of Java, Sumatra, and Bali, and to Cambodia, where he bought a house and became the adoptive father of several young Cambodians orphaned by the Khmer Rouge. Like Part I, the much shorter Part II is rich in information about the history, culture, and religion of the areas visited by the author and monuments are, as usual, described meticulously. Partly because the narrative is not diversified by the inclusion of letters, Part II is academically denser than Part I, and dealing as it does with a different geographical region could well have been published as a separate book.

*Asian Commitment* concludes with an Epilogue in which, after a few general observations on religion as both a cohesive and a divisive element in human affairs, Snellgrove offers us his reflections on Buddhism and Hinduism, on Christianity, on Dualism and the Manichean 'heresy', on Islam, and on personal religion and experience. The fruit of a lifetime of study, these reflections – the reflections of a Roman Catholic scholar who does not believe in converting Tibetan Buddhists to Christianity – will be of no less interest to students of comparative religion than the book, as a whole, will be of interest to 'Tibetan religion enthusiasts', lovers of the Himalayas, and all devotees of tales of travel and adventure in distant lands.

*This review was first published in the Times Higher Education Supplement, 25 April 2002.*

# Paths that Cross in the East

Brian Carr and Indira Mahalingam (editors)
*Companion Encyclopedia of Asian Philosophy*
Routledge, London 1997, pp. 1136.

What is philosophy? What is Asian philosophy? The definitions given by the editors of the *Companion Encyclopedia of Asian Philosophy* in answer to these questions are in both cases broad rather than narrow. Compiled 'with the intention of doing justice to the arguments, ideas and presuppositions of philosophers working largely outside the confines of western philosophical traditions,' their collection of 48 scholarly essays covers a period of some 3,000 years, from the beginning of the first millennium BCE to the present day, and discusses the life and work of thinkers from regions as far apart as Spain and Japan.

The work is divided into six parts, each of which covers a specific tradition within Asian philosophy: Persian, Indian, Buddhist, Chinese, Japanese, and Islamic. All six parts begin with a chapter on the origins of the tradition in question, and end with one sketching the contemporary philosophical preoccupations of the descendants of that tradition. Each part also includes a chapter on the philosophy's view of morals and society, and the parts covering Indian, Buddhist, Chinese, and Islamic philosophy contain chapters on logic and language and on knowledge and reality, some of these being among the most important – and most rigorous – chapters in the entire volume.

Not surprisingly, the editors have not always been able to distribute their material strictly in accordance with the headings of the six parts into which the work is divided. Buddhist philosophy not only has a sixth of the volume to itself, it also figures prominently in connection with Indian, Chinese, and Japanese philosophy. There is even a degree of overlap between Asian and western philosophical traditions. The major period of Islamic philosophy was when, in the ninth to the twelfth centuries of the common era, Islamic ideas met those of ancient Greece, while in Japan the Meiji restoration brought with it an enthusiasm for Comte and Mill. Contemporary Asian philosophy, in all six geographical areas, is probably unthinkable apart from the influence of Kant, Schopenhauer, Marx, Russell, Whitehead, and Wittgenstein.

Besides allowing them to take account of this overlap, Brian Carr and Indira Mahalingam's broad definition of philosophy enables the contributors to the volume to write from a number of different perspectives. For Philip G. Kreyenbroek, writing on morals and society in Zoroastrianism, the latter could be said to be a strongly philosophical religion even though in the extant tradition only a few texts of a predominantly philosophical nature are preserved. While A. Roy believes that most Indian philosophical thought depends for its main source of knowledge on the ancient thought of the Vedas, Upanishads, and Vedanta, Hajime Nakamura believes that the doctrine of the Buddha is not a system of philosophy in the western sense, but a path, and Chung-yin Cheng that philosophy is developed primarily to conceptualize the ideal aspirations of a people at a certain stage or under certain specific circumstances of cultural development. Some of the Asian philosophers discussed had their own perspectives on philosophy. For example it is probable, according to Ian Richard Netton, that in the mind of al-Kindi, the 'father of Arab philosophy', there was no rigid division between philosophy and theology.

Comprehensiveness is no guarantee of completeness, and despite its wealth of material the *Companion* is not guiltless of omissions. The most serious of these is in connection with aesthetics, on which there is not a single chapter in the entire volume. Apart from ten perfunctory lines on Buddhism and aesthetics in the chapter on contemporary Buddhist philosophy the subject is not even mentioned, and there is no reference to it in the index. The omission is particularly glaring in the case of Indian philosophy, which boasts a remarkably rich tradition of thought on aesthetics to which a succession of Hindu, Buddhist, and Jain thinkers made valuable contributions. Similarly in the eleven chapters of part two, covering

Indian philosophy, there is no mention of the important Trika system of Kashmir Shaivism. Nor are these the only omissions in this part. Sarasvati Chennakesavan and K. Vasudeva Reddy's rather sanitized account of the caste system, in the chapter on morals and society in Indian philosophy, makes no mention of untouchability, while A. Roy, writing on contemporary Indian philosophy, fails to mention either M. N. Roy, India's leading Marxist thinker, or her most radical reformer, B. R. Ambedkar, whose social and political ideals have affected the lives of millions of his countrymen. Roy also fails to mention Tagore, even though Sarvepalli Radhakrishnan, to whom four pages are devoted, has written a book with the title *The Philosophy of Rabindranath Tagore*. Admittedly Tagore was not a systematic thinker, but then neither were Vivekananda or Gandhi, to both of whom space is devoted in this chapter.

M. N. Roy, Ambedkar and Tagore are not the only ones who fail to receive their due. Francis Soo, writing on contemporary Chinese philosophy, mentions the names of Ouyang Jingwu and Master Taixu, the most notable of the Chinese philosophers who have devoted their efforts to the development of Chinese Buddhism this century, but he does not discuss their work, on the grounds that Indian and Chinese Buddhism are dealt with in chapters 17 and 28 of the encyclopedia. Perhaps due to an editorial oversight, not only are the two philosophers not discussed in these chapters, they are not even mentioned there, nor do their names appear in the index. There are other inconsistencies, as well as a few misprints. Although *anatta* is correctly defined in the glossary, as 'the doctrine that there exists no permanent, independent partless self underlying impermanent phenomena', the editors choose to render the term, in their introduction to part two of the encyclopedia, as 'no consciousness', which is patently absurd. They have also chosen to adhere to the convention BC and AD for all dates. In a work devoted to Asian philosophy BCE and CE would surely have been more appropriate.

According to the publishers, the volume is crucial for students and scholars working in philosophy, theology, and a variety of area studies, including Asian, Indian and Middle East studies. Probably they do not exaggerate. Many of the volume's users will no doubt be content to dip into it occasionally, whether in connection with their own academic work or simply to extend their knowledge, and indeed the encyclopedia is designed, in the words of the editors, as a reference volume for students, scholars, and others who require more than just a simple sketch of 'oriental' ideas. But perhaps the best use of the work, if one had time and the intellectual stamina, would be to read it from cover to cover, to provide a superb education in Asian philosophy. One would not only encounter many different philosophies (indeed, many different conceptions of the nature of philosophy), but also all the major religions of Asia, as well as seeing the different ways in which the philosophies and religions have interacted over the centuries. It might even be argued that the process of interaction, in Asia, between these two great areas of human experience that in the West are designated 'philosophy' and 'religion' forms the encyclopedia's major unifying theme.

Be that as it may, there is little doubt that philosophers in Europe and the Americas are beginning to take a serious interest in Asian philosophy, even as their counterparts in Asia have for a century or more taken a serious interest in the philosophy of the West. The appearance of the *Companion Encyclopedia of Asian Philosophy* is thus a sign of the times. Together with the Oxford academic *Journal of Asian Philosophy*, also co-edited by Carr and Mahalingam, and the same scholars' European society for Asian philosophy, as well as the research centre for Asian philosophy at the University of Nottingham, it will be a means of contributing to the further growth of an interest of which it is itself a manifestation. The day will soon come, I hope, when it will no more be possible for the European student of philosophy to ignore Nagarjuna, Shankaracharya, or Avicenna than it is possible to ignore Plato, Kant, or Schopenhauer

*This review was first published in the Times Higher Education Supplement, 10 October 1997.*

# Prophet and Loss Account

Mick Brown
*The Spiritual Tourist: A Personal Odyssey Through the Outer Reaches of Belief*
Bloomsbury, London 1998, pp. 309.

'Spiritual Tourism' is really a contradiction in terms, and journalist and self-styled spiritual tourist Mick Brown seems to suspect as much. Probably this is why he has given *The Spiritual Tourist* a subtitle that characterizes this story of his encounters with prophets and divine incarnations in three continents as a spiritual odyssey, as though to invest it thereby with an aura of mythic significance.

The Neoplatonist commentators on *The Odyssey* certainly saw Homer's epic as a symbolic narrative, and even gave detailed philosophical interpretations of some of its more important episodes. One therefore wonders if Brown intends us to see a parallel between the extraordinary characters he meets in the course of his travels and any of the beings, human and non-human, encountered by the wandering Odysseus. Is Mother Meera a kind of mystic Circe whose magic deprives men of their reason? Are the Western denizens of Puttaparthi and Dharamsala the Lotus Eaters?

Our spiritual tourist more than once finds himself struggling to steer a middle course between the Scylla of credulity and the Charybdis of scepticism. When a woman he meets at a dinner party tells him that he is too much the journalist, and should stop asking questions and open his heart, he reflects, 'It was what people kept telling me. I felt as I always did at such times, stranded between reason and a craving for faith, uncomfortable in the knowledge that while a spiritual life may lead you to believe in anything, a materialist outlook on life will lead you to believe in nothing.'

A spiritual life may indeed lead one to believe anything. The woman at the dinner party no more doubts that Sai Baba himself, the miracle-working *avatara* of Puttaparthi, is divine, than does Sai Baba himself, who in 1968 told a world conference of devotees in Bombay, 'In this human form of Sai, every divine entity, every divine principle, that is to say, all the names and forms ascribed to God by man are manifest.'

His faith having been exercised by *avataras* and talk of living goddesses, Brown finds it comparatively easy to believe that a ten-year-old Spanish boy might be the reincarnation of a Tibetan teacher who died in the West. He is also open to the possibility that the Dalai Lama, with whom he discusses the subject of reincarnation, may have a special connection with previous Dalai Lamas – though he reflects that identifying reincarnations seems an inexact science.

Reason is, in fact, called for from time to time and even scepticism is justified. The Crosses of Light that miraculously appear in the windows of a small church in Tennessee, and which have attracted tens of thousands of visitors, turn out to be due to natural causes. Not that it would change anything for the pastor of the church if somebody said they could prove this to him. The belief that they were witnessing a miracle had changed people's lives, and the fact that for the last year he kept the doors of his church open to them means that he became the guardian of their faith.

Our spiritual tourist has a similar attitude. He may even see the writing of *The Spiritual Tourist* as constituting him a guardian of such faith. However it may be, his account of life on the highways and back roads of spiritual tourism is both entertaining and informative. Vignettes of people and places alternate with potted histories of, for example, Tibetan Buddhism and Madame Blavatsky and theosophy. Who the book is meant for is unclear, but the professional student of contemporary religious trends and the armchair spiritual tourist can both be sure of a good read.

*This review was first published in the Times Higher Education Supplement, 20 April 1998.*

# Quiet Lives Hit Troubled Times

Damien Keown (editor)
*Contemporary Buddhist Ethics*
Curzon, Richmond 2000, pp. 217.

His Holiness the XIV Dalai Lama
*Transforming the Mind*
Thorsons, London 2000, pp. 208.

Religion is undergoing an *aggiornamento*. Christianity has perforce led the way, and other religions are increasingly obliged to follow. As a very old religion, Buddhism is probably as much in need of an update as any other, especially as it continues to spread in the West and as its views on contemporary issues are increasingly sought.

Updating is not easy. Many of the problems we face today are the result of modern social, economic, and technological developments that could scarcely have been imagined in ancient times, and to which there is no reference in the Buddhist scriptures.

Moreover, historically the Buddhist order of monks has been the backbone of the religion, and in traditional Buddhist societies the view that the monk should not be concerned with the problems of civil society and family life was and is influential.

This view cannot survive in the modern West. In his introduction to *Contemporary Buddhist Ethics*, Damien Keown points out that one of the prominent features of contemporary western Buddhism is an increased emphasis on lay organization and lay participation. As the momentum of modernization gathers pace, it is difficult to hope that the problems of modernity will go away and allow the monk to resume 'an untroubled mediaeval pace of life'.

In this innovative volume, seven scholars examine a range of contemporary moral issues from a Buddhist perspective. They address specific issues in applied ethics: human rights, animal rights, ecology, abortion, euthanasia, and business practice. Two chapters explore the sources, nature, and proper classification of Buddhist ethics, and trace its ethical teachings back to their ancient roots to discover the appropriate foundations for Buddhist ethics in the modern world. The articles will be of interest to anyone with an interest in Buddhism, comparative ethics, or contemporary moral issues.

James Whitehill conjectures that Buddhism is most likely to succeed in the West if Buddhist ethics are grafted to and enriched by the character-based 'ethics of virtue' tradition that goes back to Socrates and Aristotle. He is critical of the kind of ontological dismissal of morality preached by Robert Aitken, a contemporary interpreter of Zen who is enmeshed, according to Whitehill, in D.T. Suzuki's vigorous anti-rationalism and antinomianism. Robert Florida concludes that, traditionally, Buddhists have understood that the human begins at the instant of conception, when sperm, egg, and *vijnana* or 'intermediate being' come together. There is no qualitative difference between an unborn foetus and a born individual. Abortion is thus taking a life – a violation of the first precept.

Yet in Thailand, one of the most devout Theravada Buddhist countries, the abortion rate is high, possibly in the range of 300,000 a year. In Japan, which may have the highest abortion rate in the world, many Buddhist temples conduct memorial services for aborted foetuses – a bizarre practice that has been adopted by some North American Buddhists.

Potentially the most controversial chapters of the book are those on Buddhism and human rights and Buddhism and animal rights, by Keown and Paul Waldau respectively. Waldau shows that although the first precept prohibits intentionally killing or causing harm to animals as well as to humans, in many respects the general view of animals in Buddhism may be characterized as negative. Buddhist tradition appears to accept the instrumental use of 'other animals' such as elephants, the training of whom involved great cruelty. Waldau believes, nonetheless, that the tradition has great potential for a contribution to environmental ethics and to the benefit that increased environmental awareness entails for other animals' lives. He does not examine the notion of rights as such or ask what place, if any, it has in contemporary Buddhist discussion of ethical issues.

This is done by Keown who explores some of the issues that must be addressed if a Buddhist philosophy of human rights is to develop. While admitting that there is no word in Sanskrit or Pali that conveys the idea of 'rights', understood as a subjective entitlement, he believes that the concept of rights is not alien to Buddhist thought. Buddhism recognizes duties and because these duties are reciprocal and complementary, as between husband and wife, he argues that the fact that one of the parties has duties implies that the other has corresponding rights. For Buddhism, however, duties imply not corresponding rights but corresponding duties. It does not follow that one party's duty implies the other party's right. Buddhist ethics cannot be grounded on the concept of rights.

For the Dalai Lama, Buddhist ethics are grounded on compassion. His *Transforming the Mind: Teachings on Generating Compassion* consist mainly of the teachings he gave in London in 1999 on *The Eight Verses on Transforming the Mind*, a short but important text written by the eleventh-century Tibetan master Langri Thangpa. The book is divided into four chapters. The first three are 'The basis of transformation', 'Transforming through altruism', and 'Transforming through insight'. The fourth is a verse-by-verse commentary on Thangpa's text.

Because the basis of transformation is meditation, the teachings in Chapter One deal with such topics as meditation as a discipline, the obstacles to meditation, and the nature of consciousness, as well as discussing the 'four seals', a set of doctrinal axioms common to all schools of Buddhism, and the epistemological question of how the validity of the path is to be ascertained.

Generating compassion is dealt with in chapter two, which is as much the heart of the book as altruism is the heart of the Dalai Lama's own Mahayana Buddhism. The *bodhichitta* or 'altruistic intention' (an unavoidably weak translation) is the aspiration to attain full enlightenment for the benefit of all sentient beings. This involves both the development of compassion for sentient beings and the wish to attain enlightenment. According to an ancient authority, the practice of *bodhichitta* surpasses all ethical practices, so that, the Dalai Lama believes, 'the practice of generating and cultivating the altruistic intention is so comprehensive that it contains the essential elements of all other spiritual practices.' But compassion must be combined with the complementary factors of wisdom and insight. This is dealt with in Chapter Three, which contains a succinct account of the subtle and obscure Mind Only school that will be of particular interest to students of Buddhist philosophy.

*This review was first published in the Times Higher Education Supplement, 8 December 2000.*

# Searching for me, Me*, or I?

Shaun Gallagher and Jonathan Shear (editors)
*Models of the Self*
Thorverton Imprint Academic, Exeter 1999, pp. 524.

As one who is an author of three volumes of memoirs, and who is currently engaged in adding a fourth to the series, I have sometimes stopped and asked myself who this 'I', whose history I have been recalling and recording, really is. Did the self that I experienced as the subject of those memoirs in fact exist, and if it did, what was its nature? Was it permanent or impermanent, simple or composite, physical or mental, or both, or neither?

Questions such as these have been mooted from ancient times. While for Aristotle 'who I am' is closely tied to embodied existence and yet transcends it, for Plato and Augustine the animal elements are excluded from the human essence. In the modern era Descartes' thesis that the self is a single, simple, continuing, and unproblematically accessible mental substance came to dominate European thought, providing a background for Locke's discussion of the problem of personal identity and Hume's reduction of the so-called self to a stream of particular perceptions.

Yet Hume's analysis notwithstanding, we continue to experience a sense of self, and contemporary responses, in part, have been attempts to explain how this is possible. If the self is not an Aristotelian soul or *psyche* or a Descartian substance, why do we still believe we have a certain identity over time? The responses to the problem vary immensely. They include the assertions that there is no self, that it is a fiction, a matter of brain processes, a sociological locus, a centre of narratives (as in the case of my memoirs, for instance), or that it belongs to an ineffable category all its own. Thus there is no consensus, and both our commonsensical and philosophical notions of self have been rendered utterly problematic. This lack of consensus suggests that, like consciousness itself, the problem of the self is a complex and multi-dimensional phenomenon, and no one discipline on its own will be able to capture it in an adequate way. A cross-disciplinary approach is obviously the answer. In *Models of the Self*, Shaun Gallagher and Jonathan Shear have brought together 28 essays by 31 writers (three are co-authors). They develop divergent models of the self, grouped under six sectional headings and representative of their respective approaches, whether philosophical, psychological, or neuro-scientific, addressing such questions as what is meant by the self, whether it consists of an enduring thing or function, whether there are aspects of the self that are not reducible to such things as brain functions, linguistic and social phenomena, or consciousness, or all of them collectively.

With questions concerning the existence and nature of the self having first been debated by philosophers, it is fitting that a contemporary discussion should be inaugurated by a philosopher. *Models of the Self* opens with an essay on 'The Self' by Galen Strawson, which the editors diplomatically characterize as 'intriguing'. Most of the other authors make reference to this chapter, and Strawson responds to their comments and criticisms at the end of the volume.

For Strawson, the problem of the self arises not from an unnatural use of language but from a prior and independent sense that there is such a thing as the self. It is therefore a real problem and requires, he thinks, a metaphysical approach; but he also thinks that metaphysics must wait on phenomenology. 'One must have well-developed answers to phenomenological questions about the experience of the self before one can begin to answer metaphysical questions about the self.'

Starting, then, with the phenomenological fact of the ordinary, human sense of the self, Strawson proposes that people experience themselves as being: a thing, in some robust sense; a mental thing, in some sense; a single thing that is both synchronically considered and diachronically considered; ontically distinct from all other things; a subject of experience, a conscious feeler and thinker; an agent; and a thing that has a certain character or personality. Though admitting that most of these properties can be contested, and that the list may contain redundancy, Strawson believes that it provides a framework for discussion, and that nothing essential to a genuine sense of the mental self has been omitted. Keeping to this framework he argues for a mental self, of which the apparent necessary unity is only synchronic, not diachronic, so that each one of us is properly understandable as a sequence of many selves, existing and following each other one at a time, like a string of pearls. 'The basic form of our consciousness is that of a gappy series of eruptions of consciousness from a substrate of apparent non-consciousness.' Strawson suggests that each short-lived 'pearl' is an individual physical thing, namely a set of neurons in a certain state of activation. He also states his belief that 'the Buddhists have the truth when they deny the existence of a persisting mental self in the human case' and makes a fascinating and potentially fruitful distinction between thinking of oneself in terms of I and thinking of oneself, more fundamentally and existentially, in terms of what he characterizes as Me*.

The authors of the four essays that make up the opening section of the volume are largely critical of Strawson's approach. Kathleen V. Wilkes disagrees with his idea that 'the self', being synchronic, needs to have little or nothing to do with time-related plans and emotions; John Pickering, for whom the self is a semiotic process, takes him to task for excluding the experience of being a social self from the meaning of 'the self' in a stricter ontological sense; and Eric T. Olson, while not actually referring to Strawson, in effect undercuts his position by arguing that there is no problem of the self, discussions under the heading of 'self' being really about other things. Only Andrew Brooks is 'in complete sympathy' with Strawson's conclusions, though he wants to look at certain aspects of the framework of argument and observation used to reach them. In the section on 'Developmental and phenomenological constraints', Dan Zahavi takes issue with Strawson's understanding of phenomenology, arguing that only a phenomenology guided in a methodological fashion, of the sort initiated by Edmund Husserl, would be adequate to discover a genuine sense of self.

For me, some of the most interesting responses to Strawson's essay are found in the section 'Meditation-based approaches'. Here Steven Laycock, looking at Sartre's notion of the transparency of consciousness from a Buddhist point of view, argues that since consciousness itself is unidentifiable, and cannot be distinguished from the objective contents of one's awareness, the 'I' necessarily remains hopelessly anonymous. None of Strawson's 'pearls' can succeed in representing the self, even the self of a moment. Jeremy Hayward presents a rDzogs-chen (Tibetan Buddhist) interpretation of the sense of self. This model of self/non-self, which is grounded in the disciplined method *shamatha-vipashyana* meditation, agrees with Strawson's analysis as far as the discontinuity of the self, but elaborates the momentary self not as any kind of thing, but as an energy process having both particle-like and field-like aspects. The moment-by-moment appearance of a sense of self arises in stages over a finite duration from a background of non-dual intelligence and energy.

In the final essay, Strawson responds at length and mounts what the editors think is a convincing defence of his position, though not without strengthening his argument in certain respects and modifying it in others. Having thanked those who commented on his paper, he begins by characterizing the result as 'a festival of misunderstanding' – adding, optimistically, 'misunderstanding is one of the engines of progress'. In similar vein, he concludes by observing: 'Interdisciplinary discussion throws up a chaos of uses, but this turns out to be part of its value.' The layperson may be forgiven for thinking that the chaos thus thrown up is not so different from the dust that, according to Berkeley, philosophers raise and then complain they cannot see.

In principle, *Models of the Self* should be of interest to all thinking human beings, but I suspect that, covering as it does such a wide range of disciplines, most readers will be content to sample the volume in accordance with their particular specialist concerns. For my part, I have found many of the contributions stimulating, and in places illuminating, but I shall return to the writing of my memoirs very little wiser about the existence and nature of the self that is the subject of my narrative.

*First published in the Times Higher Education Supplement, 17 March 2000.*

# The Search for Nirvana

Richard F. Gombrich
*How Buddhism Began: The Conditioned Genesis of the Early Teachings*
Athlone, London 1996, pp. 180.

Buddhism has recently been described as Europe's fastest-growing religion. Popular as well as scholarly interest in the Buddha and his teaching has certainly increased enormously during the past few decades, finding expression in the creation of Buddhist centres and communities and the carrying on of scientific research into the history, doctrines, and institutions of Buddhism. A good deal of literature has also been produced, both popular and academic.

*How Buddhism Began* by Richard Gombrich, the Boden Professor of Sanskrit at Oxford, belongs to this latter category, though certain of his conclusions have a definite bearing on the actual practice of the Buddha's teaching and are therefore of special interest to those wishing to take that teaching seriously. Given as lectures in 1994 at the School of Oriental and African Studies, the work will be of interest to students of comparative religion and, in fact, to anyone seeking to achieve a better understanding of some of the factors conditioning the genesis of one of the world's great religions.

A Popperian nominalist by conviction rather than an essentialist, Gombrich sees Buddhism not as an inert object but as a chain of events. Such a way of seeing it is, he points out, in the spirit of the Buddha's own teaching of conditioned genesis *paticca-samuppada*), according to which things, including living beings, exist not as adamantine essences but as causally determined dynamic processes. The beginning of the chain is, however, involved in obscurity, an obscurity Gombrich seeks to dispel, at least to an extent, by a critical study of the 'earliest texts', the texts of the Pali canon, which happen to have received far less critical attention than the text of the Bible.

In studying these ancient records he follows a middle way between the extreme of deadly over-simplification and the extreme of the deconstruction fashionable among social scientists who refuse all generalization, ignore the possibilities of reasonable extrapolation – and usually leave us unenlightened.

His first point is that most of our physical evidence for the Pali canon is astonishingly recent, far more recent than our physical evidence for the western classical and biblical texts. Hardly any Pali manuscripts are more than about 500 years old, and the majority are less than 300 years old. Gombrich thinks we can apply our critical intelligence, and at least point out where they seem to be incoherent and therefore perhaps corrupt. We may even be able to suggest an emendation, even one which has no manuscript support.

As for the relation between these texts and what the Buddha taught, Gombrich insists that there are divergencies and incoherencies of significance within the *Nikayas* (the five collections of the Buddha's sermons), that doctrinal developments during the period of oral transmission were not minimal, and that his main purpose is not to stratify the texts but to trace the evolution of some of the ideas in the Buddha's teachings as reported in the Pali texts, to get a clearer idea of what they say.

The processes and mechanisms of that evolution include debate, 'skill in means', metaphor, allegory, satire, and literalism, and it is to a discussion of these that the greater part of *How Buddhism Began* is devoted. Though the Buddha's experience of Enlightenment was private and beyond language, the truths to which he had 'awakened' had to be expressed in language – not so much in the narrow literal sense, such as Sanskrit or Pali – as in that of the set of categories and concepts that language embodies. The *dharma* or teaching of the Buddha is, in fact, the product of argument and debate, the debate going on in the oral culture of renouncers and Brahmins (*samana-brahmana*), as the texts' recurrent phrase has it, in the upper Ganges plain in the fifth century BCE.

The Buddha's teaching of *kamma* or 'action' is a case in point. According to Gombrich it developed as a reaction to Brahminism. For Brahminism, 'action' (*karman*) is ritual action in accordance with the prescriptions of the *Vedas*, the typical 'action' being a sacrifice, which is normally positive. By means of sacrifice a man obtains rebirth in higher forms of life on earth and in heaven(s). For the Buddha, action is primarily ethical action, and what makes action ethical is intention. In redefining 'action' as 'intention' – a use of language which Gombrich characterizes as audacious – the Buddha turned the Brahmin ideology upside-down and ethicised the universe. 'I do not see how one could exaggerate the importance of the Buddha's ethicisation of the world, which I regard as a turning point in the history of civilisation', writes Gombrich.

Though a kind thought is good, purifying karma, it does not come naturally to call it 'action', as Gombrich admits. Yet action it undoubtedly is, karma or action being not only physical and vocal but also mental. Karma is good and bad, skilful (*kusala*) and unskilful (*akusala*), according to the nature of its motivation. The bad motivations for karma are greed, hatred, and delusion, while the good motivations include the aspect of non-greed.

At the higher stages of spiritual progress, as when one is mainly living the life of the mind in meditation, one's karma tends to be purely mental and purely skilful. Gombrich's appreciation of this fact enables him to see, not only that the practice of pervading every direction with thoughts of kindness, compassion, sympathetic joy, and equanimity (a well-known Buddhist 'meditation') constitutes mental action, but also to see that these four qualities, when cultivated to the uttermost, actually bring Enlightenment or escape from the cycle of rebirth. According to the older *Upanishads*, such escape was to be achieved by realizing the unchanging essence of man and the universe, an essence which is 'being' as opposed to 'becoming'. Ontology is merged, even confused, with epistemology.

For the Buddha, of course, there was no common, unchanging essence of man and the universe: there was no self (*anatman*). He was not an essentialist, and Gombrich sees his teaching of conditioned genesis as his answer to Upanishadic ontology. Just as 'being' lies at the heart of Upanishadic world view, so 'action' or *kamma*, in the word's primary sense of morally relevant action, lies at the heart of the Buddha's. The Buddha was concerned, not so much with *what*, as with *how*.

Forgetful of the Buddha's wisdom in bypassing ontology, an important pre-Mahayana intellectual tradition reified the concept of karma, so that good karma was turned into something that could be possessed, accumulated, and even transferred from one person to another. Whereas in early Buddhism the Buddha was a saviour only in the sense that he taught the way to salvation, in the Mahayana both Buddha and *bodhisattvas* saved more directly, by transferring merit. Gombrich sees this transfer of a reified karma as being what is crucial in turning Buddhism into a religion in which one could be saved by others.

In extreme cases, as when such karma is distributed to the wicked, it results in the original doctrine of karma being stood on its head. Reification is the child of literalism. While the Buddha himself seems to have had a lively awareness of the dangers of literalism, and even designated the literalist (*pada-parama*) as a distinct type of person, his followers did not always share that awareness. Unintentional literalism, Gombrich argues, was a major force for change in the early doctrinal history of Buddhism. He sees in some doctrinal developments what he calls scholastic literalism – which is 'the tendency to take the words and phrases of earlier texts (maybe the Buddha's own words) in such a way as to read in distinctions which they were never intended to make'.

Examples of this tendency are the Vaibhasikas' separation of act from the intention to act (for the Buddha the two were virtually synonymous), and the Mahayana's separation of nirvana from *bodhi*, or 'awakening'. More controversial still, Gombrich makes literalism responsible for the creation of Buddhist cosmology.

Scientific research of this kind is not of merely theoretical interest; it has, in some cases, a practical significance. In a fascinating chapter headed 'Retracing an Ancient Debate: How Insight Worsted Concentration in the Pali Canon', Gombrich shows how scholastic literalism played a leading role in the development of the idea that Enlightenment can be attained without meditation, by a process of intellectual analysis (technically known as *panna*, or insight) alone. This change in the soteriology took place, he believes, within at least 65 years of the Buddha's death, when the *suttas* and other texts were still being transmitted orally.

In a lengthy piece of brilliant scholarly detective work, Gombrich traces back the Theravada's sevenfold classification of moral and spiritual types to a jockeying for position among the three faculties of faith, concentration, and insight; this back to the devaluation of concentration (and faith); and this back to the differentiation between release by insight and meditation and release by insight alone, a differentiation made possible by the ambiguity of the term *panna*.

In another piece of scholarly detective work Gombrich tries to show that the famous mass murderer Angulimala, whom the Buddha converted by means of a significant play upon words, was actually a long-standing worshipper of the god Shiva and thus a Tantric. The evidence for such an identification rests upon Gombrich's emendations to the text of two canonical Pali verses. But though they make excellent sense, and resolve several difficulties, in the end one has to say of them that like a celebrated emendation of the dying Falstaff's 'a table of green fields', they are brilliant but not wholly convincing.

Despite the book's rather catchpenny title, Gombrich does not really tell us how Buddhism began. Indeed, he professes to be more concerned with formulating problems and raising questions than with providing answers. Many of his conclusions, he assures us, are tentative. Nonetheless he manages to shed a good deal of light on some of the factors conditioning the genesis of the early teachings of Buddhism, so giving us an idea of the way in which the religion (as he does not hesitate to call it) arose and developed.

On certain points his thinking is in need of clarification. In one place he says of the *dharma* that it is 'a set of truths, and as such is abstract and eternal, like all truths – think for example of the truths of mathematics. The truths exist whether anyone is aware of them or not'. Yet elsewhere he speaks of the *dharma* as having 'emerged from debate'.

Similarly, though rightly pointing out that summaries of the Buddha's teachings 'rarely convey how much use he made of simile and metaphor', he speaks at the same time of the 'language' in which the Buddha had to express his experience of Enlightenment as embodying a set only of 'categories and concepts'. That the Buddha might also have had recourse to myth and symbol is a possibility he fails to consider. These and other shortcomings do not in any way detract from the overall merits of a work in which genial scholarship is skilfully and imaginatively deployed. There can be little doubt that we have in *How Buddhism Began* as readable an introduction to a difficult and thorny subject as we are likely to find.

*This review was first published in the Times Higher Education Supplement, 4 July 1997.*

# Ways of All Buddhists

Rupert Gethin
*The Foundations of Buddhism*
Oxford University Press, Oxford 1998, pp. 333.

Of the making of many books on Buddhism there is no end. Here is yet another one. Fortunately Rupert Gethin's very readable introductory volume is a book on Buddhism with a difference. It is not a survey-type work that attempts, whether sketchily or in a more systematic manner, to cover the whole field of Buddhism and to devote the same amount of space to all the philosophical schools and popular movements that have arisen within it in the course of the past 2,500 years. Instead, Gethin seeks to identify and focus on those fundamental ideas and practices that constitute 'something of a common heritage shared by the different traditions of Buddhism that exist in the world today'.

Thus there are separate chapters on the story of the Buddha; a textual and scriptural tradition; the framework of the four 'noble truths'; the monastic and lay ways of life; a cosmology based around karma and re-birth; the teaching of 'no self' and 'dependent arising'; a progressive path of practice leading on from good conduct and devotion through stages of meditation to a higher understanding; the theoretical systems of either the Abhidharma or the Madhyamaka and Yogachara; and the path of the Bodhisattva. There is also a concluding chapter on what the author calls the evolving traditions of Buddhism, i.e. those that appear in South-east Asia, the Far East, Tibet, and the West, subsequent to Buddhism's rise and expansion in the Indian subcontinent, its original home.

One of the great merits of Gethin's approach is that it calls into question the view that tends to see the history of Buddhism in terms of a division into two major 'sects': the Hinayana/Theravada and the

Mahayana. As he is at pains to point out, many elements of Buddhist thought and practice that were once believed to be characteristic of the emerging Mahayana were simply developments within mainstream Buddhism. Although the Mahayana certainly criticized aspects of mainstream Buddhist thought and practice, much more was taken as said and done, and carried over.

Though the ideas and practices outlined by Gethin are fundamental, in that all are in some way assumed by and known to all Buddhists, some are less fundamental than others. For the Jodo Shinshu, the monk–layman dichotomy has no significance, while Zen has no time for Abhidharma studies. Nonetheless Gethin's discussion of all nine of his 'foundations' is on the whole well informed as regards ancient tradition and modern scholarship. He also has a talent for clear and succinct exposition that makes *The Foundations of Buddhism* a joy to read – a talent honed, it would seem, by his experience as a teacher of introductory courses on Buddhism at a university.

This talent is very much in evidence in the chapters on the Four Truths, the Buddhist cosmos, and the teaching of 'no self' and 'dependent arising', where it might be thought to be needed. But whereas the Four Truths and the teaching of 'no self' and 'dependent arising' have been the subject of a good deal of scholarly discussion, the subject of the Buddhist cosmos – with its 'thrice-thousandfold world-system', its hierarchy of worlds and gods, its five realms of sentient existence, and its great world mountain – have generally been passed over in embarrassed silence, especially by modern Buddhists anxious to demonstrate that Buddhism is a 'scientific' religion.

Gethin, however, succeeds in showing that the traditional Buddhist cosmology is not to be regarded as only of quaint and historical interest. On the contrary, it forms an important and significant part of the common Buddhist heritage, while the world view it embodies still exerts considerable influence on traditional Buddhist societies. The key to the understanding of the Buddhist cosmological scheme lies in the principle of the equivalence of cosmology and psychology, Buddhist cosmology being at once a map of the different realms of existence and a description of all possible experiences. Gethin explains in some detail the way in which cosmology is in essence a reflection of psychology and vice versa, and how in Buddhism cosmology and psychology, on the one hand, and the teaching about karma and rebirth on the other, dovetail into each other.

Combining as it does readability and exact scholarship, elegance and erudition, this new Oxford University Press series volume provides the novice with a solid foundation for his studies, and his elders food for reflection.

*This review was first published in the Times Higher Education Supplement, 2 April 1999.*

# Who's Who of Gurus

Andrew Rawlinson
*The Book of Enlightened Masters: Western Teachers in Eastern Traditions*
Open Court, Chicago 1997, pp. 650.

One day in the early 1960s, when I was living in India, I received a visit from a 40-year-old English doctor, a disciple of the notorious Lobsang Rampa of *Third Eye* fame. He had come to my monastery hoping I would agree to teach him how to levitate, to read people's thoughts, and to see what was happening at a distance.

Naturally I wanted to know why he was so keen to learn those things, to which he replied, 'They will be useful to me in my work.' When I enquired as to the nature of that work, he would only say darkly, 'You will be told that later.'

Subsequently it transpired that he 'knew' that he was a teacher 'with a capital T'. 'In that case you will need something to teach,' I pointed out, with a touch of irony that was lost on him. 'I suppose I will,' he replied. 'I hadn't thought of that.'

At my suggestion, he embarked on the study of Buddhism. Within a month or two, he was an authority on the subject and writing books and articles. Had he lived (he died a few years later) he would probably have become a successful guru with an international following and might well have found a place in Andrew Rawlinson's *The Book of Enlightened Masters*.

Rawlinson's 150 enlightened masters (or spiritual teachers, as he also calls them) are a mixed bunch. Not all of them claim to be enlightened, and even among the enlightened there are some who are more enlightened than others. A few were born enlightened, and two are enlightened not as individuals but as a couple. Most of them come from America, and there are more men than women teachers – though one would not suspect this from the book's politically correct front cover.

In terms of traditions, western teachers have encountered more or less all forms of Buddhism, Hinduism and Sufism. Besides moving from one tradition to another or entering more than one tradition, they may have established a western offshoot of a tradition or abandoned traditions altogether and continued as independent teachers. They may even have created completely new 'traditions'.

The phenomenon with which Rawlinson has to deal is extraordinarily rich and complex, and although the manner in which he has presented 'the entire western pantheon of gurus, bodhisattvas, swamis, scoundrels, roshis, and self-proclaimed mystics' may not enable the reader to separate the wheat from the chaff quite so easily as one of his back cover sponsors thinks, he does manage to introduce a certain amount of order into the confusion.

He does this in two ways. In Part II, 'A directory of spiritual teachers', which makes up the greater part of the book, he explains who the masters are, who influenced them, what they teach, what their personalities and personal lives are like, and the strange adventures many of them have experienced. (At this point I had better declare an interest as I am one of the teachers listed.)

In 'How to understand western teachers', Rawlinson explains what westerners are doing in all the eastern traditions. He also tells the story of how westerners have become spiritual teachers and discusses the meaning and significance of the phenomenon.

Westerners have become spiritual teachers in four stages. In the initial phase (1875–1916), the first westerners entered eastern traditions, some becoming teachers. That was followed by a consolidation of westerners in eastern traditions (1917–1945), a stage of propagation (1946–1962), when westerners became firmly established as spiritual teachers, and, finally, a stage (1963 to the present) when westerners 'do *everything*', so that 'the phenomenon of western teachers and masters is now in full bloom'.

Rawlinson believes that these people are changing western culture by making available a view of the human condition that is new to the West. According to this view, human beings are best understood in terms of *consciousness* and its modifications: consciousness can be transformed by spiritual *practice*, and there are *gurus/masters/teachers* who have done this and who can help others to do the same by some form of *transmission*. Of course, methods will vary.

Despite the links with eastern traditions, this 'spiritual psychology' is a *western* phenomenon. It has come into existence because all the eastern traditions now exist in one place: the West. Because they all exist in one place, these traditions can interact, new questions can be asked, and distinctively western forms of Buddhism/Hinduism/Sufism created. These questions cross traditional boundaries because western participation in eastern traditions is trans-traditional. Rawlinson believes that the era of self-contained traditions is over and that we need something broader and more accommodating to understand the import of western teachers.

He puts forward a fascinating model of experiential comparative religion, the starting point of which is two pairs of polar concepts: *hot* and *cool*, and *structured* and *unstructured*. These can overlap, can be combined, and can be used to highlight the four categories that are fundamental to all traditions in some form or other: ontology, cosmology, anthropology, and soteriology. The model can also be applied to a particular tradition or sub-tradition, eastern or western, as well as to individual teachers and their organizations. This gives rise to a whole range of permutations too complex to be summarized but made clear with the aid of diagrams.

Diagrams, tables, lineage trees, and photographic displays, together with a chronology of spiritual teaching in the West and thirty mini-biographies of figures of historical significance, are useful features of the work.

Rawlinson, a retired academic who remains a researcher and writer, emerges as a friendly and reliable guide to the multi-faceted phenomenon that he claims is changing western culture. His approach is balanced without being bland, sympathetic without being uncritical. He is not above letting the reader know when his information is incomplete or when, as in the case of an intra-sectarian dispute, he has heard only one side of the story.

Though we may have reservations about the value of the author's model of experiential comparative religion, there can be little doubt that this veritable encyclopedia of western gurus and their teachings is both useful and timely. Students of sociology and of comparative religion will find it a mine of information. Would-be disciples in search of a guru will be happy to browse through its pages.

As for the enlightened masters themselves, using Rawlinson's diagrams and tables they will be able to see just where they stand in relation to one another and to their own traditions.

*This review was first published in the Times Higher Education Supplement, 12 December 1997.*

# Ayya Khema: A Personal Tribute

# VII

# Ayya Khema: A Personal Tribute

Many of those who knew Ayya Khema in recent years will have known her as their beloved teacher, and most of the tributes appearing in this present volume will probably be from their pens. Others, however, will have known her simply as a very dear friend and fellow Dharma-farer, and one of these may be permitted to add his own flower to the wreath with which her memory is rightly being honoured.

Ayya Khema and I came to know each other in the autumn of 1992, in the course of the European Buddhist Union's biennial congress, which was held that year in Berlin and in which we both participated as speakers.[1] It was not quite our first meeting. We had met once before, some ten or twelve years earlier, when Ayya Khema came to see me in London not long after her ordination as a nun. Nothing came of that meeting, and perhaps nothing would have come of our meetings in Berlin had it not been for the panel discussion in which I took part on the last morning of the congress. During the discussion I happened to say something that it seems impressed her, as I discovered when with the other speakers we were entertained to lunch at Hakuin's.[2] Ayya Khema, who was seated at another table, had to leave early. As she left she came over to me and without preamble said, 'People say I am a bold woman, but I would not have had the courage to say what you said this morning.' Not being aware that I had said anything particularly courageous, I was puzzled by her words. Later the mystery was cleared up by one of her disciples, who told my companion what it was she had been referring to.

Apart from the fact that she was reputed to be a bold woman, Ayya Khema's cryptic remark told me three things about her. In the first place, it told me that she respected courage. Secondly, it told me that she was direct in her dealings with people, and did not hesitate to tell them frankly what she thought of their proceedings. Thirdly, it told me that on certain issues we were of one mind, for my supposed act of courage had consisted in my publicly dissenting, *pace* a popular fellow panellist, from a view with which she, also, happened to disagree.[3]

It was therefore not surprising that after the congress we should have remained in touch, and that whenever she came to England, which she did every year, we should have arranged to meet. In London she always stayed at the Zen Centre with Venerable Myokyo-ni (Dr Irmgard Schloegl),[4] whom I had known for many years, and when we met there her hostess would join us for afternoon tea. Ayya Khema, I noticed, on such occasions did not hesitate to partake of a biscuit or a piece of cake. Though a strict observer of the Vinaya in all essentials she was no formalist, and was critical of Western bhikkhus who believed that they could eat chunks of cheese and bars of chocolate in the afternoon without technically breaking the 'no solid food after mid-day' rule. 'It's very bad for their stomachs,' she would say disapprovingly. For her, spirituality and common sense were not incompatible.

At one of our meetings she apologized for having been a little confused when I had telephoned the previous day. She had been deep in an Agatha Christie detective novel, she explained, and it had taken her a minute or two to realize who was speaking and what the call was about. Ayya Khema was in fact an Agatha Christie fan, a fact that showed there was a human side to her character, and that she was not quite such an austere figure as one might have thought. I was *not* a fan of the famous Queen of the Detective Novel and had never read any of her books, but I was at least able to tell my Dharma-sister that I had met her once or twice during the War.[5]

As we saw each other only once a year, Ayya Khema and I kept in touch principally by means of letters. I quickly discovered that she was an excellent correspondent, who rarely kept me waiting for more than a week or two before replying to my latest budget of news and views. As she wrote in one of her earlier letters, 'It is my habit to answer all letters almost immediately, as otherwise I would not be able to cope with them.' Believers in astrology might attribute her methodical ways to the fact that she was a Virgoan, her birthday falling the day before my own. Personally, I like to think that her fidelity as a correspondent was due to the fact that she believed, with Dr Johnson, that one should keep one's friendships *in constant repair*.[6] She was a good correspondent because she was a good friend.

In the course of the letters that passed between us we touched on a variety of topics. Apart from keeping each other informed about our movements and activities (we both travelled a good deal), and about the progress of our respective organizations, we discussed questions relating to the teaching of the Dharma in the West as well as more personal matters. Writing on 16 January 1993, Ayya Khema expressed her concern that a leading Buddhist teacher seemed to steer away from the truth of *dukkha* and make statements which seemed to contradict the Buddha's teaching in a fundamental way. One such statement was that you should 'embrace your rage', on which Ayya Khema tersely commented, 'Embracing means loving and drawing near. To my mind that is nonsense, but the way to purification is: Recognition, no blame, change.' This was very much my own opinion and parallelled what I had repeatedly said in connection with the popular New Age belief that one should 'accept oneself.'[7] Another well-known teacher had maintained that 'Enlightened Beings could still have cravings.' With this proposition, too, we both disagreed, if by an Enlightened Being one meant an Arahant, as the teacher in question apparently did.

In the same letter, dated 28 August 1993, in which she had written about the second of these aberrations, Ayya Khema observed, 'I don't think it is surprising, if we have strange outcrops of the Dhamma in our times. We are not living in a spiritual age and the majority of Europeans have lost their connection with their own religious background, whereas Americans have probably never had such a connection. To superimpose a totally strange culture and utterly different social mores on people in the name of spirituality (or religion) seems to me a psychological disaster. An example is the assumption ... that EVERYONE will meet peaceful and wrathful deities after death. I would assume that a devout Catholic would encounter Jesus or the Virgin Mary, whereas practising Jews might have visions of Moses or such like. Not to speak of Theravadins who might encounter a vision of Buddha, or Ananda or whatever. Peaceful and wrathful deities are not exactly part of a Central European mental culture. The same applies to the inordinate importance given to Japanese eating habits (chopsticks) and cultural implements in some of the Zen courses.' Once again, these were very much my own sentiments.

Ayya Khema belonged to a German Jewish family that had emigrated as a result of Nazi persecution. Writing to her about the VE Day commemoration[8] in Britain I therefore commented that for people of Jewish origin the occasion was no doubt one of special poignancy, adding, 'Like many others I still cannot understand how a civilized people like the Germans, who through their philosophy, music, and literature have made such an important contribution to world culture, could have produced the monster of Nazism.' To this she replied on 11 May 1995, with sadness for the past but also hope for the future, 'When the Nazis were persecuting the Jews here in Germany, my father said the same thing you wrote in your letter, namely that he could not believe that a civilized people like the Germans, who had produced Bach, Beethoven, Schubert, Wagner, Goethe, Schiller, Lessing, Kleist, Kant, etc., etc., could go along with an uneducated man like Hitler. But eventually he had to believe it and emigrate to China, where he died in a Japanese prisoner-of-war camp, five days before the end of the war. I fully agree that only the Dhamma will and can bring true peace and am directing all my efforts and energy to propagate this, which especially here in Germany finds many willing ears.' Thanks to Ayya Khema, there are now many more such willing ears – both in Germany and elsewhere – than there might otherwise have been.

In her teaching Ayya Khema dwelt more on practice and personal experience than on theory and speculation, and it was therefore not surprising that in her letter of 29 November 1994, she should have written, 'My whole emphasis has been on the Suttas, although I did study the Vinaya for some years...' In similar vein, on 11 May 1995, she wrote that she considered the work of producing a new German version of the *Majjhima Nikaya* to be more important than translating the Abhidhamma. She also believed in the value of spiritual friendship, and in the same letter agreed with me that it was lacking among the Western Theravadin Sangha. Not that Ayya Khema always agreed with me, or I with her. This was far from being the case. But she possessed the rare virtue of being able to disagree without rancour, so that differences of opinion between us on such controversial topics as the nature of tolerance and the relation between Buddhism and Christianity were never allowed to disturb our friendship even slightly. She indeed was a remarkably fair-minded, balanced, and rational person.

The last letter I received from Ayya Khema was written in her own hand on 1 October 1997 – a month and a day before her death. In it she wrote, 'My health is not really improving, rather the contrary. I am trying in all ways to safeguard the teaching, so that my death will not be too disruptive.' It was typical of her that even at such a time she should think not of herself but of the teaching to which she had dedicated the last twenty years of her life, as well as of those who relied on her spiritual leadership. Though she now has gone the way we all must go, she lives on in her books, in the Order she founded only a week before her death, and in the memories of all who came in contact with her. While those who knew her as their beloved teacher will surely miss her supportive and inspiring presence, one who knew her as a very dear friend and fellow Dharma-farer will miss her friendship – and her letters – no less. May she attain Nibbana!

*This tribute was originally published in German translation in 'Grenzenloses Sein: Gedenkschrift für Ayya Khema', Jhana-Verlag, 1998. ISBN 3-931274-12-8.*

**Notes**

1. The European Buddhist Union, founded in 1975, is an umbrella association for Buddhist groups and organizations from all Buddhist schools. In 1992 it organized a congress on the theme of Unity in Diversity which was attended by leading Buddhist teachers in Europe including Ayya Khema, Sogyal Rimpoche, Thich Nhat Hanh, and Sangharakshita and which drew some 2,000 visitors. The congress was held in former East Berlin in the Werner-Seelenbinder-Halle shortly before it was demolished.

During the event with its talks and discussions and its many stalls representing the different Buddhist groups and schools, Sangharakshita gave a talk on 'Buddhism and the West: the Integration of Buddhism into Western Society'. See www.sangharakshita.org/online_books.html.

2. A vegetarian restaurant founded in 1982, run by Rinzai Zen practitioners and specializing in Japanese food.

3. The panel discussion on Emptiness and Compassion took place on 27 September and was chaired by Sylvia Wetzel with Rewatta Dhamma, Sangharakshita, Sogyal Rimpoche, and Thich Nhat Hanh. In responding to a question from the floor, Thich Nhat Hanh emphasized the importance of being happy. Sangharakshita pointed out that one cannot always be happy – not even Dharma teachers – but one can always be friendly. See: https://vimeo.com/26795496.

4. Venerable Myokyo-ni (Dr Irmgard Schloegl) (1921–2007) was an Austrian-born Rinzai Zen nun. She was a member of the Zen group associated with Christmas Humphreys at whose London house she lived after undergoing Zen training in Japan. She went on to become head of the London Zen Centre and author of a number of books on Zen.

5. Dennis Lingwood's first job when he left school in late 1940 was with Parkes' Coal Company in Torquay. One of their customers was Agatha Christie (*RR*, p. 60).

6. R. M. Hutchins et al (eds), *Great Books of the Western World, Volume 44: Boswell*, Encyclopedia Britannica 1952, p. 83.

7. See for example *A Stream of Stars*, Windhorse Publications 1998, p. 31; and 'Fifteen Points for Old and New Order Members', a talk given on the 25th anniversary of the founding of the Western Buddhist Order in 1993. See www.freebuddhistaudio.com/talks/details?num=180.

8. 8 May 1945: the Nazi forces surrendered to the forces of the Allied armies bringing the war in Europe to an end. c.f. VJ Day, see note 15, p. 145.

An Apology

# VIII

## An Apology

*We live in the Age of Apologies. Here is an apology that is much more meaningful than many being made today.*

Mankind owes a profound apology:

To the Birds, for having polluted the air through which they fly,

To the Ape and the Tiger, for having destroyed the forests in which they live,

To the Deer and the Bison, for ruthlessly hunting them almost to extinction,

To the Rivers and Streams, for poisoning them with chemicals,

To the Earth itself, for greedily pillaging its riches of silver and gold,

To the Ocean, for slaughtering the greatest of her children, the Whale, 'for scientific purposes',

To the Mountain Peaks, for defiling their virgin snows with our trash,

To the Moon, for rudely invading her sacred space,

To the Stars, for obscuring their brightness with the smoke of our cities,

To the Sun, for not gratefully acknowledging our dependence on his bounty,

To the truly great Men and Women of the past, for not honouring their memory as we should and for not walking in their footsteps.

## Written after Hearing a Radio Programme on Dementia

My mind is a theatre
Where every kind of play
Is staged with lights and music
All night and half the day.

I myself am all the actors
In gold and red and blue,
Myself the fickle audience
Myself the critics too.

One day that mad theatre
Will show a red-nosed clown,
And mournful placards will announce
'Last performance. Closing Down.'

## Mr Wireless

Meet my best friend, Mr Wireless,
I've known him years and years.
We've laughed a lot together;
Together we've shed tears.

He wakes me in the morning
With news from round the world,
News of earthquakes and agreements,
Troop withdrawals, rockets hurled.

He talks to me of people,
Of lands both near and far,
Plays me tunes on the piano,
Or conducts an orchestra.

Yes, we grew up together,
And I remember yet
The days when Mr Wireless
Was Little Crystal Set.

Accumulators then he had,
And did in valves rejoice;
And I had to put on headphones
To hear his muffled voice.

Now I hear him very clearly,
He doesn't need to shout.
From sitting room to kitchen
He follows me about.

Meet my best friend, Mr Wireless.
The last sound I shall hear
Will be that well loved voice of his
Receding from my ear.

## The Twin Towers

Proudly they stood, those towers, a monument
To money, and the power that money brings.
But hate was stronger. Now they lie in dust,
And impotent hands a mighty nation wrings.

## Political Correctness Goes Mad Again?

"Racist!" they cried when she said 'golliwog',
And Carol Thatcher wondered what had changed
Since her childhood in the fifties, when she played
With dolls both white and black, and loved them both.

## The Beguiling of Merlin

*After the painting by Burne-Jones*

From his own book of spells she chants, and lo
The charmed earth opens. Sadly, Merlin thinks
How vain is wisdom. The last sight he sees
Is Vivian's smile of triumph as he sinks.

## The Brahmas and the Sages

The Brahmas sit on thrones of light
Immersed in meditation.
For them there is no day, no night,
No worldly perturbation.

Above the lesser gods they dwell,
Immaculate, sublime.
Their bliss no mortal tongue may tell;
They have no sense of time.

Age after age they sit, until
At last their life-span ends.
Each Brahma then, against his will,
To lower realms descends.

Some wake on earth, and find their light
Obscured by mortal clay,
Though still there struggles through that night
A faint celestial ray.

Beside it streams a second ray,
A glittering ray of gold
From Buddha's hand. It shows the way
To wonders manifold.

It points beyond the Brahma-realms
To realms of pure delight.
It points beyond the Brahma thrones,
To Light beyond their light.

'Nirvana' it those sages call
Who dwell on Himalay.
It is their hope, their life, their all,
Their Way beyond the way.

Upright upon their seats of grass
They sit when death is near.
Released, their spirits slowly pass
Beyond, and disappear.

## The Family Reunion

Full twenty years I stayed away.
My father grew thin; my mother grey;
And my young sister went astray.

Now, I see them in my dreams;
A mystic light about them gleams.
They have become my Muse's themes.

My mother and I in an orchard strolled.
Her looks were neither young nor old,
And she was wearing a gown of gold.

Apple blossom was overhead;
Sunlight on the green grass was shed.
At peace we walked, and no word was said.

In front of his cottage my father stood;
Before him a stream, behind him a wood.
He has lived his life as a true man should.

Black his hair as the fur of mole;
He beckoned me in to share a bowl,
And I saw that his withered arm was whole.

My sister had lived with a gypsy man
In a gaily painted caravan
Drawn by a horse. So the story ran.

Now she was dancing the 'Dying Swan'.
Snow white the plumage that she had on,
And joy from her every movement shone.

# Index

*Poems and book reviews are not indexed. n indicates a note*

# Other Ibis Titles by Sangharakshita

DEAR DINOO: LETTERS TO A FRIEND

Sangharakshita's letters to Dinoo Dubash published here for the first time cover a wide range of subjects: from an exploration of meditation to an account of Sangharakshita's experiences when addressing the hundreds of thousands of followers of Dr Ambedkar immediately after their great leader's demise. Art, travel and books are topics that recur, as well as mutual friends and teachers including Dr Dinshaw Mehta of the Society of Servants of God and Bhikshu Jagdish Kashyap, Sangharakshita's first Buddhist teacher.

Reading these letters we find ourselves listening in to a private conversation and are afforded a glimpse of an unusual friendship.

152 pages
£8.99 or £5.39 plus p&p direct from lulu.com
ISBN 978-1-4478-5581-1

BEATING THE DRUM: MAHA BODHI EDITORIALS

The editorials collected here were composed between 1954 and 1964. The themes are diverse and surprising: the effects of horror comics (for which read computer games), the plight of animals, the evils of Hindu casteism or the apathy of the Buddhist world. More than anything the editor is concerned with the need of the world for the Dharma, and the need of the individual to practise it. His unique voice combines clarity, humour, compassion and, above all, challenge.

The book includes an extended introduction with a vivid and readable account of the history of the Maha Bodhi temple, the life of the inspiring Anagarika Dharmapala and his bid to restore the temple to Buddhist hands, and the founding of the *Maha Bodhi* journal. There is also a short and accessible account of Sangharakshita's life up to the time of becoming editor of the *Maha Bodhi*.

*Beating the Drum* will appeal to anyone who wants to know how the Dharma can be applied to the realities of human life and society today and to those interested in the history of Buddhism in the twentieth century.

294 pages
£9.99 or £5.99 plus p&p direct from lulu.com
ISBN 978-1-291-10922-1

ANAGARIKA DHARMAPALA: A BIOGRAPHICAL SKETCH
& Other Maha Bodhi Writings

The life of the great Dharmaduta who was the first to 'girdle the globe
with the Master's Message' is told here by Sangharakshita with a vividness
and passion that has inspired generations of Buddhists. It is followed by
sixty-five of Anagarika Dharmapala's 'Immortal Sayings'; and a short
article about his great patron, Mrs Mary E. Foster of Honolulu.

The volume also includes a series of pieces written under the
pseudonym 'Himavantavasi' which were first published in the *Maha Bodhi*
journal in the 1950s. Often witty, they were a resounding challenge to
the Buddhist world: the writer does not fail to point out the undesirable
and unacceptable – as well as giving praise where it is due.

The final section consists of fifteen book reviews on titles ranging from
*Buddhist Jataka Stories and the Russian Novel* by Martin Wickramsinghe to
Eugen Herrigel's *Zen in the Art of Archery*.

Taken together these remarkable writings from one of the leading
figures in the modern Buddhist world are spiritually invigorating and
deeply inspiring.

194 pages
£10.00 or £6.00 plus p&p direct from lulu.com
ISBN 978-1-291-43071-4

EARLY WRITINGS 1944–1954

From the earliest prophetic or visionary pieces written when the author was still in his teens to those composed a decade later with their exceptional clarity and inspiration, these early writings are crucial in the development of Sangharakshita's thought and expression.

They cover a wide range of subject matter from explorations of the entire field of Buddhism to the encounter of Buddhism with western culture and modern life; and penetrating explorations of the implications for humanity of the Buddha's teaching of anatta or selflessness.

Among the Early Writings is a dramatic dialogue: 'Is Buddhism for Monks Only?'; and 'Krishna's Flute', a piece of literary criticism exploring the life and work of Indian poetess Sarojini Naidu. Articles written during Sangharakshita's first years living in the East show how Vedanta and Christian mysticism were all seeking a place in his understanding of human and spiritual life.

Those fascinated by the emergence of Sangharakshita as a major figure in the Buddhist world, who have been curious about his development as a thinker and writer, as well as teacher, will find themselves stimulated – and perhaps surprised. But there is more to be discovered here: in every piece are springs of inspiration; and through it all there is that characteristic call that is Sangharakshita's, distilled in a line from one of his poems: 'O Man, aspire!'

294 pages
£9.99
ISBN 978-1-291-78614-9